HONOR, POLITICS, AND THE LAW IN IMPERIAL GERMANY, 1871–1914

Honor in nineteenth-century Germany is usually thought of as an anachronistic aristocratic tradition confined to the dueling elites. In this innovative study Ann Goldberg shows instead how honor pervaded all aspects of German life and how, during an era of rapid modernization, it was adapted and incorporated into the modern state, industrial capitalism, and mass politics. In business, state administration, politics, labor relations, gender and racial matters, Germans contested questions of honor in an explosion of defamation litigation. Dr. Goldberg surveys court cases, newspaper reportage, and parliamentary debates, exploring the conflicts of daily life and the intense politicization of libel jurisprudence in an era when an authoritarian state faced off against groups and individuals from "below" claiming new citizenship rights around a democratized notion of honor and law. Her fascinating account provides a nuanced and important new understanding of the political, legal and social history of imperial Germany.

ANN GOLDBERG is an associate professor of History at the University of California, Riverside. She is the author of *Sex, Religion, and the Making of Modern Madness* (1999).

NEW STUDIES IN EUROPEAN HISTORY

Edited by

PETER BALDWIN, University of California, Los Angeles
CHRISTOPHER CLARK, University of Cambridge
JAMES B. COLLINS, Georgetown University
MIA RODRÍGUEZ-SALGADO, London School of Economics and Political Science
LYNDAL ROPER, University of Oxford
TIMOTHY SNYDER, Yale University

The aim of this series in early modern and modern European history is to publish outstanding works of research, addressed to important themes across a wide geographical range, from southern and central Europe, to Scandinavia and Russia, from the time of the Renaissance to the Second World War. As it develops the series will comprise focused works of wide contextual range and intellectual ambition.

A full list of titles published in the series can be found at:
www.cambridge.org/newstudiesineuropeanhistory

HONOR, POLITICS, AND THE LAW IN IMPERIAL GERMANY, 1871–1914

ANN GOLDBERG

University of California, Riverside

CAMBRIDGE
UNIVERSITY PRESS

CAMBRIDGE UNIVERSITY PRESS
Cambridge, New York, Melbourne, Madrid, Cape Town, Singapore, São Paulo, Delhi

Cambridge University Press
The Edinburgh Building, Cambridge CB2 8RU, UK

Published in the United States of America by Cambridge University Press, New York

www.cambridge.org
Information on this title: www.cambridge.org/9780521198325

© Ann Goldberg 2010

First published 2010

Printed in the United Kingdom at the University Press, Cambridge

A catalogue record for this publication is available from the British Library

Library of Congress Cataloguing in Publication data
Goldberg, Ann.
Honor, politics and the law in imperial Germany, 1871–1914 / Ann Goldberg.
p.   cm. – (New studies in European history)
ISBN 978-0-521-19832-5 (hardback)
1. Honor – Germany – History.   2. Political culture – Germany – History.   3. Libel and
slander – Germany – History.   4. Germany – History – 1871–1918.   I. Title.   II. Series.
BJ1533.H8G65   2010
306.20943'09034–dc22
2009045832

ISBN-13: 978-0-521-19832-5 Hardback

Contents

Acknowledgements   *page* ix
List of abbreviations   xi

Introduction   1

1   The development of the law   19

2   Honor disputes and everyday life   37

3   The state   81

4   Politicization   115

5   Popular mobilizations: Jews and lunatics   157

Conclusion: Beyond 1914   193

Index   213

Acknowledgements

The research for this book was enabled by the generosity of several institutions and funding organizations, whom I would like to thank. The idea for the section of chapter 5 dealing with mad people first emerged years ago as a result of an initial research foray at the Landeshauptarchiv Koblenz, during a visiting fellowship at the Friedrich-Ebert-Stiftung in Bonn. Subsequent trips to German archives were partially funded by the University of California, Riverside and the National Endowment for the Humanities. Many thanks, as well, to the following institutions for access to their research holdings and for their helpful staff: Geheimes Staatsarchiv Preussischer Kulturbesitz; Bundesarchiv Berlin-Lichterfelde; Brandenburgisches Landeshauptarchiv; Nordrhein-Westfälisches Hauptstaatsarchiv; Stiftung Neue Synagoge Berlin; Institut für Geschichte der Medizin, Berlin; Staatsbibliothek, Berlin. In Düsseldorf, the Heinrich-Heine-University supplied a place to stay and the company of a terrific group of international scholars. In Berlin, Roswitha Gronich, Ilan Gronich, Uschi Hoffmann, and Max Hoffmann provided lodging and, much more importantly, their friendship and company.

Earlier versions of parts of the book were presented at the European Social Science History Conference; Association for Jewish Studies Conference; German Studies Association Conference; a forum on German history at U.C. Berkeley; and U.C. Riverside's Legal Studies Workshop. I thank for their comments, suggestions, and probing questions Margaret Anderson, James Brophy, Darcy Buerkle, Eric Engstrom, Kenneth Ledford, Kees Gispen, Atina Grossmann, Paul

Lerner, Peter Loewenberg, Glenn Penny, Richard Wetzell, and the members of U.C. Riverside's Legal Studies Workshop.

Special thanks go to Peter Baldwin, who read the entire manuscript and offered insightful advice. Other colleagues and friends who have helped over the years are Sharon Gillerman, Benjamin Hett, Steve Loewenstein, Guenther Roth, Emmanuel Saadia, David Sabean, Heinz-Peter Schmiedebach, Dana Simmons, Jonathan Sperber, Kathy Stuart, and Ulrich Raulff. My very warm thanks go to Michael Watson at Cambridge University Press, whose professionalism and cordiality were extremely important to me; it was a pleasure working with him. At Cambridge University Press I would also like to thank Joanna Breeze, Joanna Garbutt, and Laurence Marsh.

Abbreviations

BA	Bundesarchiv, Berlin-Lichterfelde
BLA	Brandenburgisches Landeshauptarchiv
CJA	Stiftung Neue Synagoge Berlin – Centrum Judaicum, Archiv
GStPK	Geheimes Staatsarchiv Preussischer Kulturbesitz
HdR	Handwörterbuch zur deutschen Rechtsgeschichte
IdR	*Im deutschen Reich*
IR	Irrenrechts-Reform
NWHSA	Nordrhein-Westfälisches Hauptstaatsarchiv
SBR	*Stenographische Berichte über die Verhandlungen des deutschen Reichstags*
SBPA	*Stenographische Berichte über die Verhandlungen des Preussischen Hauses der Abgeordneten*
StPO	Strafprozessordnung (code of criminal procedure)

Introduction

Germans have long been a thin-skinned people, easily insulted and, when provoked, exceptionally ready to sue. Three anecdotes, spanning the seventeenth and twentieth centuries, give a sense of what was at stake in their lawsuits. The first is of a Saxon blacksmith in 1671 whose wife was called a "whore" (allegedly she had had sex for money with her male servant).[1] For the dishonoring remark, made by a drunken tanner, the blacksmith filed charges and the tanner was called to court to account for his insult (though eventually acquitted). The second case, over 300 years later, is of the Berlin court actor Siegwart Gruder, a man whose successful career peaked during the Kaiserreich (1871–1918). Now, in 1927, aging, ill, and living off a meagre pension, he goes to the telephone exchange to complain about service, and has a fit when the woman at the desk fails to treat him with the respect he thinks he deserves (allegedly she didn't heed the sign he had made (*Blinkzeichen*) calling for her attention). Having called in her supervisor, Gruder blusters, "I am an academic [sic] and I don't have to let myself be treated like this by an uneducated vagrant street girl and daughter of a [mere] postman [*Postschaffner*]." This tiny moment of rancour became the basis subsequently of a court case, the state charging and convicting Gruder of insulting a civil servant (*Beamtenbeleidigung*).[2] The third case took place in the 1950s in West Germany between an agricultural worker, who had recently moved from East Berlin, and his employer, a farmer who was also the worker's landlord. During a disagreement over rent

---

[1] Eileen Crosby, "Claiming Honor: Injury, Honor, and the Legal Process in Saxony, 1650–1730" (PhD diss., Cornell University, 2004), pp. 264ff.

[2] I. HA Rep. 84a, Nr. 58224, GStPK.

and wages, the farmer called the worker a "jailbird" (*Zuchthäusler*) and a "Communist." The worker promptly turned around and sued for insult (whether he prevailed in court is unknown).[3]

Despite some important differences,[4] what is most striking about these cases is the continuity – the tenacity over centuries and within vastly different settings – of an honor culture litigated in the courts. Honor was serious business. The time and monetary risk of bringing a lawsuit over even a trivial insult was taken in stride by many Germans because, as the anthropologists tell us, what they were defending went to the heart of their sense of self and social identity, honor being "the value of a person in his own eyes and in the eyes of his society. It is his estimation of his own worth, his *claim* to pride, but it is also the acknowledgment of that claim, his excellence recognized by society, his *right* to pride," – namely, respect and deference.[5] And that value, symbolic as it was, translated into all the important material things in life – social status, jobs, credit, marriage, and power – honor being a kind of currency that could be turned into goods and services, or, to the contrary, squandered and lost. The extravagant disproportion of Gruder's reaction to an inattentive telephone employee, strange as it seems, did have a certain logic and pathos, that of a man whose world no longer recognized him – a man of honor and status – as he saw himself.

Neither the devotion to honor nor the use of defamation law for policing speech was unique to Germany. To this day, England's notoriously restrictive libel statutes continue to inhibit free speech in that country and, via a globalized publishing industry, increasingly in the US as well. The French were obsessed in the nineteenth century with issues of honor and respect, and elite men dueled just as avidly there as in Germany.[6] But legally and historically, the honor cultures

---

[3] Hans-Georg Doering, *Beleidigung und Privatklage* (Göttingen, 1971), pp. 41–42.

[4] For example, it would have been illegal for a seventeenth-century worker to bring an honor lawsuit against his master.

[5] Julian Pitt-Rivers, "Honour and Social Status'" in J. G. Peristiany (ed.), *Honour and Shame: The Values of Mediterranean Society* (Chicago, 1966), p. 21.

[6] Robert Nye, *Masculinity and Male Codes of Honor in Modern France* (Berkeley, 1993); William Reddy, *The Invisible Code: Honor and Sentiment in Postrevolutionary France, 1814 – 1848* (Berkeley, 1997); Edward Berenson, *The Trial of Madame Caillaux*

of those countries developed along different lines – both from each other and from Germany. The result was that in France the mechanisms regulating civility and respect (i.e. behavior according with a person's honor and status) developed outside of the court system – in the schools and bourgeois voluntary associations, according to a recent study[7] – and thus did not juridify interpersonal conflicts as they did in Germany. In England and the US, a property-oriented view of defamation had long largely decoupled honor and the law of slander, setting, accordingly, high standards of legal proof (a plaintiff was required to show evidence of material harm to his or her financial existence) that minimized such lawsuits.[8] And, in the US, particularly since a 1964 Supreme Court decision, defamatory speech has been significantly narrowed in order to protect First Amendment rights.[9]

By contrast, since at least the late Middle Ages, Germans have been successfully suing one another for not only public speech that harms reputation, but for insults (*Beleidigungen*) that make them *feel* disrespected, irrespective of whether their reputations have actually

(Berkeley, 1992). On Italian honor, see Steven C. Hughes, *Politics of the Sword* (Columbus, OH, 2007).

[7] James Whitman, "Enforcing Civility and Respect: Three Societies," *Yale Law Journal* 109 (2000), 1279–398. Whitman's comparative study of France, Germany, and the US is extremely useful and thought-provoking. I do take issue with a number of his factual assertions and interpretations (see Conclusion). For more details on French and British libel statutes, see below (ch. 1).

[8] Very good discussions of comparative defamation law can be found in Mittermaier et al. (eds.), *Vergleichende Darstellung des deutschen und ausländischen Strafrechts: Besonderer Teil* vol. 4 (Berlin, 1906). For a recent analysis of British and US law, see Paul Mitchell, *The Making of the Modern Law of Defamation* (Oxford and Portland, OR, 2005). For comparison of German and US defamation law, see Georg Nolte, *Beleidigungsschutz in der freiheitlichen Demokratie* (Berlin, 1992); Pawel Lutomski, "Private Citizens and Public Discourse: Defamation Law as a Limit to the Right of Free Expression in the US and Germany," *German Studies Review* 24 (2001), 571–92.

[9] The majority ruling in this case, *New York Times v. Sullivan*, raised the bar very far for plaintiffs, requiring them to "prove actual malice on the disseminator's part": Ian Loveland, *Political Libels* (Oxford, 2000), p. 69. The case derived from a lawsuit brought against the *New York Times* for publishing an advertisement (containing minor factual errors) critical of Alabama's harassment of civil rights activists.

or potentially been harmed.[10] Indeed, in modern German insult law – a kind of "rudeness regulation"[11] – no knowledge of the insult by a third party is required for the complainent to sue (as in the worker-farmer case above) and to do so successfully. In the Kaiserreich, moreover, such lawsuits became actionable in criminal law – a situation that in effect "criminalized" disrespectful behavior[12] – and Germans were given the right to bring these actions themselves in private prosecutions (_Privatklage_). This _Privatklage_ provision of German law, perhaps more than any other single factor, kept honor intensely alive in popular culture and ensured that the interpersonal conflicts of daily life became lawsuits on an unparalleled scale. To this day, Germany is a country that guarantees in its _Grundgesetz_ a "right" to honor; it still has an "insult" provision of its defamation laws regulating respectful treatment such that, under certain circumstances, one can be prosecuted for, say, giving the finger to a driver as he cuts you off on the road.[13]

The nineteenth century played a critical role in perpetuating Germany's juridified honor culture. Indeed, judging by the numbers, it was the Kaiserreich in particular that massively expanded that culture. An epidemic of libel litigation characterized this era. There were 52,645 criminal indictments for libel in 1883. By 1910, that figure

---

[10] For early-modern German defamation litigation, see, in addition to Crosby, "Claiming Honor," in Ralf-Peter Fuchs, _Um die Ehre: Westfälische Beleidigungsprozesse vor dem Reichskammergericht, 1525–1805_ (Paderborn, 1999); Klaus Schreiner and Gerd Schwerhoff (eds.), _Verletzte Ehre: Ehrkonflikte in Gesellschaften des Mittelalters und der frühen Neuzeit_ (Cologne, 1995); Martin Dinges, "Die Ehre als Thema der Stadtgeschichte: Eine Semantik im Übergang vom Ancien Regime zur Moderne," _Zeitschrift für historische Forschung_ 16 (1989), 409–40; idem, _Der Mauermeister und der Finanzrichter_ (Göttingen, 1994).

[11] Whitman, "Enforcing Civility," 1295.   [12] Ibid., 1296.

[13] Whitman, "Enforcing Civility," Doering, _Beleidigung und Privatklage_, and Rüdiger Koewius, _Die Rechtswirklichkeit der Privatklage_ (Berlin, 1974) are sociological studies of insult litigation in West Germany. On East German honor litigation: Paul Betts, "Property, Peace, and Honor: Neighborhood Justice in Communist Berlin," _Past and Present_ 201 (2008), 215–54.

had grown to 84,058.[14] This was an increase of over 59 percent at a time when the population, itself rapidly expanding, grew at a rate of 41 percent. These figures, moreover, do not include the tens of thousands of libel actions that were settled out of court each year. Indeed, contemporaries estimated that in Prussia, for example, more than half of all insult proceedings were settled through pretrial mediation.[15] The comparable figures for France, for example, are miniscule by comparison, even when one factors in that country's smaller population.[16] Finally, it was the Kaiserreich that granted almost all Germans the extraordinary right of the *Privatklage*.

This should not have been happening according to a body of scholarship on honor reaching back to the turn-of-the-century work of sociologist Max Weber. Honor was central to Weber's typological distinction between traditional corporate and modern class societies.[17] Corporate societies, according to Weber, categorize people according to hierarchically ranked, exclusive estates (*Stände*) in which membership and status is determined by honor, a quality displayed in a particular lifestyle (*Lebensführung*) – dress, comportment, titles – that distances and elevates higher, more honorable estates and individuals from lower ones. By contrast, modern market

---

[14] 1883 is the first year for which there are libel suit figures in the Reich's official statistics. I calculated the rate of increase using the years 1883, 1890, 1900, 1910. In all of these decades, libel indictments outstripped population growth, but the gaps varied by decade. 1890–1900 saw the smallest gap – ca. 1.5%; the period of 1883–1890 saw the largest (ca. 9%). *Statistisches Jahrbuch für das deutsche Reich*, vols. 6, 13, 23, 33.

[15] Heinrich Gerland, "Die systematische Stellung des Privatklageverfahrens im Strafprocess," *Der Gerichtssaal* 60 (1902), 161. The numbers are opaque in some respects. For example, they do not normally tell us what proportion of these cases were prosecuted by the state. They also do not reveal much about the litigants' social backgrounds.

[16] France recorded its defamation statistics somewhat differently and thus the comparison is not exact, but the French figures for 1897 give a sense of the wide gap between it and Germany. In that year, the French criminal courts (cours d'assises and the tribunaux correctionnels) adjudicated ca. 2,400 cases of public defamation and insult; an additional 4,017 cases of private insult were brought at a lower level as police misconduct charges (akin to a parking ticket violation) in the tribunaux de simple police: *Annuaire Statistique* 20 (Paris, 1968), 117, 129.

[17] Max Weber, *Wirtschaft und Gesellschaft* vol. 2 (Tübingen, 1956), pp. 534ff.

societies are governed by "objective criteria" and have "no idea about honor,"[18] grouping people instead in social classes that are purely economic, determined by a person's "relations to production."[19]

Weber's distinction between modernity and honor entered recent scholarship via the work of anthropologists in the mid-twentieth century. Their ethnographic studies of Mediterranean societies closely associated an abiding attachment to the values of honor with rural, preindustrial settings.[20] As Peristiany put it, "Honour and shame are the constant preoccupation of individuals in small scale, exclusive societies where face to face personal, as opposed to anonymous, relations are of paramount importance ..."[21] It is such settings, structured by rank and the power of the social group, where reputation and respect, displayed and fought over through the rituals of honor, are of paramount importance.[22] In this view, by contrast, modernization erodes the value of honor by developing differentiated, complex structures and non-overlapping social roles that undermine the power of the small group over the individual. An external and group-defined sense of self, status, and respect is replaced by an individualized, internal identity that makes "honor," as a social value, less relevant or irrelevant.[23] Accordingly, urban gangs, the

---

[18] Ibid., p. 538.

[19] Weber's historical (as opposed to theoretical and ideal-typical) analysis of market societies was in fact much more nuanced and complex, viewing honor-estatist values as continuing to coexist and be intertwined with economic classes: for example, ibid., p. 535. For a historical narrative, based on Weberian ideas, on how modernization "brought about the decline of honour and its replacement by the notion of dignity," see Peter Berger et al., *The Homeless Mind: Modernization and Consciousness* (New York, 1974); Pat O'Malley, "From Feudal Honour to Bourgeois Reputation. Ideology, Law and the Rise of Industrial Capitalism," *Sociology* 15 (1981), 79, offers a critique of modernization theory that continues to use the dichotomy of modernity and honor but reformulates it within a Marxist paradigm.

[20] Classic work done by Pitt-Rivers, Peristiany, and others. See, e.g., Peristiany, *Honour and Shame*.

[21] Ibid., p. 11.   [22] Ibid., pp. 21ff.

[23] An influential analysis of the development of Western honor within this Weberian modernization mode is Peter Berger's "On the Obsolescence of the Concept of Honor," *Archives Européennes de Sociologie* 11 (1970), 339–47. A modernization view applied to German honor in the nineteenth century can be found in Ute Frevert, "Ehre – männlich/weiblich. Zu einem Identitätsbegriff des 19.

Sicilian Mafia, and immigrant Turks[24] in the modern West, groups whose values continue to be structured around honor, have a whiff of archaism about them, being seen as holdovers from the past or displaying signs of deprivation and underdevelopment.

It is difficult to fit Germany's honor culture into this schema, given that it continued unabated even as the country rapidly modernized, developing in the nineteenth century social and political structures – impersonal cities, bureaucracies, industrial workforce, mass voting and mass press – that should have undermined the role of honor. Even as far back as the sixteenth and seventeenth centuries, honor in Germany was not progressing along the lines set out by modern anthropologists. In her study of early-modern guild honor, the historian Kathy Stuart found that, contrary to the "anthropological assumption ... that the significance of honor recedes as societies become more complex and diversified," in Germany "the larger the city, the more stringent the honor code" among municipal craft guilds.[25]

Perhaps the contradiction in Germany is reflective of the continued strength of traditional values and preindustrial elites? This is the conclusion one inescapably gets from studies of the duel, which dominate the scholarship on nineteenth-century honor. A dramatic but minor phenomenon compared to the defamation lawsuit, the duel in Germany was nevertheless spreading downward before World War One via university student fraternities and the reserve officer corps to encompass wide swaths of the educated bourgeoisie. This development, to be sure, was occurring elsewhere, most notably in republican France and liberal post-Risorgimento Italy. It thus does not, as one scholar clarifies, signal any uniquely illiberal features on

Jahrhunderts," *Tel Aviver Jahrbuch für deutsche Geschichte* 21 (1992), 22, 28; and, implicitly, in Whitman, "Enforcing Civility."

[24] Clementine van Eck, *Purified by Blood: Honour Killings amongst Turks in the Netherlands* (Amsterdam, 2003), a fascinating anthropological study that traces present-day honor killings among Turkish immigrants to the Mediterranean values they are bringing and re-adapting from rural Turkish village culture.

[25] Kathy Stuart, *Defiled Trades and Social Outcasts: Honor and Ritual Pollution in Early Modern Germany* (Cambridge, 1999), p. 11.

the part of the German bourgeoisie that would support the notion of a German *Sonderweg* – a pathological departure from the developmental norms of the West.[26] And yet, given the duel's aristocratic-military ethos, it is hard to interpret this form of honor (whether in Germany, France,[27] or the US South[28]) as anything but a reflection of the persistence of preindustrial norms and practices of old elites into the modern era.

Perhaps, as in one recent study,[29] the modern German defamation lawsuit should be seen, accordingly, as an anachronism reflecting the continued power of traditional hierarchical values? Certainly, there were strong links in Germany between honor and premodern or even anti-modern values. One sees this in the defense of entrenched corporate interests in the military and the civil service, and in the way professional disciplinary courts (*Ehrengerichte*) defined honor in opposition to the maligned values of the marketplace (chapter 2). The authorities' use of defamation prosecutions on a massive scale to censor political dissent (chapter 3), furthermore, certainly reflected resistance to a modern liberal state guaranteeing freedom of speech and opinion.

This said, the notion of a dichotomy between honor and modernity is far too simplistic.[30] It does not begin to capture the complexity of how Germany's honor culture interacted with the transformations

---

[26] It is "doubtful whether it is possible to interpret [German bourgeois dueling] as a drive towards feudalization on the part of the middle class." Ute Frevert, *Men of Honor: A Social and Cultural History of the Duel*, trans. Anthony Williams (Cambridge, 1995), p. 7. By contrast, a *Sonderweg* argument is explicitly the point of Kevin McAleer, *Dueling: The Cult of Honor in Fin-de-Siècle Germany* (Princeton, 1994).

[27] Robert Nye's study of French honor in the nineteenth century, *Masculinity and Male Codes of Honor*, shows that the French bourgeoisie were just as passionate about dueling as their German counterparts.

[28] The literature on honor for both the antebellum and postbellum South is too large to cite here. A good starting point is the work of Bertram Wyatt-Brown, *Southern Honor: Ethics and Behavior in the Old South* (Oxford, 1983) and *The Shaping of Southern Culture: Honor, Grace, and War, 1760s–1880s* (Chapel Hill, 2001).

[29] Whitman, "Enforcing Civility."

[30] Weber himself understood this and wrote about a complex overlapping of the values and practices of corporate and class societies. See fn. 17.

of modern life. This culture was woven into the social fabric as an idiom of social relations with multiple functions and tremendous adaptability to new conditions and interests. Honor codes were flexible, multipurpose, and, far from anachronistic, being incorporated into the modern state, industrial capitalism, and mass politics in the age of democracy. Professional honor courts, for example, were not holdovers from the past but the creations of the late nineteenth century and part of the professionalization (modernization) of medicine, law, and other areas of professional life. The state's draconian libel prosecutions of its opponents were tremendously controversial, producing, in the age of parliaments and a mass press, a vigorous and "modern" debate about state power, free speech, political and administrative accountability, and the role of honor in a Rechtsstaat (constitutional state). Even the conservative courts were of different minds on these issues. Finally, the institution most responsible for maintaining and expanding insult and libel litigation, the *Privatklage*, far from being an extension of aristocratic "private prosecutions,"[31] was the product of the liberalization of Germany's criminal justice system in the nineteenth century.

Privatklagen, which made up the majority of libel actions, were breathtakingly pervasive and multifunctional. Anywhere one looks at German society at the turn of the twentieth century – politics, business, the Churches, professions, press, daily life, gender and labor relations – one finds clashes over competing honor claims that ended up in court. No social interaction, no gesture or statement, however trivial, seemed immune from denunciation and litigation. The motives and interests behind these lawsuits were extremely varied: revenge, rage, jealousy, setting the record straight, restoring one's reputation, defeating an opponent, shaming an enemy. So were the circumstances that brought people to litigation: land disputes, rude behavior, drinking and gossip, bad reviews, contested business deals, hostilities between strikers and strikebreakers, to name just a few.

What underlay all of these suits was the propensity of Germans to turn their disputes into lawsuits, and what this entailed was the

---

[31] Whitman, "Enforcing Civility," 1321.

articulation of material and symbolic interests within a language of honor, an idiom embedded in the legal terms of the defamation lawsuit itself. The political and social flexibility of this idiom is striking, providing as it did a language of dispute at all levels of society and among both reactionaries and socialists, defenders of corporate interests and rebels against those interests, the powerful and the powerless.

On the one hand, there was the continuation of traditional corporate notions of identity and honor and sharp class distinctions. On the other hand, industrial capitalism and the democratization of German society were undermining the paternalistic and deferential relations that had been the basis of a hierarchical corporate society. Indeed, the fact that so many Germans were feeling disrespected suggests a society in massive transition where firm markers of status were being undermined or challenged, and where geographical mobility, urbanization, and industrial capitalism were bringing more and more strangers and mixed classes into contact, causing anxiety and confusion about social roles and the norms of behavior.

Accordingly, many of these suits, particularly those of the middle classes, were shot through with status anxiety. As early as the 1850s, at least one legal expert was making precisely this point, arguing that "the loosening of the firm fundament of the bourgeoisie is gradually making necessary a more touchy honor and strengthening its weight in public opinion," with a resulting "epidemic" of defamation litigation.[32] Still other lawsuits were from marginalized or outsider groups – Jews, workers, women, psychiatric patients – people (with the exception of the latter) who had long defended their honor in court, but who were doing so now in new ways, filing suit against superiors, organizing in political groupings as pressure groups, adopting and reshaping honor ideas for new purposes related to the claims of citizenship rights. They were also addressing the public in new ways with a barrage of inventive pamphlet writing that appealed in print to the court of public opinion.

---

[32] C. Reinhold Köstlin, *Abhandlungen aus dem Strafrechte* (Tübingen, 1858), pp. 71, 79.

This was an extraordinary move in the history of honor. To put it in technical terms, while most libel lawsuits remained "horizontal" (i.e. those between social equals), "vertical" lawsuits between unequals, which had always been brought by superiors because of their higher honor and social status, could also now involve legal actions of inferiors against their social superiors and even against government officials. At the same time, defamation lawsuits were more and more likely to involve press libels outside the area of interpersonal, face-to-face relations, to reflect, in other words, the growth of a mass press, which tremendously expanded the opportunities, kinds and publicity of insults, as well as offering new venues for individuals to defend their honor.

What was coming into existence in the Kaiserreich, in other words, was a hybrid legal culture that harnessed a traditional idiom of honor to a democratic politics of rights. The association of honor and rights, to be sure, was neither new nor unique to the Kaiserreich. As the anthropologist Frank H. Stewart puts it, all assertions of honor cross-culturally are in some way "rights claims" to a certain status and respect.[33] But what was new in the German nineteenth century was the association of these "claim rights" with those of modern citizenship and equal rights, together with practices associated with mass, participatory politics.[34]

This democratization of honor reflected the social changes brought about by industrial capitalism, liberalism, urbanism, and mass politics. It was also the product of changes within honor itself. Alongside the continued strength of collective, corporate honor ideas, honor, in the course of the nineteenth century, was becoming fragmented and individualized. Traditionally, honor was based on a person's membership in a hierarchically ranked corporation (*Stand*). It was defined in terms of the person's reputation and standing in his or her community and demonstrated through group-defined external

---

[33] Stewart, *Honor*, pp. 75–78, 146–47; Crosby, "Claiming Honor", pp. 5–6.
[34] For an excellent study about politics and honor in an earlier period in the US, see Joanne Freeman, *Affairs of Honor: National Politics in the New Republic* (New Haven, 2001).

markers: birth and lineage, profession, guild membership, religion, sexuality and gender. Towns, for example, treated Jews, criminals, the illegitimately born, non-citizens and members of tainted trades as dishonorable. Beginning in the eighteenth-century Enlightenment, a new bourgeois notion of honor arose – a moral, internalized, and *vernünftige* concept of the man or woman of virtue, whose honor was defined and determined not by the group or *Stand*, but by the individual himself through the cultivation of a rational and moral life. As Fichte put it:

I do not in any way base my judgment regarding the honor of my behavior according to the opinion of others …, rather on my own opinion. My opinion of my behavior depends on whether it accords with who I am or whether this behavior brings me in conflict with myself. In the first case I can approve the behavior. In the second I would have dishonored myself and all I can do to re-establish my honor is to candidly, and with all my strength, retract and correct [my behavior].[35]

It was this new kind of honor – (ideally) self-determined and freed from the strictures of rank, hierarchy, and birth – that, like modern citizenship itself, opened new possibilities for claiming honor rights and that underlay the new uses of defamation litigation discussed in this book.[36]

Despite its democratizing and liberalizing trends, imperial Germany remained constrained within illiberal forms of government and the outsized power of an authoritarian monarchy, military, and bureaucracy. Since the 1980s,[37] historians have been rethinking that illiberalism, and one effect, after years of debate, is the possibility of less polemical and teleological treatments of the era, ones that seek to understand the society on its own terms without the pitfalls associated with reading back into the Kaiserreich Germany's later history (i.e., the Third Reich). We now know, for example, from a study of the

[35] Fichte (1862), quoted in Zunkel, "Ehre, Reputation," in Otto Brunner et al. (eds.), *Geschichtliche Grundbegriffe* vol. 2 (Stuttgart, 1975), p. 27.
[36] See ch. 2 for an in-depth discussion of this issue that problematizes the notion of modern honor.
[37] For an influential book within and about these debates, see David Blackbourn and Geoff Eley, *The Peculiarities of German History* (Oxford, 1984).

Kaiserreich's electoral politics that, alongside its authoritarianism, democratic ideas and practices – a "legalistic culture" in Anderson's term – were making deep inroads into German society.[38]

That culture of legalism is the topic of this book. Focusing on the interactions of culture and politics, it shows the way Germans experienced the changes of modernization through the lens of an entrenched but evolving culture of honor and extreme litigiousness.[39] It analyzes German litigiousness in the context of both mass political institutions (press, parliaments) and the authoritarian state. On the one hand, it shows honor lawsuits to be tools of state repression and the defense of corporate interests. In this sense, honor and its litigation functioned to reinforce existing hierarchies and power structures. On the other hand, the defamation suit was becoming a tool of democracy, one that made sense in a society where status and identity remained closely bound up with honor. Taken together, these two aspects of libel litigation had the effect of massively juridifying conflict, creating a society of surveillance and censorship that, to an extraordinary extent, brought the state at every turn into the lives of private citizens, politicians, and public officials.

The vast majority of court records were destroyed, but several hundred still exist in the archives. Libel litigation also left its traces in many other places. Newspapers regularly carried notices about individual cases, as well as commentaries about the legal, social, and political controversies surrounding honor and defamation law. I have culled information from published collections of legal judgments, the scholarly legal literature, and the record books of court mediators, a small number of which still survive in the archives. A type of popular

---

[38] Margaret Lavinia Anderson, *Practicing Democracy: Elections and Political Culture in Imperial Germany* (Princeton, 2000). Among the many other excellent works in a post-*Sonderweg* mode that I have found useful for the topic of this book is Kevin Repp's *Reformers, Critics, and the Paths of German Modernity* (Cambridge, MA, 2000).

[39] That litigiousness was not confined to libel lawsuits. It also manifested itself, for example, in conflicts over welfare claims. See, Greg Eghigian, *Making Security Social: Insurance, Disability, and the Birth of the Social Entitlement State in Germany* (Ann Arbor, 2000).

memoir written in pamphlet form by litigants themselves was essential reading for understanding experiences and mentalities. On the political aspects, the essential sources, besides the press, were the minutes of parliamentary debates in the Reichstag and the Prussian lower house, reports of the meetings of the Prussian Ministry of State, and other government records.

Chapter 1 traces the long-term development of defamation law. The origin and purpose of libel laws were always about state attempts to limit violent clashes in the population, including those of the aristocratic duel. But the dueling link has been so overemphasized in the scholarship that it has blinded us to the existence of a parallel but quite different story: libel law's connections to the history of German liberalism. This is the focus of chapter 1, which traces the efforts of liberals to limit arbitrary and absolutist state power. In the process, those reformers ended up democratizing libel law while, ironically, helping to perpetuate Germany's traditional honor culture.

Whereas chapter 1 is interested in the long-term development of defamation law, chapter 2 focuses synchronously on one slice of time – the years of the Kaiserreich before World War One (1871–1914) – and the multiple meanings and uses of honor litigation in that era's popular culture. These lawsuits offer a kaleidoscope of the Kaiserreich's social history. They show a distinct culture of complaint and interpersonal conflict revolving around the honor idiom and the practices of the defamation suit. They also suggest the complex, tension-ridden ways that honor values were embedded in a society undergoing rapid modernization. As a marker of social status and a mode of behavior, honor was a critical component of Germany's highly rationalized bureaucracy. I analyze the status anxieties and forms of institutional self-disciplining that manifested themselves among officials and would-be officials around clashing honor claims and defamation litigation. In the economic realm, honor was both crucial to business relations and, as a result of the defamation litigation it spawned, a disruption of the free flow of information necessary to market capitalism. Labor relations were likewise stamped by such litigation, the battles of labor and management, employee and employer, often playing out in the courtroom in a language of reputation, insult, and honor. Among professionals – doctors, lawyers, journalists, and the like – the idiom of honor, institutionalized in the honor courts and codes of conduct of newly formed professional organizations, accompanied and under-girded the modernization of academic and professional expertise. Gender roles were defined around competing conceptions of male and female honor. And, while the latter, defined in terms of sexual chastity, was historically bound up with preserving women's inferior status, I show the remarkable ways in which women also appropriated notions of female honor to unmask and punish sexual harassers and rapists – in one case with tragic results for the woman herself. The chapter ends with the day-to-day mechanics of politics. Defamation litigation, I show, not only pervaded electoral campaigning and parliamentary practices; it formed a distinct method of doing politics.

The Kaiserreich's authoritarian political system, established under its architect, the conservative first chancellor of Germany, Otto von Bismarck, at the time of German unification in 1871, granted universal manhood suffrage in the lower house of the national parliament (Reichstag). But it was intentionally constructed to limit democracy and the power of the Reichstag in the interests of conservative forces within the Prussian bureaucracy, military, and landed elite – a regime headed by the Kaiser and his ministers with only minimal oversight of the Reichstag. This system, which had bought off many erstwhile liberal critics with the promise of national unification, was riven by political and social tensions associated with nation-building (religious divisions between Protestants and Catholics; political divisions between the federal states and the Prussian-dominated central government) as well as the rapid modernization of the German economy. The system became increasingly unstable with the growth in particular of a militant labor movement and Socialist political party (Social Democratic Party – SPD), whose Marxist rhetoric and social-democratic demands were anathema to the propertied classes and the powers that be.[40] Government attempts to stem the Socialist tide

---

[40] For a classic structuralist account of this history, see Hans-Ulrich Wehler, *The German Empire, 1871–1918*, trans. by Kim Traynor (Providence, RI, 1985).

and democratic reform – most famously with the repressive anti-
socialist laws of 1878–1890, the granting of social insurance to workers in the 1880s, and the *Sammlungspolitik* of a defensive alliance of
capitalists and landowners[41] – formed one of the most important
political dynamics of the era. The war against social democracy (by
1912, the SPD had become the largest political party in the Reichstag)
was complicated by the shift in these years from an elitist form of
notable politics in the 1860s and 1870s to mass democracy after 1880,
a phenomenon reflected not only in the SPD on the Left, but in the
rising influence of extra-parliamentary interest groups, many repre-
senting a new rightist populism of nationalism, xenophobia, and
antisemitism.

These elements form the political context of the state's repressive
libel policies (chapter 3) and the intense politicization of libel jurisprudence under the Kaiserreich (chapter 4). Chapter 3 – on the
policies, debates, and practices of the government, the bureaucracy,
and the courts – examines the libel suit as a form of state rule. It
emphasizes the extent to which an idiom of state honor underpinned
the authoritarian practices of the government and the lengths to
which it and the courts went in repressing allegedly libelous speech
by government opponents. This was most prominently the case in a
massive campaign of censorship – via the defamation lawsuit – of the
Socialist press. But repression in the interests of state honor went
much further, pervading the daily life of citizens, as officials at all
levels enforced their rights, as representatives of the state, to respect
and obedience (*Beamtenbeleidigung*). Large areas of speech, including
not only the press but citizen petitions, letters of complaint, and
speeches at public meetings, were subject to this logic of state authority. The chapter begins at the top, with the policies of Bismarck and
his successors, and with the Prussian Ministry of State strategizing
about ways to deal with the problem of public libels against the state.
From there, it moves out to the world of lower officialdom and
clashes between citizens and state in daily life. The chapter ends

---

[41] Geoff Eley, *Reshaping the German Right: Radical Nationalism and Political Change
after Bismarck* (Ann Arbor, 1980), p. 4.

with a consideration of the courts, particularly the very narrow interpretation by the Reichsgericht (Supreme Court) of "legitimate interest" in a clause of the defamation laws (§193) that would otherwise have protected the oppositional press from prosecution. The courts, as I show, played a critical role in legitimizing state repression, but they were at the same time split from within over libel law and free speech rights.

Chapter 4 focuses on the great political controversies attending libel law and state prosecutorial practices. The debates – from the seemingly technical and abstruse (e.g. interpretations of "legitimate interest" in the penal code) to the special honor status of state officials (*Beamtenbeleidigung*) and a revised lèse-majesté bill – constituted important (and hitherto unexamined) forums in which battles over free speech, civil rights, and state power took place. In the press and the parliaments, the debates pitted roughly two very different conceptions of honor: one traditional, corporate, and hierarchical; the other, most radically and forcefully articulated by Socialists, egalitarian and democratic. This division corresponded with broadly different conceptions of civil society and the state. Thus, the debates, whose intensity drew from the high political stakes involved and the way they intersected with popular culture, divided the political class and the public along ideological lines that in part mirrored and reinforced the broader rifts in German society. Certain high profile defamation trials that stamped German public life, most notably the Eulenburg Affair, formed the backdrop to these events and the shifting political dynamics analyzed in the closing section of the chapter.

Part of the expansion and transformation of libel litigation in the nineteenth century was the seizure of a juridical honor idiom by outsider and disempowered groups. This went back at least to the early nineteenth century in individual cases. But by the later decades of the century, injured honor was being mobilized in grassroots movements, two of which are explored in chapter 5: those of Jews and lunatics. Here, I discuss the rise in the 1890s among Jews and lunatics of a bourgeois politics from "below" that appropriated and modernized an old corporate language of honor in order to make democratic claims for the rights of citizenship. The multiple responses of Jews to the rise of political antisemitism, from conversion and assimilation to Zionism, have been explored at length in the scholarship. Less understood is the role of honor in the politics of Jewish emancipation, which, I argue, formed a cultural lens or framework through which Jews experienced and sought to resist antisemitism in their daily lives and in contests with political antisemites. I follow this history in the defamation cases of individual Jews and in the literature and practices of Germany's first organized Jewish defense league.

The second part of the chapter charts the contemporaneous rise of "lunatic's rights" (*Irrenrechtsreform*), a movement spearheaded by the "mad" themselves, whose horror stories of wrongful incarcerations and legal incapacitations became the subject of widespread media coverage, parliamentary debate, and an organized pressure group. Lunatics' rights, a species of bourgeois populism, built a protest movement around merging questions of honor, law, and the asylum issue, with a new style of grassroots politics that extended the democratic functions of the public square. They did this, I show, through adopting the tools of political organizing; just as importantly – and perhaps more interesting for social and cultural history – was their use of the self-revelatory pamphlet, which, in the interests of defending and recovering an individual's reputation and honor, commodified private experience and ended up politicizing madness.

The conclusion briefly takes the story past the Kaiserreich through the Weimar Republic, the Third Reich, and into the present. It is a story of both transformation and tremendous continuity – despite political upheaval and reform, across the regime changes of the twentieth century – in Germany's litigious honor culture. The conclusion ends with a return to the historiography and the broader question of tradition and continuity in German history.

CHAPTER I

The development of the law

German modernization, far from loosening the hold of a culture of honor, strengthened and expanded it. The law itself was crucial in this respect. In the course of the nineteenth century, German law was liberalized as it moved from an adjudication system based on estate (*Stand*) to one of formal equality and civil rights. Defamation law followed suit and was reconstituted along more democratic lines. But this transformation, rather than undermining the old values of honor, provided them with a new lease on life. The result, by the Kaiserreich, was a hybrid legal culture that merged key liberal legal principles – the *Rechtsstaat*, legal equality, civil rights – with a jurisprudence that assumed and protected the social hierarchies and status differences embedded in the concept of honor. In so doing, it provided the institutional basis for the vast expansion of defamation lawsuits, as the conflicts of modern society came to play themselves out in honor disputes. Legal developments in Prussia were key here, since it was Prussia's criminal code that formed the basis for the statutory laws regulating defamation after German unification in 1871. Two critical developments determined the shape of the Kaiserreich's defamation laws: (1) the end of a jurisprudence based on legally unequal estates; (2) the liberal rediscovery of the *Privatklage*, which was part of the broader fight against an arbitrary, politicized justice system – a cause that profoundly stamped mid-century liberalism.

Medieval and early-modern justice looked very different from what it would become in the nineteenth century. The state did not monopolize all judicial functions; litigants were subject to different legal jurisdictions depending upon their corporate estate, and many legal functions were privately administered in patrimonial courts by lords of the manor (*Gutsherren*).[1] Under the inquisitorial court system, many of whose features lasted into the nineteenth century, criminal trials were secret and written, employed torture, and presided over by jurists who combined the functions of both prosecutor and judge. Lacking all transparency, such trials did not grant defendants the ability to confront their accusers or see the evidence against them. Judges lacked political and administrative independence, being subject to arbitrary dismissal or their verdicts being overruled by monarchs and other heads of government.

The notion of legal equality was foreign to this society, organized as it was by estate, a legal classification based on a person's birth or profession. Honor litigants, accordingly, received differential justice — the type of court, level of punishment, and even the cost of litigation — based on their corporate status.[2] Under Prussia's law code, the Allgemeines Landrecht (1794), modified by a December 30, 1798 circular, all cases of minor insult were heard before a civil magistrate, but plaintiffs of birth and position (the upper echelon of commoners or *höher Bürgerstand*, the aristocracy, and military officers), were given the option of an appeal in the regular courts with a court-appointed *fiskalischer Bedienter*[3] (a kind of proto-state prosecutor) and a thorough judicial investigation of their cases.[4]

There could be no clearer message that the honor of the privileged was more valuable than that of their social inferiors. The message was

---

[1] W. Sellert, "Standesgerichtsbarkeit," in Adalbert Erler et al. (eds.), *Handwörterbuch zur deutschen Rechtsgeschichte* vol. 4 (Berlin, 1990), pp. 1916–17.

[2] Berlin Kammergericht to King, May 27, 1799, I. HA Rep. 84a, Nr. 49524, GStPK, pp. 1a–1f, and passim (pp. 16–22).

[3] The *Fiskalat*, which lay outside of but intertwined with the regular court system, was a kind of nascent state attorney, whose job it was to represent the state in court cases affecting the state treasury ("soweit das Vermögensinteresse des Fiskus bei Geldstrafen und Vermögenseinziehungen in Betracht kam."): Conrad Bornhak, *Preussische Staats- und Rechtsgeschichte* (Berlin, 1979), pp. 186–87.

[4] I HA Rep. 84a Nr. 49524, GStPK p. 4ff; Evers, "Erörterungen über den preussischen Injurien-Prozess," *Archiv für preussisches Strafrecht* 8 (1860), 609–17.

reinforced by the disparate sentences meted out by estate. Legal redress for insult came in two forms: the *Privatgenugtuung*, a formal ritualized apology, retraction, and/or declaration of respect (*Abbitte*, *Widerruf*, and *Ehrenerklärung*); and the public punishment for violation of state laws. In the latter case, "minor insults" among people of the same estate or between parties belonging to the "peasant or the lower commoner estates," for example, brought sentences of the workhouse or prison of between 24 hours and 3 days. The same offense among people of the higher third estate (*Bürgerstand*) and aristocracy, and military officers brought, respectively, jail time of 8–14 days and 2–4 weeks.[5] The *Privatgenugtuung* differed as well by estate.[6] When, for example, the violator belonged to a higher estate than the injured party, the former was allowed to perform the *Ehrenerklärung* in writing rather than in person before witnesses and a judge. Those found guilty of insulting their direct superiors (e.g. children their parents; pupils their teachers; servants their masters) were required to perform the *Abbitte* kneeling in court.[7] Perversely, in this system, court costs were set in inverse proportion to a plaintiff's ability to pay. When plaintiffs from the privileged orders (upper *Bürgerstand*, the aristocracy, and the military) lost their cases, the costs were paid out of a state fund (*Kriminal Fond*). Plaintiffs from the lower orders, by contrast, paid out of their own pockets; this applied even when the plaintiff won his or her lawsuit, if the convicted defendant lacked the means to pay.[8]

By the early nineteenth century, meanwhile, the Prussian government was busy enacting a series of laws and regulations intended to shield the military and bureaucracy from popular lawsuits by progressively undermining the jurisdiction of the regular courts. An 1808 decree, for example, required the courts to petition the

---

[5] ALR, II Theil, 20. Titel, §607–609.

[6] Friction surrounding the *Privatgenugtuung* requirement was often itself the cause of further defamation litigation; it was abolished in 1811. I. HA Rep. 84a, Nr. 49524, GStPK, p. 76.

[7] ALR, II. Theil, 20. Titel, §584ff.

[8] Oberlandesgerichtspräsident Lent, March 6, 1842. I. HA Rep. 84a, Nr. 49528, GStPK.

government in advance before filing charges against a public official accused of wrongdoing, and, in cases of insult lawsuits against officials, required the courts to inform the government beforehand. An 1835 law went further, preventing insult complaints against officials from being brought directly to the courts; they were required to be lodged beforehand with the official's superiors who would determine whether or not an offense had occurred and thus whether the lawsuit could proceed. This trend was strengthened by the *Disziplinargesetz* of 1844 and the creation in 1847 of a *Kompetenz-Gerichtshof* to decide matters of jurisdiction between the administrative and the regular courts.[9]

Unequal, secretive, and politically repressive, this judicial system was helping to fuel the discontent that broke out in revolution in 1848. It also drove liberal attempts to reform defamation law in the decades leading up to the Reich legal statutes of the 1870s. Liberal outrage drew from abundant firsthand experience. Two causes célèbres at mid-century indicate what reformers faced in these years. In the 1840s, the liberal leader Johann Jacoby was charged with treason and lèse-majesté (*Majestätsbeleidigung*) for his famous pamphlet *Vier Fragen* (1841) that had the audacity to call for a constitutional state in Prussia.[10] In the 1860s, the parliamentary deputy Karl Twesten, a champion of judicial and constitutional reform, was tried and convicted of calumny for a speech he gave on the floor of the Prussian parliament in which he condemned at length the "systematic corruption" of the courts, by which he meant their lack of impartiality and their use as a tool for persecuting government critics. Twesten's was a particularly egregious case, still cited decades later, because his prosecution violated the supposed legal immunity of statements made by politicians in parliament.[11]

---

[9] *Stenographische Berichte über die Verhandlungen des Preussischen Hauses der Abgeordneten* (SBPA) (Berlin, 1861), p. 901.

[10] He was eventually acquitted. The pamphlet and other documents in the case can be found in Johann Jacoby, *Gesammelte Schriften und Reden* (Hamburg, 1872).

[11] Veronika Renner, "Karl Twesten, Vorkämpfer der liberalen Rechtsstaatsidee" (PhD thesis, University of Freiburg, 1954), pp. 150ff.

Before 1848, legal reform had very limited success. To be sure, torture had been abolished.[12] In defamation law, the absolutist state's rationalization of the courts had incrementally expanded equality by lowering and equalizing penalties, for example, for all "minor defamations among people of the same estate."[13] A 1911 decree ended the humiliating and much-hated *Privatgenugtuung*.[14] But overall, these changes had done little to ameliorate the system's fundamental problems.

Then came 1848/49, an event that swept away the old legal order, bringing with it legal equality; the end of patrimonial jurisdiction; the introduction of direct, public, oral, and jury trials;[15] and measures to end the special legal protections of state officials.[16] Another extremely important development were reforms to create an independent judiciary through the separation of judicial and prosecutorial functions, as well as the creation of a public state attorney's office (*Staatsanwaltschaft*) modeled after the French Criminal Code of 1808.[17] Legal equality, in turn, forced on the Prussian regime, which was otherwise doing its best to crush the revolution, the democratization of defamation law. On December 18, 1848, just weeks after Prussian troops occupied Berlin, forcing the breakup of

[12] This development did not affect defamation litigation. On, more generally, the centralization and rationalization of the legal systems of the absolutist German states, see Erich Döhring, *Geschichte der deutschen Rechtspflege seit 1500* (Berlin, 1953). On Prussia's patrimonial courts, see Monika Wienfort, *Patrimonialgerichte in Preussen* (Göttingen, 2001).

[13] The punishment was set at 2–6 hour jail time. Decree of December 30, 1798, Section 4, §17. Carl Ludwig Heinrich Rabe (ed.), *Sammlung preussischer Gesetze und Verordnungen* vol. 5 (Halle and Berlin, 1817), p. 269.

[14] Laws of 1798 and 1811, respectively.

[15] Wienfort, *Patrimonialgerichte*, pp. 322ff. The key royal decree for reforming trial procedure and introducing a state prosecutor's office was that of January 3, 1849.

[16] This included the declaration that "no prior authorization from the government is necessary" for bringing lawsuits against the civil and military authorities: Article 95 of the Constitution of December 5, 1848.

[17] In Prussia, these reforms were instituted in two stages in 1846 and 1849. In southwestern Germany – the Rhineland (1810), Baden (1832), and Württemberg (1843) – they had occurred before the revolution. M. Frommel, "Staatsanwaltschaft," in Erler, *Handwörterbuch zur deutschen Rechtsgeschichte* vol. 4 (Berlin, 1990), pp. 1809–10.

the new parliament, the king issued a decree that took a big step toward granting equality in insult proceedings.[18] Henceforth, these actions (excepting those against state officials and those involving grievous physical harm), irrespective of the litigants' social class, were to be heard before a civil magistrate. Punishments were likewise equalized.[19]

Most of the reforms of the revolutionary period remained in Prussia's revised 1851 legal code. Yet, the law was still far from fully liberalized, and the defeat and conservative backlash against the revolution brought with it the reassertion with a vengeance of the old order, in the form of a reactionary 1854 law that gave the authorities a tool to block or complicate lawsuits against military and administrative officials.[20] Libel offenses against state officials, moreover, continued to be treated in the 1851 code as separate crimes meriting much more severe punishments than libels against private citizens.[21]

It was in the repressive political environment of the 1850s that liberals began to critically reassess an institution that had once looked so promising, indeed for which they had passionately and successfully advocated as a way of checking the arbitrary influence over the courts of politics and the state: the public prosecutor's office. Far from creating judicial fairness, the *Staatsanwaltschaft* was proving to be eminently corruptible: many of its prosecutions were discriminatory and highly selective, based on political and other extra-legal considerations. By the early 1860s, momentum was thus building in legal and political circles for reforming the

---

[18] I. HA Rep. 84a, Nr. 49528, GStPK, pp. 161ff.

[19] They were set at a maximum of 300 Thaler or 6 months' detention.

[20] The law gave the official's superiors or the central government an authorization *Konflikte zu erheben*, which then forced a special judicial hearing of the merits of the case: "Bericht der Kommission über den Gesetz-Entwurf, betreffend die gerichtliche Verfolgung von Beamten ...," *SBPA, Anlagen* 6 (Berlin, 1861), pp. 959–61.

[21] Defaming an official, a member of a political body, a "religious servant" or a member of the military got a defendant one week's to one year's incarceration. The same offense against a private citizen was punishable with a maximum fine of 300 Thaler or incarceration up to six months: *Das preussische Straf-Gesetzbuch nebst dem Einführungs-Gesetz* (Berlin, 1851), pp. 78, 101.

Staatsanwaltschaft by ending its monopoly over prosecutions. In searching for a way at once to check its power but not dismantle its progressive aspects, reformers seized on a device with a long-standing tradition in Germany: the *Privatklage*.[22] The *Privatklage* was poised in the next few years to become a crusade of liberal legal reformers.

The norm for centuries in ancient Germanic law, *Privatklage* trials, initiated by the accuser him-/herself, were originally "confrontational, oral, and public" events in which "adversaries [we]re brought face to face in a contest" resembling a duel.[23] The development of the state in the late Middle Ages gradually began to replace this procedure with the inquisitorial trial, but the tradition was far from lost.[24] By the nineteenth century, the *Privatklage*, in which plaintiffs brought and tried their own lawsuits before a magistrate, had migrated to the area of the law dealing with minor civil offenses, in particular insult and bodily harm.[25] This was the case in Prussia's 1851 Criminal Code, which incorporated the *Privatklage* for those two

---

[22] Another model for liberal reform of the *Staatsanwaltschaft* came from British law, which had retained an accusatory trial system. A. Esmein, *A History of Continental Criminal Procedure* (Boston, 1913), pp. 571, 580, 588–90. For British defamation law in comparative perspective, see Carl Kade, *Die Privatklage in den Strafprozessordnungen der Jetztzeit* (Berlin, 1900).

[23] Esmein, *History of Continental Criminal Procedure*, p. 6; Rainer Schröder, *Rechtsgeschichte* (Münster, 2004), p. 7. Roman law also had a form of *Privatklage* for civil trials, about which there is scholarly disagreement over whether it was the ancestor of the modern German *Privatklage*.

[24] G. Buchda, "Anklage," *Handwörterbuch zur deutschen Rechtsgeschichte* vol. I, pp. 171–74.

[25] For example, Baden (GBG, March 6, 1845, p. 71f.); Württemberg (StPO, April 17, 1868, section 413); Braunschweig (law of August 22, 1849, sections 2, 2a); Oldenburg (law of Nov. 2, 1857, section 446); Frankfurt (law of May 15, 1856, section 48); Saxony's *Privatklage* provisions were the most extensive (StPO, August 11, 1855), cited in Heinrich Gerland, "Die systematische Stellung des Privatklageverfahrens im Strafprocess," *Der Gerichtssaal* 60 (1902); *Motive, Anlage IV*, in C. Hahn (ed.), *Die gesammten Materialien zur Strafprozessordnung* vol. I (Berlin, 1880), pp. 431ff; pp. 182ff. On the development of defamation law in the German states, see also: Helmut Rannacher, *Der Ehrenschutz in der Geschichte des deutschen Strafrechts* (Breslau-Neukirch, 1938); C. Reinhold Köstlin, *Abhandlungen aus dem Strafrechte* (Tübingen, 1858).

offenses because of their "everydayness" and their triviality as purely personal offenses deemed lacking relevancy to the public interest.[26]

Although not a source of controversy in 1851, the *Privatklage* would become so just a decade later when liberal jurists spearheaded a movement to massively expand that institution in order to limit state power. Criticism of the state's prosecutorial monopoly in the public prosecutor's office, mounting in the 1850s, came to a head at the first two all-German conferences of lawyers and jurists (Juristentag) in 1860 and 1861. The meetings saw extensive debate and an affirmative vote on a resolution supporting, with a very extensive *Privatklage* right, the end of the state's prosecutorial monopoly. This resolution, although entirely unbinding on governments,[27] reverberated in legal and political circles,[28] making an immediate appearance in legislative discussions within the Prussian Landtag in 1861, and leaving its imprint on subsequent statutory law – on Prussia's 1867 Criminal Code, which increased the kinds of offenses that could be tried as *Privatklage*, and, most importantly, on the 1877 Reich Code of Criminal Procedure.[29]

From the beginning, the drive for an expanded *Privatklage* right was tied in reformers' minds to the goals of ending abuses of state power and promoting civil rights. At the first Juristentag in 1860, Lewald, the Berlin lawyer who introduced the *Privatklage* resolution, gave a speech about the "*Privatanklage* question" as a right of citizenship, equivalent to the burning matters of "censorship and press freedom."[30] His proposal, based on the work of the legal scholar Julius Glaser,[31] was not about eliminating the public prosecutor's ability to pursue an offender "who has harmed another in his honor or liberty," he assured

---

[26] Hahn, *Gesammten Materialien zur Strafprozessordnung* vol. I, pp. 277, 422ff.

[27] The aim of the conference participants was to set out general legal principles, which members would then seek to implement in the different German states.

[28] For example, the 1861 debates of the Prussian Diet.

[29] This law of February 1, 1877 went into effect in October, 1879.

[30] *Verhandlungen des ersten deutschen Juristentages*, p. 147.

[31] Glaser was a Viennese professor and author, among many other works, of "Das Princip der Strafverfolgung" in his *Gesammelte kleinere Schriften über das Strafrecht* (Vienna, 1868), pp. 429–67. Glaser was, according to Rüdiger Koewius, *Die Rechtswirklichkeit der Privatklage* (Berlin, 1974), p. 22, the intellectual "originator" of the subsidiary *Privatklage*.

his colleagues in the audience. Rather, this was about giving "every harmed individual the ability to protect himself" within a modern *Rechtsstaat*. No one, argued another *Privatklage* advocate, wanted to go back to the days before a public prosecutor, let alone revive the ancient *Privatklage* when the harmed individual alone was responsible for pursuing the prosecution of an offense.[32] Such a direct ("principal") *Privatklage* right should only be allowed for a very limited number of offenses – namely, insult and *Körperverletzung* – "where the overwhelming interest is not that of the *Gesammtheit* [the community as a whole], but directly [and alone] that of the harmed individual."[33]

There was in fact wide consensus, both at the conference and in the society at large, that such offenses (insult and minor bodily harm), precisely because of their ubiquity and their personal nature, were best left to the responsibility of the injured party to pursue directly as a *Privatklage*. Indeed, this "principal" *Privatklage* right, in which the harmed individual, without any involvement of a state prosecutor, presented his/her case in court, already existed, as noted, within civil law in Prussia, as well as in many other German states. The aspect of the Juristentag's resolution, on the other hand, that would prove controversial in subsequent years, was its call for a very broad "subsidiary" *Privatklage* right. Here, the ability of the harmed individual to pursue justice would only kick in if and when the district attorney declined to take up his or her case. The person would then have the right to a court hearing, and if the court agreed with the merits of the case, the accuser could proceed in pressing charges with the use of a court-appointed lawyer functioning as an *ersatz* state prosecutor. Although less immediate and direct than the principal *Privatklage*, the subsidiary *Privatklage* was potentially much more radical because, according to the resolution adopted by the Juristentag, it would be allowed in all civil and criminal cases.[34] As such, the

---

[32] Speech by Schwarze at the second meeting, *Verhandlungen des zweiten deutschen Juristentages*, pp. 660–61.

[33] Ibid., p. 661.

[34] *Verhandlungen des ersten deutschen Juristentages* (Berlin, 1860), p. 71 provides Lewald's original proposal, which was debated at length and partially amended. See, also, *Verhandlungen des zweiten deutschen Juristentages*, p. 363 and passim.

subsidiary *Privatklage* right would, as envisioned, function as a kind of watchdog or *Überwachung* of the district attorney's office.[35]

Almost immediately following the Juristentag resolution, the *Privatklage* issue moved into the legislative realm, surfacing in the Prussian lower house of parliament (Abgeordnetenhaus) within the context of liberal attempts to impose controls on arbitrary state power. What was most on the minds of left liberals were the recent laws (above) protecting officials from citizen lawsuits. These laws more than anything drove sentiment in the 1850s and early 1860s for the *Privatklage* right and the view that the state's prosecutorial monopoly was not serving justice. As liberal deputies in the Prussian parliament debated dissolving the 1854 law and the special legal protections of officials, they began calling for even more radical measures. Invoking the Juristentag's resolution, they demanded the empowerment of citizens with a subsidary *Privatklage* right for all misdemeanor and criminal offenses.[36] Freiherr von Vincke opined that any progress through abolishing the 1854 law would prove "illusory" without the simultaneous end to the state's prosecutorial monopoly: offical misconduct could still evade justice, since the Justice Ministry would retain the right to direct district attorneys not to proceed with indictments of certain officials. He cited the case of a Berlin police chief, a request for whose prosecution had been sent to the Minister of Interior by the governing police authority, but was never acted upon by the district attorney.[37]

Yielding to such sentiment, the Prussian government was forced in 1862 to bring before the parliament a draft resolution for a *Privatklage* law, one, however, that fell far short of liberal demands. Vincke, Waldeck, and other left liberals did succeed at this time in ending the 1854 law, but were unable to prevail with their version of the *Privatklage*. Prussia's 1867 Criminal Code, which was extended to all of Germany in 1872, expanded the *Privatklage* for minor offenses, but did no more.[38] In the mid-1870s, thus, the *Privatklage*

---

[35] Koewius, *Rechtswirklichkeit*, p. 22.   [36] Ibid., p. 962.
[37] *SBPA* (1861), pp 904–05.
[38] S. Mayer, *Zur Reform des Strafprozesses* (Frankfurt a.M., 1871), pp. 1–2; Hahn, *Materialien*, p. 424ff.

issue resurfaced in Reichstag legislative debates during the drafting of a unified Imperial Code of Criminal Procedure (StPO).

The concerns driving reformers had shifted in the dramatically altered political landscape of the 1870s. To be sure, they continued to call for an extensive (subsidiary) *Privatklage* right to counter arbitrary state power. But now what was foremost in their minds was Bismarck's ruthless persecution of dissident (or perceived enemy) political and religious organizations, most notably, the *Kulturkampf* against the Catholic Church and the repression of a rapidly growing socialist and labor movement. Arguments for the subsidiary *Privatklage* thus now revolved around the need for legal protections of whole groups and political parties, not merely of individuals. Left liberal Friedrich Arthur Eysoldt, from the Progressive Party, argued for putting into the hands of citizens and organizations a legal tool (the *Privatklage*) to mitigate the "unequal treatment of parties in politically agitated times," a situation in which "police measures are applied against one association but not against another that has the favor of the government."[39] Windthorst, leader of the Catholic Center Party, wondered if, under the proposed *Privatklage* provisions of the StPO, individual members of a "corporation" would have the right to sue when they believed themselves to be "encumbered" (*beschwert*) by actions taken against a corporation to which they belonged, say, in the case of the "slandering of a religious society" (a reference to the abuse being heaped on Catholics during the ongoing *Kulturkampf*).[40] Von Schwarze, whose advocacy of the *Privatklage* went back fifteen years to his work on the Juristentag resolution,[41] did not know the answer, but he was sure that "if an association is shut down, every member would be considered the harmed party" and allowed to take legal action.[42]

---

[39] "... der der Regierung bequem ist." *SBR*, vol. 47, December 21, 1876, p. 983.
[40] Ibid., p. 982. This was a paraphrase of Windthorst's thoughts by deputy von Schwarze.
[41] He was an active participant and advocate of a broad *Privatklage* right in the conferences' discussions. See, *Verhandlungen des zweiten deutschen Juristentages* (Berlin, 1861), pp. 657ff. He continued to fight for this in the mid-1870s as Reichstag deputy and *Berichterstatter* of the Reichstag committee preparing draft legislation for the new StPO.
[42] Ibid.

This was the majority sentiment of the justice committee drafting the legislation, and, as a result, the Reichstag's initial draft proposals included provisions affording an extensive subsidiary *Privatklage* right, one moreover that broadly defined the harmed party to allow for the kinds of group lawsuits made urgent by the aforementioned political developments and debates.[43] Liberals were to be disappointed. Their version of the *Privatklage*, originating in the 1861 *Juristentag* resolution, never became law, being rejected by the government as an unacceptable incursion by private citizens into the jurisdiction of the state attorney's office.[44] But liberals did succeed on one fateful front, putting into the hands of private citizens an extraordinary legal tool. For by the time of the final passage of the 1877 StPO, defamation, including simple insult (as well as minor bodily injury), had become criminal offenses to be pursued by private citizens wielding the principal *Privatklage* right.[45]

The possibility of the Reich criminalizing insult law was greeted with jubilation by the *Magdeburgische Zeitung*, a voice of the educated liberal middle class. When, in 1876, von Schwarze, as *Berichterstatter* of the Reichtag's Justice Committee, proposed this move, the newspaper enthusiastically endorsed it.[46] In its article, one finds articulated at length the hybrid legal culture – a mixture of democracy and corporatism – that was both cause and product of the historical forces shaping Germany's honor culture and laws. There were, in the article's analysis, two troubling inequities in present defamation law. First, with reference to Prussia, was the unequal

---

[43] It gave citizens a substantial subsidiary *Privatklage* in the form of the right of appeal in decisions by state prosecutors to suspend or stay charges. The relevant documents, including the various Reichstag drafts and committee reports, can be found in *SBR*, 2. Legislatur-Periode, IV Session 1876. Vol. 3, Anlagen (Berlin, 1876).

[44] "Bericht der Kommission zur Vorberathung der Entwürfe … einer Strafprozessordnung über den Entwurf einer Strafprozessordnung …," ibid., pp. 382–83.

[45] This move built upon and incorporated into national law the existence already in some German states of a *Privatklage* right in the criminal courts. James Whitman, "Enforcing Civility and Respect: Three Societies," *Yale Law Journal* 109 (2000) 1324, fn.131.

[46] *Magdeburgische Zeitung* 119 (1876).

treatment of defamatory offenses, on the one hand, against state officials which (together with grievous physical defamations) were prosecuted as criminal offenses by the state attorney, and, on the other hand, those against regular citizens and for minor (verbal) defamation offenses. Since the latter were treated as civil offenses, citizens seeking justice for honor damages were at a grave disadvantage because, unlike criminal trials, where the district attorney was able to call the plaintiff as a witness to the crime, civil proceedings did not allow plaintiffs to testify as their own witnesses. Yet verbal insult cases required just that when, as often was the case, at issue were insulting statements exchanged between two people without the witness of a third party. This made it all the more galling that decisions about whether a citizen's dishonor qualified as "grievous" (criminal) or "minor" (civil) were left to the whims of the public prosecutor's office. Moreover (secondly), insult had very different ramifications for the citizen depending upon his "level of education":

the educated, sensitive [*feinfühlende*] person feels just as deeply insulted by a stray remark as does an uncouth, uneducated person by a grievous, violent insult.[47]

And, it added, the resulting feeling of "lack of rights" (*Rechtlosigkeit*) on the part of the sensitive, who often lacked the ability to achieve satisfaction (*Genugtuung*) through the civil courts, was forcing them to resort to self-help (*Selbsthilfe*, i.e. dueling), as well as personal acts of revenge. The article's position, in other words, thought in the language of "rights" and "equality" while calling for honor laws to, in effect, police the boundaries of the social hierarchy and the refined sensibilities of the privileged. Such sentiment, which was helping to drive forward the liberalization of defamation law, suggests how that process occurred not despite (outdated) honor notions, but *because* of them and the need, therefore, to modernize institutions to expand access to new groups (i.e. the middle classes) claiming that honor.

[47] Ibid.

As it turned out, the final version of the StPO, while failing to achieve the newspaper's desire for a vast expansion of state prosecutions of defamation, did end by criminalizing insult law, turning the *Privatklage* for insult and bodily injury offenses into matters linked to the criminal courts.[48] The Kaiserreich's defamation laws thus managed to preserve and extend traditional honor notions within the modern constitutional state (*Rechtsstaat*). It was possible to file a civil defamation suit, but, unlike in Britain, individuals rarely used this option because there was no possibility of receiving a monetary award to make the effort worthwhile.[49] Indeed, "hostility to money damages" was later purposefully built into the German Civil Code (coming into effect in 1900).[50]

Honor and punishment, not money, were the point of German insult and defamation lawsuits, a fact made clear in the penalty for public and/or published libels (§200), which required that the convicted libeler publish at his or her expense a notice of the court judgment – an updated form of the *Ehrenerklärung*, whose purpose was the public restoration of the plaintiff's reputation.[51] Indeed, so tainted was monetary pursuit in the honor codes of many members of

---

[48] As for the subsidiary *Privatklage*, the StPO (§§169–175) provided a very weak substitute for what liberals had sought: in cases where the state prosecutor failed to pursue the case of an injured party, that person was given the right to lodge a complaint with the prosecutor's superiors and to appeal in court the latter's decision. For a decent overview of the *Privatklage*, see Glaser, "Privatanklage," *Encyklopädie der Rechtswissenschaft*, 2. Theil, vol. 3 (Leipzig, 1881), pp. 175–85.

[49] Prussian State Ministry report, November 30, 1908. GStPK, Rep. 90a, vol. 157. §823 of the Civil Code (*Bürgerliches Gesetzbuch*, BG). According to a 1913 Reichsgericht ruling, §249 could in certain circumstances provide the plaintiff with the basis for demanding other remedies beyond money in the restitution of his/her honor, namely, an *Ehrenerklärung*. The high court also interpreted the *Unterlassungsklage* [action for an injunction] (§§12, 864, 1004 of the BG) to allow in civil suits the broader ability of the plaintiff to sue for an injunction to stop the defamatory statements of his/her opponent. In depth on this issue: "Der Schutz der Ehre," *Berliner Tageblatt*, April 9, 1914.

[50] Whitman, "Enforcing Civility," p. 1318, who makes much of this point as part of a broader argument about the central and continuing role played by aristocratic honor values.

[51] Only in the 1950s did it become possible for plaintiffs to receive monetary awards in insult cases: ibid., p. 1302.

the middle and upper classes that statements to this effect were themselves considered cause for libel actions.

Those actions were overwhelmingly pursued as criminal offenses under §§94–104 (honor offenses against the Kaiser, princes, and foreign ambassadors and heads of state) and §§185–200 of the Criminal Code (StGB). Simple insult (*Beleidigung*) under §185 was punishable with a fine of up to 600M or incarceration of up to one year; punishments substantially increased when the libel involved physical violence.[52] The majority of actual sentences meted out, however, seemingly involved fairly small fines. Notably, §185 was extremely broad: it did not even attempt to define insult, leaving this difficult task entirely to the courts; nor did it require proof of intention to harm or that the insult be untrue.[53] §§186–187 dealt with the more serious charges of defamation proper: respectively, calumny and calumny with malicious intent, the latter defined as intentionally spreading a false statement that could potentially make a person "scorned" (*verächtlich machen*) in public opinion or harm his/her credit; §187 was punishable with up to two years jail or, when the statement was "public" (i.e. known beyond a limited circle of people) or spread in print, with no less than one month's incarceration. §189 made it a crime to intentionally defame the "memory of a dead person." The Code of Criminal Procedure (StPO), which came into effect in 1879, allowed the *Privatklage* in defamation actions brought under §§185–87 and 189; for bodily harm offenses; and, beginning in 1896, for unfair competition. Corporations, associations, and certain groups were also entitled to bring *Privatklage* lawsuits.

Two other sections of the law played important roles in the story of defamation politics. §193, probably the most politically contested issue of all (chapter 4), formally protected defamatory speech in certain circumstances: scholarly, artistic, and professional critiques for the purpose of "defending rights or legitimate interests";[54] the reprimands against subordinates by their superiors; and, official denunciations of

---

[52] A maximum fine of 1,000M or prison up to two years.
[53] By contrast, §539 of the ALR had required intent.
[54] My emphasis added.

and judgments about state officials where such statements were not libelously phrased. On *Beamtenbeleidigung* (the offense of libeling an official), liberals had won an important victory: its formal abolition. What remained was merely §196, which gave the superiors of a libeled official the right to bring defamation charges in his name. Yet, as we will see, *Beamtenbeleidigung* managed to live on in the practices of the courts and the state attorneys, with controversial effect.

Given the importance of the *Privatklage* in German insult law, it is worthwhile considering this legal feature in comparative context. There were European countries – Austria-Hungary, Denmark, Finland, some Swiss Cantons, Norway, Sweden, Spain, and Russia – that had some version of a *Privatklage* right for a variety of minor offenses, although it is not clear how these laws impacted the practices of honor disputes.[55] The British had in principle a kind of *Privatklage* right, but in practice, by the late nineteenth century, this right was exercised not by private individuals, but by corporations, communities, and associations. Unlike Germany, British defamation law, moreover, was oriented toward civil proceedings and the issue of material harm (as opposed to honor per se). Anglo-American law, unlike its continental European counterparts, distinguished between written (libel) and spoken (slander) defamation. Libel was treated as a criminal felony but cases where the victims were private citizens tended to be prosecuted not as honor insults but as offenses endangering the public peace.[56] Slander, by contrast, was a civil not a criminal offense, and the laws governing it were not directed at protecting an individual's honor so much as his or her professional and financial existence. Hence, convictions in slander cases usually required evidence of material harm (that the plaintiff had been harmed in "his office, profession or employment")[57] – a much higher level of proof than in Germany.

[55] On comparative *Privatklage* laws, see Gerland, *Systematische Stellung des Privatklageverfahrens im Strafproceß* (Stuttgart, 1901), pp. 12–13 and, especially, Carl Kade, *Die Privatklage*.

[56] Lilienthal, "Üble Nachrede und Verleumdung," in Mittermaier et al. (eds.), *Vergleichende Darstellung des deutschen und ausländischen Strafrechts: Besonderer Teil* vol. 4 (Berlin, 1906), p. 440.

[57] Liepmann, "Die Beleidigung," ibid., p. 307.

In France, the Criminal Code of 1808 (and the law codes else-where in Europe, e.g. Italy, modeled after it) provided a private person no right to bring a criminal lawsuit; it granted the injured party only the right to bring a civil lawsuit for monetary damages. On defamation, French law differentiated between defamation proper (*diffamation*) and insult (*injure*). Both were actionable in criminal law if the offending statement was public (widely diffused in print or in a speech). But such suits, unlike in Germany, required the intervention of the state attorney, who, however, was unlikely to take legal action in cases involving private citizens and everyday insults. The only path open for those defamed by non-public insults – i.e., the kinds of disrespectful conduct and cursings that drove seemingly the majority of *Privatklagen* in Germany – was to bring the dispute before a very low-level police court, which treated such offenses as minor infractions, akin to a parking ticket today and punishable by a maximum fine of 5 francs.[58]

Germany's *Privatklage* was an anomalous institution that blended criminal and civil-law features. Cases were brought and tried under criminal law before local magistrates by private-citizen plaintiffs with no involvement of the state attorney. At the same time, following civil law, plaintiffs did not have the right to testify as witnesses on their own behalf. A state prosecutor had the right to take over and litigate a pre-existing *Privatklage* if it deemed the case important to the public interest.[59] In such cases, the original plaintiff could choose to remain as co-plaintiff.[60] In reality, the state almost never intervened in the *Privatklage* of private citizens.[61] They did so, however, on a routine basis when the libeled party was a state official. Finally, there were safeguards built into the system that attempted to prevent

---

[58] Ibid., pp. 279–84.

[59] Karl Binding, *Die Wirkungen des Eintrittes der Staatsanwaltschaft in das Privatklageverfahren* (Leipzig, 1908), pp. 4–5.

[60] The official aims of the co-plaintiffs, however, would be different, the state's being 'punishment', while the *Privatkläger*'s was, via the punishment, "Genugtuung": ibid., p. 11.

[61] It was estimated this happened in one out of 2–3,000 cases: Rudolf Beinert, *Die Ausdehnung der Privatklage* (Halle, 1906), p. 35, fn.2.

citizens from abusing the *Privatklage* right with trivial disputes and personal vendettas. Litigants living in the same city district were required to submit to pretrial mediation before an officially appointed mediator (*Schiedsmann*), one of hundreds of laymen presiding over an extensive system of lay courts established for settling minor daily conflicts.[62] Only when and if mediation failed to produce a resolution could the case proceed to trial;[63] plaintiffs could be required to appear in person in court, they had to pay a hefty deposit to cover initial court costs and were responsible for all of the court costs if they lost the case.

The liberalization of German law re-anchored honor along lines consistent with a modern constitutional state, preserving, indeed strengthening, defamation law in accord with the democratizing tendencies of the era. Honor and defamation had been a part of but not central to the political discussions on legal reform. With the reconstituted *Privatklage*, however, they emerged with a new force in the Reich's legal system, providing citizens with ready access to the criminal courts. The institutions were in place for a vast expansion of honor lawsuits as the conflicts of modern life moved into the courts.

---

[62] These mediation courts were originally established in Prussia in 1827: "Entwurf eines Justiz-Verfassungs-Gesetzes für das deutsche Reich: Reform des Schiedsmanns-Instituts," I. HA Rep. 84a, Nr. 625, GStPK, p. 3.

[63] Pretrial mediation was specifically not required for charges brought under §196, i.e., those related to defamation of a state official.

CHAPTER 2

Honor disputes and everyday life

"It is not only a right but a duty for anyone with claims to a
respectable position in society to defend his honor when it is in any
way attacked or called into question."[1]
"Don't be so sensitive!"[2]

Judges in the Kaiserreich were driven to distraction by the landslide of
defamation suits, most of which were the *Privatklage* of private citizens.
Those with firsthand experience wrote in disgust about their daily
encounters with insult suits that "stem from gossip and revolve around
[legally] invalid issues," most of these being "petty suits" dealing with
"ludicrous tongue lashings ... pettiness ... [and] squabbling without any
deeper meaning."[3] Overburdening the courts, these suits were "poison-
ing" social relations in whole communities:

The worst aspect of defamation suits is ... that they poison the social climate of
small towns more than all other lawsuits. Thus witnesses are hauled in for
whom the whole matter, for personal reasons, is highly embarrassing; thus, old
friendships are destroyed, old long forgotten matters are dug up and hostilities
are provoked which otherwise would never have broken out.[4]

---

[1] Emil Schulze, *Ein militär-ehrengerichtlicher Prozess* (Würzburg, 1879), p. 3. "Es ist
nicht blos ein Recht, sondern eine Pflicht für jeden, der Anspruch darauf macht, in
der Gesellschaft eine geachtete Stellung einzunehmen, seine Ehre zu vertheidigen,
wenn dieselbe von irgend einer Seite angegriffen oder in Frage gestellt wird."
[2] "Die Beleidigungsklage: Nicht so empfindlich!" *Berliner Abendpost*, August 24, 1913.
[3] "Beleidigungsprozesse im Kriege," *Berliner Tageblatt*, February 5, 1915. This was
also the view of Kade, *Privatklage*, who, as member of a Berlin appellate court for
Privatklage cases, had extensive firsthand experience.
[4] "Die Beleidigungsklage," *Berliner Abendpost*, August 24, 1913.

Commentators in the press and the parliaments likewise bemoaned German "sensitivity" (*Empfindlichkeit*), the hypersensitivity to the tiniest slights, and the readiness to turn those feelings into lawsuits: "every swear-word uttered in back courtyards or on the street leads ... to a solemn official proceeding," complained the right-wing writer Richard Nordhausen.[5] They speculated about quarrels intensifying in the modern "struggle for existence,"[6] and commented on the deleterious effects of the era's "nervousness" and of a population wasting away its "energy" (*Energieverschleuderung*) in the courtroom.[7]

Still, the tide of lawsuits kept rising. This was happening, moreover, despite the considerable personal risks and social consequences involved in bringing such a suit. Filing a lawsuit was not cheap, and it was even more expensive to lose. The accuser was required to post in advance a bail (*Sicherheit*) of 10M to cover the initial court costs.[8] There were lawyers' fees, a service which, though not required (and some litigants did without this to save money),[9] was strongly advisable, not only for the expertise, but because only lawyers had access to certain legal documents (*Akteneinsicht*).[10] By the eve of World War One, lawyers were charging 50–100M in such cases.[11] If, furthermore, one lost the case, one faced the punishment of a fine or jail time, as well as paying for the very steep court costs (including the legal fees of the defendant),[12] which could amount to five times the penalty fine.[13] On top of all of this, one faced numerous hassles: filing the court papers,

---

[5] "Die Beleidigungsklage," *Der Tag*, February 19, 1914.   [6] Ibid.

[7] "Energieverschleuderung," *Berliner Morgenpost*, February 28, 1914. This was a term used in a Reichstag speech by Eugen Schiffer; its affinity with Monism struck the author of the article.

[8] Carl Kade, *Die Privatklage in den Strafprozessordnungen der Jetztzeit* (Berlin, 1900), p. 14.

[9] "Beleidigungsprozesse im Kriege," *Berliner Tageblatt*, February 5, 1915.

[10] Julius Glaser, "Privatanklage," in Holtzendorff (ed.), *Encyklopädie der Rechtswissenschaft* (Leipzig, 1881), p. 182.

[11] The view of Nordhausen, "Die Beleidigungsklage," *Der Tag*, February 19, 1914.

[12] *Sammlung der Entscheidungen bayerischen Landesgerichten* I (1902), p. 11.

[13] §419 of the StPO. Special provisions applied to the indigent, whose court fees were paid out of Armenfonds, as set out in the Zivilprozessordnung, §§114–127 and §119. *Berliner Zeitung*, June 24, 1885.

the time and income lost from work to appear at a mediation hearing, and subsequently, if the case failed to be settled, at court. Even so, there was always the distinct possibility that the accused simply failed to show up at scheduled hearings, which could force indefinite postponements. Or, not uncommonly, countersuits.

Defamation suits were increasing because of people like Cologne Generalsekretär "St." In 1910, St. wrote to the *Kölner Tagesblatt* to complain about the outrageous obstacles a "good citizen" like himself faced in trying to redeem his honor through the courts. In the process of telling his story, he revealed to posterity not only his legal difficulties, but the extraordinary mindset of a man who turned a tiny slight into a months-long legal crusade. It all began in February, 1910, when St., arriving home from a business trip, found a letter waiting for him from the baker "H.," a renter in St.'s house, whose wife had been a maid there.[14] The letter contained an unspecified "insulting expression." St. demanded a written apology, and when this was not forthcoming, he took what in his culture was the next obvious step: he went to the law, applying for a mediation hearing (*Sühnetermin*) with the local mediator (*Schiedsmann*). Striking is not only St.'s willingness to take this step, given the circumstances, but his dogged persistence. Three times the hearing was scheduled, and three times H. failed to show up.[15] Postponements, reschedulings, headaches, and lost time ensued, including an added round of phone calls and complications when H. moved to another *Schiedsmann*'s district. Still St. persisted. The dispute, beginning with an offensive word choice in a private letter, was taking on its own dynamic and snowballing. St. disbelieved an excuse H. gave for cancelling one of the scheduled hearings, so he wrote a letter to a high justice official, the *Landgerichtspräsident*, denouncing H. for "contempt of court." Six months later, the conflict between St. and H., having failed to be settled at the mediation level,

---

[14] The use of initials instead of full names is original to the source: "Wie es um den Rechtschutz des Staatsbürgers als Beleidigten in Preussen und im Reiche steht," *Kölner Tageblatt*, August 20, 1910.

[15] Such cancellations on the part of the defendant were legal and, it seems, a common ploy. Complainants, by contrast, were required to show up at such hearings or forfeit their case, a fact St. bitterly complained about.

had moved into the courts. Once again, H. tried to postpone, arguing a new (and, to St., pathetic) excuse in a pretrial hearing. When the judge sided with H., St. lodged another formal complaint with the *Landgerichtspräsident*, this time against the trial judge himself for "bias toward the defendant and inappropriate stance toward me." St. also requested the judge's replacement, which took him off into a whole new set of legal maneuvers. When his article went to press in August of that year, he was still at it, not having gotten his trial.[16]

Not every insult was litigable. To be sure, the criminal statute on simple insult (*Beleidigung*, §185) was extremely murky and ripe for popular exploitation since it left "insult" entirely undefined. The commentary for an 1877 edition of the Criminal Code did not help much when it defined *Beleidigung* very broadly as "the expression of disdain [*Geringschätzung*] toward another person or official."[17] Yet, legal opinion seems to have been in agreement that a prosecutable insult required in addition, if not actual premeditation, then at least that the insulter was aware of the defamatory nature of his statement and its "unlawfulness."[18] The statutes on libel and calumny, which dealt with insults of a public nature, were clearer about the parameters, requiring that the offending statement make the victim appear "contemptible [*verächtlich*] or degrade" him in public opinion (§186) and to do so with malicious intent (§187). More specifically, according to Karl von Lilienthal, Heidelberg law professor and a leading authority on libel law, a person's honor could be judged debased in public opinion (the person's peer group) by a libel only if the libel had the effect of interfering with the "fulfillment of [his or her] life's work [*Lebensaufgaben*]."[19] Simply calling someone "dumb" was not

[16] H. had failed again to appear in court. St. went on to appeal to the highest judicial authority, the Reich Ministry of Justice.
[17] *Strafgesetzbuch für das deutsche Reich* (Berlin, 1877), p. 370, fn. 1.
[18] Ibid., p. 375, fn. 24ff.
[19] Lilienthal, "Üble Nachrede und Verleumdung," in Mittermaier et al. (eds.), *Vergleichende Darstellung des deutschen und ausländischen Strafrechts: Besonderer Teil* vol. 4 (Berlin, 1906), p. 397. This study was commissioned by the government as part of a multi-volume comparative study of law for the purpose of preparing a new criminal code.

litigable, in other words; it became so only when and if the epithet was taken seriously as true by the victim's peers, thus damaging the insultee's reputation and, in turn, his or her ability, say, to function in professional life. Likewise, in many circumstances, curse words, as in "robber" and "murderer" uttered during an angry interchange, did not qualify as criminal slanders since in this context they were not meant to be taken literally as objectively true.

Given the limited number of surviving trial records, it is impossible to generalize about the extent to which judges actually followed such principles in practice. But there are indications that some did not, applying instead a rather looser definition of insult that failed to consider the subtleties of context and that thus allowed many simple curse-word insults to go forward as litigation. Moreover, judging both by the kinds of petty lawsuits (many about curse words) that the population sought to file and by the views of legal scholars, it is clear that there was a significant gap between popular and learned legal opinion.[20] Still, many of these *Privatklagen* were by definition ruled out of court, irrespective of the judges' inclinations, by the regulation that plaintiffs in *Privatklage* suits were not allowed to testify on their own behalf as witnesses. The result was to substantially limit the volume of private slander cases involving two individuals and no third-party witnesses.

Jurist-critics tended to blame the out-of-control litigiousness on uneducated, lower-class rural and small-town folly. But, as St.'s case suggests, the *Privatklage* was far from confined to the "scoldings of market women."[21] These lawsuits spanned the entire social spectrum. They included even the *satisfaktionsfähig* (those upper- and upper-middle-class men qualified to give satisfaction in a duel). To be sure, these men of the elite, particularly military officers, favored the more manly duel and had a certain contempt for the *Privatklage* precisely because it was available to all classes.[22] Still, elite men were not infrequently plaintiffs in libel litigation. In such cases, one can see the transference into the courtroom of the thinking and practices of the duel.

---

[20] See, e.g., Aschrott and Liszt (eds.), *Die Reform des Reichsstrafgesetzbuchs* (Berlin, 1910), pp. 309ff.
[21] Kade, *Privatklage*, p. 49.   [22] Ibid., p. 50.

A good example comes from the life of Max Weber, whose theoretical writings on honor seem to have been deeply grounded in his own life in imperial Germany. Weber's student-day dueling is well known, but not his libel litigation. In 1911, Weber was enraged by a newspaper story that, quoting an anonymous source, claimed he had refused a duel with a Heidelberg colleague, the philosopher, antisemite, and antifeminist Arnold Ruge, whose honor dispute with Weber had begun with Ruge publicly insulting Weber's wife Marianne, the feminist activist.[23] In Weber's world, to let the duel rumour stand would have been to surrender to the dishonorable charge of cowardice. Weber's face-saving maneuver, however, was not to challenge the anonymous source – whose identity had since surfaced as the Heidelberg historian Adolf Koch – to a duel. Perhaps because of Koch's marginal status (as an *Extraordinarius* he had failed to achieve full-professor status), but more likely because of Weber's distaste at this point in his life for dueling, the latter chose to issue a different sort of honor challenge: he wrote an inflammatorily insulting letter to Koch and sent copies to a newspaper editor and to Koch's department at Heidelberg University. An act intentionally calibrated to force a courtroom confrontation (there was no way Koch could avoid suing for libel and hope to maintain a respectable reputation according to the honor logic of the day), Weber's letter was the legal equivalent of a dueling challenge. At the subsequent trial, Weber pressed his "battle of annihilation"[24] against Koch so hard that the latter, turned into the de facto defendant standing accused of being a libeler and coward, not only lost his trial but, stripped of his ability to teach at the university, was financially and professionally ruined.[25]

---

[23] Joachim Radkau, *Max Weber: die Leidenschaft des Denkens* (Munich, 2005), pp. 633–39. The primary sources, which deserve their own article-length analysis, can be found in "Anhang: Dokumente zu den gerichtlichen Auseinandersetzungen Max Webers 1911–1912," in M. Rainer Lepsius et al. (eds.), *Max Weber Gesamtausgabe* 2 (Tübingen, 1998), pp. 816ff. Many thanks to Guenther Roth for bringing this material to my attention.

[24] Radkau's term (*Max Weber*, p. 633).

[25] Radkau, ibid., p. 638, rightly suggests the presence of latent antisemitism in Weber's pitiless attacks on the already marginal Koch.

Views varied among contemporary commentators on the strategic thinking of plaintiffs in *Privatklage* suits. There were those like the Munich Oberamtsrichter Meikel, for whom "often the issue for the insulted party was less the punishment of the defamer than the restoration of [the former's] honor."[26] Other commentators emphasized the revenge aspect of the *Privatklage*, the purpose of which was to force the insulter to pay a "fitting" cost.[27] Still other commentators made the opposite point: the indifference of many plaintiffs to the insult itself. Such people took legal action only because they felt compelled to by the widespread public belief that "if one doesn't file suit then one admits in a way that the insulter is in the right."[28] Half a century later, the anthropologist Pitt-Rivers articulated this social compulsion in more general terms: "To leave an affront unavenged is to leave one's honour in a state of desecration and this is therefore equivalent to cowardice."[29] One journalist noted that a majority of complainants in the 1910 statistics were between the ages of 30 and 40, an age preoccupied with the "struggle" to establish oneself financially and professionally; in these circumstances, he argued, such a person had no choice but to take legal action against an insult since failure to defend oneself "endangered" both one's honor and one's material existence.[30]

Either way – whether from belief or compulsion, revenge or anxiety over impugned honor – these disputants acted within the parameters of Germany's litigious honor culture, a culture in which personal disputes were regularly fought out in the courts and in which, whatever one's personal feelings, social pressure and the laws themselves dictated the turning of these conflicts into questions of honor. The relationship between honor and the law was one of mutual reinforcement and influence. It was not simply that the

---

[26] "Der Schutz der Ehre," *Berliner Tageblatt*, April 9, 1914.
[27] "Die Beleidigungsklage," *Der Tag*, February 19, 1914.
[28] "Die Beleidigungsklage," *Berliner Abendpost*, August 24, 1913.
[29] Julian Pitt-Rivers, "Honour and Social Status," in J. G. Peristiany (ed.), *Honour and Shame: The Values of Mediterranean Society* (Chicago, 1966), p. 26.
[30] "Die Beleidigungsklage: Nicht so empfindlich!" *Berliner Abendpost*, August 24, 1913.

laws – e.g., the easy access to the *Privatklage* – gave people an accessible legal remedy for insult and violated honor.[31] The laws themselves helped shape the experience of being dishonored, both encouraging and sometimes requiring the transformation of slights and quarrels into legally actionable honor disputes.

That honor language was permeated with the fine gradations of status and class. The adjudication of libel disputes in the courts was always contextualized and individual since, as the legal experts agreed, standards of honor (and hence the kind of respectful treatment a person could legally claim) varied by class, profession, gender, age, and a host of idiosyncratic factors like the litigants' relationship and the circumstances of the insult. There did exist a "universal human honor" (*allgemeine Menschenehre*) that was inherent and inalienable in all people, even in the insane or the convicted felon who, by virtue of his conviction, had lost his civil rights (literally, "honor rights": *Ehrenrechte*) to vote or hold office.[32] Legal and other learned opinion, however, differentiated that universal honor from the social honor, derived from status and the fulfillment of one's social functions and duties, at issue in most defamation proceedings.[33] Thus, judges, according to one expert, were always forced to be mindful of the "individuality and position of the particular honor that has been attacked."[34] Addressing a person with the personal "Du," for example, was libelous only under "certain conditions"[35] (read: only in relation to people in the middle and upper classes). Needless to say, the effect of all of this was to make the libel courts in many cases mechanisms for the reproduction and enforcement of Germany's stratified social order. At the

---

[31] This is the approach taken, for example, by Nancy Shields Kollmann, *By Honor Bound: State and Society in Early Modern Russia* (Cornell, 1999).

[32] Hans Lemme, *Der Verlust der bürgerlichen Ehrenrechte* (Halle, 1910).

[33] A lengthy discussion of the jurisprudential and philosophical issues, together with an extensive bibliography, can be found in Hans Joachim Hirsch, *Ehre und Beleidigung: Grundfragen des strafrechtlichen Ehrenschutzes* (Karlsruhe, 1967).

[34] *Strafgesetzbuch für das deutsche Reich*, p. 370, fn. 1. See also Lilienthal, "Üble Nachrede," p. 396.

[35] Ibid., p. 371, fn. 2.

individual level, of course, this was precisely the point: to reclaim a level of respect consistent with the individual's status and thus re-establish a status quo brought into disequilibrium by the affront.

How, in turn, Germans thought about their honor was, as contemporaries noted, extremely "fluid,"[36] differing by social milieu; it could even change within a single individual depending upon circumstance. Class constituted perhaps the most important social factor determining a person's sense of his/her honor. Over the centuries certain distinct cultures of honor had developed in the estates: an aristocracy with its titles and lineages, its fine manners, military ethos, and disdain for commerce and manual labor; guild members and a newer bourgeoisie with their ethic of work, thrift, honesty, moderation, and sexual chastity; a peasantry, by contrast, that allowed premarital sex within defined parameters and that, by the eighteenth century, put a premium on the honor of the free landowner.[37] The imprint of these differences persisted and were refined into different cultures of honor in the Kaiserreich. This was most clearly the case in the continuing social chasm between a *satisfaktionsfähig* dueling elite and everyone else. The manly honor values of the officer corps – "bravery, loyalty and knightly conduct"[38] – differed from the prized qualities of an honorable businessman, qualities centered around "promptly fulfilling one's obligations" and living an upright, "solid" life. State officials differed in turn, emphasizing "incorruptibility, punctuality und 'strict scholarly seriousness in the understanding of his official duties.'"[39]

[36] Aschrott and Liszt, *Reform*, p. 311.
[37] Zunkel, "Ehre, Reputation," in Otto Brunner et al. (eds.) *Geschichtliche Grundbegriffe* vol. 2 (Stuttgart, 1975). In general, for early-modern popular honor, see Eileen Crosby, "Claiming Honor: Injury, Honor, and the Legal Process in Saxony, 1650–1730" (PhD diss., Cornell University, 2004); Kathy Stuart, *Defiled Trades and Social Outcasts: Honor and Ritual Pollution in Early Modern Germany* (Cambridge, 1999); Richard van Dülmen, *Der ehrlose Mensch* (Cologne, 1999); David M. Luebke, "Serfdom and Honour in Eighteenth-Century Germany," *Social History* 18/2 (1993): 143–61; Ann Goldberg, *Sex, Religion, and the Making of Modern Madness* (New York, 1999), on the norms of gender and sexuality in nineteenth-century peasant society.
[38] A nineteenth-century source cited in Ute Frevert, "Ehre – männlich/weiblich. Zu einem Identitätsbegriff des 19. Jahrhunderts," *Tel Aviver Jahrbuch für deutsche Geschichte* 21 (1992), 25.
[39] Ibid.

At the same time, a certain cultural amalgamation and homogenization was taking place. One sees it in the spread downward of the duel to the educated middle classes. More importantly, this amalgamation involved the dissemination of an honor ethic attached to state service, an ethic of obedience and loyalty, disinterested impartiality and devotion to the public good, which reached from the aristocracy through the professions and far down into the petit bourgeoisie. One also sees the spread into the middle classes of a contempt for business and profit, pursuits that were dishonorable, a view, originating from both aristocratic snobbery and anti-free-market craft guilds, reinforced by decades of Romantic thought and increasingly attached in the Kaiserreich to antisemitic sentiment.

There was also a certain sameness across classes in the continuing power of externalist, social definitions of honor. To be sure, the Enlightenment, as explained above (see the Introduction), had evolved an internalized, rationalist definition of honor – a notion of personal virtue divorced from rank and birth – and that new kind of honor was critical in the practices of Germans discussed below.[40] But the idea of a new rationalized honor has to be kept in perspective. The dichotomies on which it was based – inner vs. external honor, virtue vs. rank – were more ideological constructs than positive truths. Arising in the eighteenth century, this construction of the honor issue was a powerful polemical tool of a new bourgeoisie in battles against aristocratic privilege and the inequities of the corporatist order.[41] It became a pervasive trope of German literature. From Lessing's *Minna von Barnhelm* (1767) and Schiller's "Verbrecher aus Infamie" (1786) to Fontane's *Effi Briest* (1894), German writers critical of the corporatist order thematized "the loss and the assertion of corporate honor in conflict with 'internal honor' and ultimately the redemption of corporate honor by bourgeois honor."[42] One finds a

---

[40] The actual legal distinction between external and internal honor predated the Enlightenment by several centuries. Hans-Heinrich Dressler, *Das deutsche Beleidigungsrecht des 16. und 17. Jahrhunderts* (Frankfurt am Main, 1967).

[41] Zunkel, "Ehre, Reputation," pp. 25–27.

[42] Wolfgang Frühwald, "Die Ehre der Geringen: Ein Versuch zur Sozialgeschichte literarischer Texte im 19. Jahrhundert," *Geschichte und Gesellschaft* 9 (1983), 71–72.

similar trope in nineteenth- and early twentieth-century legal scholarship, among jurists devising theories to reconcile internal honor
with the continuing practice of the defamation lawsuit. Complex
formulations were theorized in order to explain why, if honor was
an internal, personal quality, an insulted person was still justified in
defending his honor in court vis-à-vis the external world. A leading
expert on insult law, Moritz Liepmann, devised the distinction
between "objectified" (reputation) and "subjectified" (internal feeling) honor, arguing that both comprised individual honor and
needed legal protection.[43]

Further, the actual honor practices of Germans tended to blur
any distinctions between internal and external, corporate and bourgeois honor. Honor litigation had its own logic that transcended
individual feelings and ideas. In an honor culture like Germany's, "to
leave an affront unavenged is to leave one's honour in a state of
desecration ... and jeopardy ... [the insult] requires 'satisfaction' if
[the offended person's honor] is to return to its normal condition."[44]
Within this logic, an insult left unchallenged, moreover, risked
appearing true, and while the upper classes – military officers and
university students especially – generally settled their honor disputes

---

[43] A good discussion of this can be found in Stewart, *Honor*, p. 15ff. Hans Joachim
Hirsch, *Ehre und Beleidigung: Grundfragen des strafrechtlichen Ehrenschutzes*
(Karlsruhe, 1967). One contemporary example of the contradictions within the
thought about honor: a 1914 *Berliner Morgenpost* article making a liberal argument
for Germans to cease with their (mostly trivial) honor obsessions and, at the
political level, for the state to tolerate free speech. It offered an internalized
definition of honor as one argument against German litigiousness: "Die
persönliche Ehre ist ein so wertvolles und so hochstehendes Rechtsgut, dass wir
überzeugt sein sollten, dass sie durch ein unvorsichtiges Versehen eines anderen ...
gar nicht verletzt werden kann ..." In other words, it asserted that a person's sense
of honor should be anchored in the self and not subject to harm by the whims of an
external world. But the author went on in the very same sentence to use a quite
different notion of honor that focused on a person's reputation and its need to be
defended from external attack: "und wir sollten nur dann nach Rache oder
Vergeltung [e.g. filing a *Privatklage*] rufen, wenn positive Beweise dafür vorliegen,
dass der andere, der vermeindliche Beleidiger, unseren Charakter wider besseres
Wissen verdächtigen gewollt hat": "Energieverschleuderung," *Berliner Morgenpost*,
Feb. 28, 1914.
[44] Pitt-Rivers, "Honour and Social Status," p. 26.

with the duel, for most Germans the courtroom was the forum for resolving personal disputes. And, given a world in which a tainted reputation spelled social disaster, the logic of honor pushed even the most progressive and most hostile to corporate honor – e.g., Socialists – into libel litigation.

Thus, whatever the philosophers and moralists said about the integrity of inner honor (virtue), everyone knew what really counted: one's reputation and standing in the eyes of society, a type of honor, conferred and denied by the outside world, that was thus always deeply vulnerable and easily lost. Going to court was often an inadequate solution at best. Even for those in the non-dueling population who did not view honor litigation as a form of cowardice, going to court, as in St.'s case, potentially opened one up to further humiliations through court delays, thus "advertis[ing]" the vulnerability of one's honor.[45] Moreover, losing the case and long months and years of countersuits and appeals were always possibilities.

This being so, the next step, while often shocking, was somehow logical: the humiliated and desperate, their honor lost or in jeopardy, their social standing plunging, not infrequently took their cases directly to the public. Sometimes, as in St., they published newspaper articles. More often, the medium of choice was a pamphlet laying out the TRUE FACTS of their stories. Hence the birth of a new popular pamphlet literature that developed around German litigiousness – what could be called the legal defense memoir-sourcebook. Their authors' contribution to a modern mass reading public was in forging around honor a personalized politics of complaint. The pamphlets were hybrids, borrowing from a range of literary genres (the epistolary novel, pulp crime stories, memoir, legal brief, political polemic, the philosophical tract) and coming in an infinite variety of personalized combinations (more on the form and function of these pamphlets in chapter 5). They were self-revelatory narratives of the most extraordinary kind. Trying to set the record straight, they ended up narrating in often painstaking (and painful) detail the most private details of the authors' personal lives – stories of divorce,

---

[45] Ibid., p. 30.

sexual molestation, loss of employment, insane asylum incarcerations, bankruptcy – and doing so with a great passion for documentary proof in the form of court verdicts, letters, petitions, and other primary sources.

An army doctor (Emil Schulze) was fired from his post and stripped of his officer's uniform in 1878 after a military honor court determined that he had "made a false statement" (later, he learned the real reason was his refusal of a dueling challenge). Jobless, utterly dishonored, a social outcast ("contact with [someone stripped of his uniform] is avoided"), "without prospect of any other way of rehabilitating myself with my acquaintances and friends," Schulze set out to tell the world the "unbiased ... truth" of a chain of events that had begun with a jealous best friend and the deterioration of their friendship.[46]

Elise Hessels, allegedly molested by Berlin's police chief, went public after years of fruitless litigation, including a conviction against her for defaming her attacker.[47] Alfred Schulze, a former law student and tutor at the Berlin home of Dresdner Bank director Gutmann, wrote his bitter confessional pamphlet in the wake of a conviction for attempted blackmail of the Gutmann family and other personal disasters related to the case.[48]

A sense of violated rights and outsized entitlement permeated these acts of press folly. "St.," the man offended by a private letter, went public to proclaim his outrage over a "legal situation in which an insulted citizen is faced with unbelievable vexations" and finds himself "defencelessly facing the rudest improprieties from the defendant."[49] Schulze, the fired army doctor, was sure that it was a man's "duty," not just his "right," to "defend his honor when it is attacked or placed in question."[50]

---

[46] Schulze, *Ein militär-ehrengerichtlicher Prozess*, pp. 20–21, 24. In Schulze's convincing narrative, the "false report" was a word-of-honor assurance to a superior officer that he had not used curse words in a quarrel with a fellow officer; a third officer – an ex-best friend turned enemy – contradicted Schulze's statement and the court believed the former.

[47] Elise Hessels, *Frauenloos in Preussen* (Bern, 1882).

[48] Alfred Schultze, *Für Ehre und Recht* (Zurich, 1903).   [49] Ibid.

[50] Schulze, *Ein militär-ehrengerichtlicher Prozess*, p. 3.

There was also a crusading mentality to these works, a tendency of their authors to turn personal woes into broader narratives of injustice. The clearest example is in the writings of "lunatics" battling the psychiatric system and articulating their plights within stories about nation-wide social injustice (chapter 5). Clara Hahn's confessional about her messy divorce was written not merely as an "indictment against" her husband, but against a society, "whose lack of feeling for the law, of rationality, [and] chivalry allowed these events to come into being."[51] A. Collmann, a Protestant minister removed from his position, wrote not merely to defend the honor of a "simple village pastor" (himself), but to enlighten the public about a widespread "sickness" of bureaucracy and authoritarianism in the Protestant church and public life.[52]

The following discussion gives a sense of the great variety of circumstances narrated in the pamphlets and in the other sources available on defamation litigation. It is neither a definitive nor an all-encompassing analysis. Rather, its purpose is to suggest the widespread role played by and the social dynamics surrounding honor in German everyday life. Those dynamics were in large part about the many fine permutations of status anxiety – class, gender, professional – in a modernizing society whose structural tendencies (industrial capitalism, urbanization, democratization) were undermining fixed social roles. The social dynamics of honor were at the same time about the incorporation of hierarchical, corporate values into modern institutions: the state, business, labor and gender relations, politics, and the professions.

BUREAUCRATS: SOCIAL STATUS AND CLASS ANXIETY

In a sense, honor was a method of governing. It influenced the state's treatment of its opponents (chapter 3). It was also a tool of self-disciplining within the governing class itself. It is the latter aspect that concerns me here. Nowhere was the strict conformity of honor values more apparent than in the Prussian bureaucracy. The rigid,

---

[51] Clara Hahn, *Mein Ehescheidungsprozess* (Vienna, 1895), p. 1.
[52] A. Collmann, *Mein Disciplinarprozess* (Cleve, 1873).

punctilious, rule-obsessed Prussian bureaucrat is a familiar figure in German literature.[53] His mentality came out of the longstanding interpenetration of the military and civil bureaucracies,[54] as well as the peculiar mixture of modern and corporate thought that characterized state service. Germany's civil and military bureaucracies were, on the one hand, highly efficient modern institutions organized along functional lines of authority and run by a cadre of specialized, professional, tenured experts. These institutions were also, however, classic *Stände*. To be an official in the Kaiserreich was to belong to an exclusive, privileged status group whose honor claims were central to state power and the legitimation of its authority.

The lives of officials were governed, accordingly, by elaborate codes of etiquette – titles, address, dress, comportment, the proper social circles – involving an endless discipline of lifestyle and protocol, whose underlying values of status and honor were thoroughly internalized. The particularity of their honor values can be traced to the functional requirements of state service, the inherently hierarchical and authoritarian nature of bureaucracy, and a Hegelian view of the state as an impartial, transcendent authority acting in the interests of the common good. Most familiar is the military's honor code – manifested in officer duels and the judgments of military honor courts – of physical courage, loyalty, obedience, self-sacrifice, and comradeship.[55] In the civil administration, the service ethic translated into an honor code that equally reified an obsessive observance of regulations and rank, honesty, sobriety, respectability in private and social relations, and, above all, impartiality and disinterestedness.[56]

---

[53] A classic portrayal can be found in Henrich Mann, *Der Untertan* (1918).

[54] Hans Rosenberg, *Bureaucracy, Aristocracy, and Autocracy: The Prussian Experience 1660–1815* (Boston, 1958).

[55] Ute Frevert, *Men of Honor: A Social and Cultural History of the Duel* (Cambridge, MA, 1995); Kevin McAleer, *Dueling: The Cult of Honor in fin-de-siècle Germany* (Princeton, 1994).

[56] The sociologist Max Weber, living and writing in imperial Germany, wrote the classic work on the characteristics of modern bureaucracy. Though formulated as an "ideal type" applicable to all modern societies, Weber's modern bureaucrat possesses characteristics that closely resemble the German type with which he was most familiar. See, *From Max Weber*, pp. 196ff.

There was no more dishonoring charge against a German bureaucrat than that of self-interested corruption, such as favoritism, bribery, and graft.

A stark example of this can be seen in the 1897 disciplinary hearing against the explorer Karl Peters, the imperialist who helped found German East Africa. As a Reichskommissar in German East Africa in the early 1890s, Peters's brutality against the native community was notorious, provoking uprisings, military intervention, and ultimately a government investigation that led to his firing. Yet, the disciplinary court was most disturbed not with his cruelty against the natives: beatings and executions could be justified by the need to maintain order under dangerous conditions. What was inexcusable was the "self-interest" behind Peters's actions, namely, that his cruelty involved acts of personal revenge related to his relationship with a native woman whom he had taken as his concubine. Peters's "mistakes" made it impossible for him to continue as a state official, the judgment proclaimed:

> Someone who, like the accused, has used the power of his official position to advance his own personal interests and who disavows the foremost principles of administration, justice, decency and truthfulness, and who has proved himself unable to exercise self-control – this official may not remain in office regardless of his successes.[57]

A more typical case shows the way honor codes infused the bureaucracy in its everyday workings, functioning as a form of intra-institutional self-disciplining. Here status anxieties manifested themselves in a fetishized attachment to bureaucratic forms and protocols. The case involved breaches of bureaucratic protocol in the Prussian district of Spremberg, an event that led in 1893 to the libel convictions of two of the district's most important notables.[58] The scandal revolved around the word *"ergebenst"* (most loyally) – when to write it and when not to. The first breach occurred when the

---

[57] My emphasis. N.a. *Die Urteile der Disziplinargerichte gegen Dr. Karl Peters* (Munich, 1907), pp. 60–61.

[58] Many of the documents have been preserved in I. HA Rep. 84a, Nr. 58199, GStPK, from which the following discussion is taken.

word failed to appear on a letter sent to Spremberg's magistrate's court (*Amtsgericht*). The court had written to an official in a nearby town requesting information about a pending trial. The official, Amtsvorsteher General-Major von Hagen, wrote back answering the question but signing the letter simply "Der Amtsvorsteher von Hagen." For reasons unknown – his own excuse does not merit mention – von Hagen had left out from his signature the properly respectful *ergebenst*. The recipient of von Hagen's soon-to-be notorious letter, magistrate Oscar Müller, testily replied with a polite admonishment to observe the official writing "style." Hagen was insulted – being lectured to like that by a (low-level) magistrate – and sent copies of the correspondence to the district's highest official, Landrat Ernst Falkenthal. Falkenthal, in turn, forwarded Hagen's complaint to Müller's boss, the president of the county court (*Landgericht*) in Cottbus, who, after back-and-forths about the proper jurisdiction, asked Falkenthal to reprove Hagen for not following the "required style" and for seeking "satisfaction" with the wrong authorities. Falkenthal, already manifesting that less-than-reverent attitude that would later cause him legal grief, refused to do so, saying that Hagen's writing style was entirely correct. Cottbus let the matter drop, but one month later saw another of Spremberg's magistrates, a Dr. Schneider, consulting with the Landrat at his office about the complaint against von Hagen. A friend of the Landrat, Robert Freytag (*Standesbeamte*, *Rittergutsbesitzer* and reserve officer), was also present at the meeting. At some point, while filling out an official form, Freytag wrote down *ergebenst* followed by the place and date. It was an allusion to the original complaint, a joke, the two explained later in their interrogation. But Schneider did not think it was funny; he saw it as "mocking" him and his office's complaint, in other words, as an insult and affront to his honor. He denounced Falkenthal and Freytag, and the authorities agreed, trying and convicting them of criminal libel and meting out the huge fines of 400M and 300M, respectively.

This absurd story of a signature's reverberations offers a window onto the internecine battles over status that took place around the baroque intricacies of bureaucratic forms. If bureaucratic honor codes were critical to the outward assertion of state power, they were, at the individual level, essential to an official's place and authority within the state. Honor was a deeply serious matter in a world obsessed by the fine gradations of rank and authority – hence the worshipping of protocol and "correctness" and the symbolically devastating affect on Schneider of Falkenthal's and Freytag's playful disparagement of these rules.

Heinrich Mann immortalized the mentality in his scathingly satirical novel *Der Untertan* (1918). At university, Diederich Hessling, the novel's tyrannical, jingoistic protagonist, is swept up by the wonders of membership in a student fraternity, the Neo-Teutons. No longer small and alone – one of the anonymous "herd" – he is now part of a select elite and thrilled to defend its "honor." The fraternity teaches him to live like a man of honor: besides drinking and fencing, he learns the importance of precise "observance of prescribed forms and mutual deference":

A fellow student, with whom Diederich had hitherto had only official relations, once bumped into him at the door of the lavatory, and although both of them were in a great hurry, neither would take precedence over the other. For a long time they stood bowing and scraping – until suddenly, overcome by the same need at the same moment, they burst through the door, charging like two wild boars ... knock[ing] their shoulders together.[59]

As in Hessling and his fellow fraternity members, honor was critical to those seeking entrance into the governing classes. An honorable reputation ranked with a university (usually law) degree and the right social contacts as part of the entrance ticket to a secure, mid-level civil service job and membership in privileged social circles. Alfred Schulze, a 23-year-old law student from modest circumstances, was one such social striver in turn-of-the-century Berlin. Except Schulze played his cards spectacularly poorly, ending up a fugitive felon banished from Berlin society and his country. As a poor law student, Schulze had had the extraordinary fortune of landing a job in one of the great households of Berlin high society,

[59] English translation: Heinrich Mann, *Man of Straw* (London, 1984), p. 25.

that of Dresdner Bank director Eugen Gutmann, whose elder sons Schulze tutored. But, in events that unfolded like a pulp novel, Schulze got himself involved in a disastrous love affair with Gutmann's 35-year-old wife. Pregnant with his child and fearing, one presumes, the severely compromising position she was in, she at some point broke off relations with Schulze and ordered him to leave Berlin. A catastrophe for Schulze on many levels (personal, social, professional, and financial), it was here that his life plans began to fall apart and that he began the schemes that would lead several years later to a felony conviction for blackmail. He attempted to extort money from the Gutmanns by threatening to go public with Frau Gutmann's love letters, was sent off to the "orient" to work for the railway with a promise of a payoff that never arrived, and returned to Berlin years later, embittered and impoverished, to once again take up his blackmail scheme for hush money. He sued Herr Gutmann, who countered with a defamation *Privatklage* and a criminal suit for blackmail. Tried and convicted, Schulze fled to Switzerland before his jail sentence began.[60]

Schulze's notions of honor were key both to how he lived and how he self-destructed. Honor framed his story in the most literal sense: the narrative of his published pamphlet – a poisonous mix of self-pity, misogyny, and class resentment – was constructed as a revenge piece and as an entreaty to the public in defense of his reputation. His life and thinking entirely conflated honor and social status. As his troubles mounted, facing dismissal from his job, mounting debts, withdrawal from law school, and exclusion from whatever contacts he had made in high society, he began to feel "dishonored." That feeling must have been acutely reinforced when Herr Gutmann, although deeply insulted by Schulze's actions, refused to challenge him to a duel because, in his eyes, Schulze was no longer *satisfaktionsfähig* (i.e., honorable enough to duel).[61] Other people's

---

[60] Schulze, *Für Ehre und Recht.*

[61] Ibid., pp. 37–39. Following Schulze's narrative strategy (revenge and defending his honor), he sought to turn this fact into a stain on Gutmann's honor, arguing that the latter actually did not possess the courage and manliness to duel.

reactions to Schulze were likewise mediated by honor ideas: implicitly understanding the psychology of a man with honor pretensions riven by rage and insecurities, they began avoiding him for fear of becoming the target of an insult lawsuit.[62] Schulze's litigiousness, so bound up with class resentment and slighted honor, was what ultimately did him in. When Herr Gutmann offered him a sum of money to, essentially, go away and drop a lawsuit Schulze had filed regarding an earlier unfulfilled money offer, he refused because "I wanted justice!" (*Recht*) and was above accepting "a gratuity."[63] There ensued Gutmann's lawsuits that destroyed him.

BUSINESS

Honor was integrated into German capitalism in complex and sometimes contradictory ways, being at once integral to the economy and disruptive of it. On the one hand, honor was an essential part of doing business. Merchants, entrepreneurs, and bankers worked diligently to maintain honorable reputations of probity and trustworthiness. They did so not only through staying solvent and maintaining honest business dealings but by displaying markers of bourgeois respectability, cultivating the proper (Weberian) "lifestyle" in their social and personal relations. Hence, the porousness of the personal and the professional, the private and public aspects of a businessman's life. Perhaps the most important structural reason for this situation was the persistence of personalized credit institutions within Germany's modernizing economy. Sperber's study of the Palatinate shows how most loans in the nineteenth century were taken not from financial institutions like banks but within a "face-to-face relationship, in which the creditor could assess both the personality and the property of the debtor."[64] Whether it was running up a tab at the local store or borrowing from a family member, credit relations were "ubiquitous," forming "a dense network running from individual

---

[62] Ibid., p. 33. At least this was Schulze's impression.   [63] Ibid., p. 47.

[64] Jonathan Sperber, *Property and Civil Society in South-Western Germany*, 1820–1914 (Oxford, 2005), p. 107.

to individual [and] family to family."[65] As such, credit involved trust and reputation – in short, honor.

Potentially, then, businessmen with besmirched reputations were in deep trouble. This is why Schulze, the aggrieved tutor at the home of Gutmann, Dresdner Bank director, felt he had a chance of getting away with blackmailing the Gutmann family, and why a man of Gutmann's stature, in turn, worked so hard to silence his lowly, outcast opponent (above, p. 55). It is also why the pro-business *Ostsee Zeitung* was so upset over a 1912 court ruling that acquitted an employee of a Saxon firm who, after being fired, had slandered his former boss in a job interview with another firm, claiming he had left his earlier job because his boss had tried to get him to falsify the firm's books (*falsche Buchung*). The boss, having learned second-hand about this claim, promptly took his former employee to court for slander, since, as the article explained, such an accusation, "is one of the worst things that can be done to a businessman," having the ability to make him "forever, in all honorable business circles, unacceptable and unworthy of his social position [*standesunwürdig*]."[66] The court, however, saw things differently, brushing aside such concerns and granting the employee-defendant's speech the protection of §193. Outraged, the article cited this case as one more example of how out of touch "legal circles" were with "business affairs," a sentiment helping to fuel widespread discontent with the laws and efforts to reform them (chapter 4).

The significance of honor and reputation for the credit market is also reflected in the enormous amount of contemporary writing devoted to the topic, and to the fact that unlike the otherwise vague libel statutes, defamation threatening a person's credit was specifically referenced in the law (§187) and treated as a serious offense. In at least one instance, a businessman deliberately used the link between credit and reputation to coerce the repayment of a loan,

---

[65] Ibid., p. 106.
[66] "Weltfremdheit der Richter und kaufmännisches Ehrgefühl," *Ostsee Zeitung*, August 17, 1912.

orchestrating a public shaming of his debtor with a newspaper ad. (The debtor sued for insult.)[67]

But honor also disrupted business. First, because the expansion of trade and the modernization of the economy were increasing economic transactions between people who did not necessarily share the same honor codes. On the one hand, the structural trend in industrial capitalism was toward the depersonalization of business and the relaxation accordingly of a social etiquette born in an earlier, face-to-face, corporatist world; on the other hand, there were plenty of people who remained deeply attached to that etiquette and its attendant markers of rank and status. The result was bruised egos and lawsuits. One can see the underlying clash between a *ständisch*-military and a capitalist ethos that, for example, poisoned the business relations between Y and X. As reported in *Reichsfreund*, X, a military officer, sent Y insufficient funds in a transaction over the transport of some furniture. Y, angry but wanting to avoid further trouble, responded with a curt letter: "Since we have no desire to go on about our legitimate claim in court, we are giving you the six marks [money Y owed] and request the remittance of the residual amount."[68] Granted, the letter was impolite by contemporary standards; perhaps it even merited a *Privatklage*. But what followed startled even the authors of the article: X denounced Y to the state prosecutor, who, sharing X's military ethic, filed formal defamation charges against Y for the insult of offering a soldier a present, a violation of X's "corporate honor."[69]

Another reason for the economic disruptiveness of honor was its tendency to clash with the free flow of information and goods on which capitalism depended. One sees this in, for example, a 1914 *Frankfurter Zeitung* article condemning a recent defamation ruling of the Frankfurter Oberlandesgericht against the newspaper.[70] In 1911 the newspaper reprinted an article from the *Münchner Neueste*

---

[67] "Darf man eine ausgeklagte Forderung durch Annonce zum Kauf ausbieten?" *Schlesswiger Nachrichten* August 26, 1902. The businessman was convicted and fined 5M; this ruling was reversed on appeal, the court citing §193.

[68] "Staatsanwalts-Anklagen," *Reichsfreund*, August 23, 1890.

[69] Y was eventually acquitted, see chapter 3.

[70] "Die Freiheit der Finanzkritik," *Frankfurter Zeitung*, March 7, 1914.

Nachrichten that had accused the banker Max Ansbacher of unethical behavior, namely, of withdrawing the dividends of Bayerische Bodenkreditanstalt stock, a bank in which he was the leading influence, shortly before a company meeting. Ansbacher sued the *Frankfurter Zeitung* for defamation. The court's ruling supported, in principle, the legitimacy of a §193 defense by the financial press, which, the newspaper's commentary pointed out, was more than could be said for the justice system's treatment of the political press. But the court ruled against the *Frankfurter Zeitung* in this case, denying it §193 protection, because the paper had failed to check the facts of the case before reprinting them. This principle, the *Frankfurter Zeitung* argued, placed an undue burden on newspapers, which was bad for business. The freedom of the press to inform its business public is essential for the capitalist economy: a critical and conscientious financial press "is essential both in the interests of the individual capitalist, whose investments need to be protected, and in the general interest keeping the national economy clean of unstable and socially harmful enterprises." And it felt compelled to point out that, far from serving some "irrelevant private curiosity" (i.e. illegitimate critical speech), such articles played a very important "public function."

LABOR RELATIONS

Libel lawsuits were endemic to the unionized sectors of the economy. Employers fought labor battles with defamation litigation, suing pro-labor newspapers,[71] organizations, and, probably, unruly workers. In one case, a group of Alsatian quarry owners sued a local priest after the latter wrote a series of articles claiming that the owners were undermining the health and finances of their workers by plying them with copious amounts of schnapps and beer.[72] Workers, in turn, used

---

[71] For example, the libel lawsuit of a Hanauer mill owner against the Frankfurt *Volksstimme.* "Hanauer Justiz," *Vorwärts,* April 14, 1911.

[72] "Beleidigung oder Ausübung seelsorgerlicher Pflichten durch die Presse?" *Tägliche Rundschau,* December 31, 1913. The quarry owners argued in their suit

the libel lawsuit in intra-labor struggles. Christian and independent-Socialist unions (their officials, newspapers, and political representatives) sued one another.[73] Strikes sparked animosities between strikers and strikebreakers that produced libel lawsuits. After a successful factory strike of piano makers, a strikebreaker, Möller, cursed one of the workers, Ralikowski, who had participated in the strike, with: "you scoundrel, you blackguard ... you should have your skull smashed." Ralikowski sued for insult; Möller countersued, saying that, as a strikebreaker, he had been insulted by Ralikowski during the strike.[74] A dockyard worker was given the extraordinarily harsh three-month jail sentence for yelling "strikebreaker, Heidelberger, scoundrel."[75]

Workers also sued their employers. The cases I have found reported in the press, however, were from non-industrial sectors of the economy, where, as in servants and masters, relations between employer and worker were close and personalized. If it is true (and it is not yet clear if this was the case) that industrial workers were less likely to bring libel suits against their employers,[76] then it should be attributed both to the more depersonalized relationship of industrial labor relations and to the fact that industrial workers were likely to be unionized and thus have at their disposal collective means of complaint and resistance like the strike.

There is a long history in Germany of subordinates bringing lawsuits against their superiors, as in peasant-lord legal disputes. But, in a world where honor was distributed hierarchically by estate,

---

that matters outside of the church were none of the priest's legitimate business. The priest's initial conviction was overturned on appeal. The appellate court accepted the church's argument (higher church officials intervened in defense of the priest) that the well-being of his parishioners was indeed a church concern.

[73] One example is a series of defamation suits between the right-wing Reichstag deputy Franz Behrens (1872–1943), who was a leader in the Christian workers movement, and the SPD. *Tägliche Rundschau*, November 22, 1912.

[74] Möller was convicted and fined 10M. "Gerichts-Zeitung: Gleiches Recht," *Vorwärts*, March 12, 1911.

[75] On appeal, the sentence was reduced to two weeks. "Gerichts-Zeitung: Abgemilderte Klassenjustiz," *Vorwärts*, March 9, 1911.

[76] My conclusion is based primarily on a scanning of the court section of *Vorwärts* for the years 1902 and 1911, an admittedly unscientific sample.

a libel suit by a worker against his master was neither legal nor cognitively intelligible.[77] It took the liberalization of libel law and the democratization of German society in the nineteenth century to make such lawsuits possible.

But, while workers now had the means and motivation to bring honor suits against their employers, both the law – e.g. §193 which protected certain harsh and insulting employer/master speech – and the corporate notions of honor rife in the courts made it difficult for worker plaintiffs to succeed. When, in a rural area of Bavaria, a master chastised his two female laborers for being late to work, saying to them: "Aren't you at all ashamed of yourselves? First you go to confession and then you commit sacrilege [*begeht einen Gotessraub*]," they sued for libel. The court, however, sided with the employer, citing §193 and other sections of the law codes protecting employer reprimands and requiring servant obedience.[78] A maid sued her mistress after the latter, responding to the maid's attempt to share her meal with a dog, contemptuously declared her a "dumb broad." The court found the utterance both insulting and done with said intent, but it acquitted, citing the employer's low "educational level" (and, implicitly, the plaintiff's low social and educational status) and arguing that an "invective does not in all circumstances involve a punishable insult."[79]

THE PROFESSIONS

Medicine, law, and other areas of knowledge were being radically retooled in this era as they became modern professions. Fields of knowledge were more strictly delineated and monopolized by specialists whose expertise rested on formalized university training and degrees. State-sanctioned independent professional organizations, as well as specialized journals and conferences, were founded for the

[77] Crosby, "Claiming Honor," p. 129 and passim.
[78] Ferdinand Kurz (ed.), *§193: Beleidigung und berechtigte Interessen* (Nuremberg, 1909), p. 13.
[79] Ibid., pp. 14–15.

exchange of ideas and the promotion and regulation of the professions. As in the modernization of the state bureaucracy, this "professionalization" took place by incorporating, not undermining, the
values of honor. The promotion of a profession's status and its
monopolistic claims of expertise, as the sociologists tell us, required
not only the regulation of academic qualifications of practitioners.[80]
It also required systems of internal policing by professional associations of its membership to ensure adherence to appropriate standards
of conduct. In imperial Germany, this self-policing was accomplished
largely within the language and practices of honor. The result was
that the professions were at once modernizing and functioning as
classic Weberian corporate status groups.

The regulations and disciplinary courts set up by the professions,
which were partially modeled upon the earlier military courts,[81]
aimed above all at protecting the corporate honor of the group.
The bylaws of Germany's first professional writers' organization,
the Leipziger Literaturverein, founded in 1842, stated the goal of "a
collective observation, investigation, consultation, and resolution
with respect to all circumstances relating to honor and the interests
of the literary class."[82] A similar bylaw decades later in the Verband
Deutscher Journalisten- und Schriftstellervereine (VDJS), founded
in 1895, as an umbrella organization of nineteen writers' associations,
placed the protection of journalist and writer "professional honor and
general professional questions" third in its declared goals, after
copyright law (number 1) and press rights (2).[83]

Disciplinary courts established for lawyers in 1878, which spread
later to doctors and other professions, were called literally "honor

---

[80] For the medicial profession, see, e.g., Eliot Freidson, *Profession of Medicine: A
Study of the Sociology of Applied Knowledge* (New York, 1970); Jeffrey Lionel
Berlant, *Profession and Monopoly* (Berkeley, 1975). For an historical study of the
German medical profession that uses the professionalization model, see Claudia
Huerkamp, *Der Aufstieg der Aerzte im 19. Jahrhundert* (Göttingen, 1985).

[81] Erik Nils Voigt, *Die Gesetzgebungsgeschichte der militärischen Ehrenstrafen und der
Offizierehrengerichtsbarkeit im preussischen und deutschen Heer von 1806 bis 1918*
(Frankfurt, 2004).

[82] Friedhelm Kron, *Schriftsteller und Schriftstellerverbände* (Stuttgart, 1976), p. 32.

[83] Ibid., p. 38.

courts" (*Ehrengerichten*).[84] These courts were not holdovers from the past; they were direct products of the professionalization process. Their self-regulating functions were an essential tool enabling the professions to assert autonomy from the state (before 1869, for example, doctors were little more than civil servants),[85] the status of the profession, and the trust of the public. Enforcing honor codes was a key aspect of what these courts did.

It involved policing of member behavior in ways that dissolved the boundaries of professional and private life. The responsibility of each VDJS member to uphold an honorable reputation was a prerequisite of membership. "Loss of civil rights [*Ehrenrechte*]," the result of a criminal conviction, or engaging in "insulting" (*ehrenrührig*) behavior was cause for expulsion from the Deutscher Schriftsteller-Verband.[86] Attorney honor courts had the right to discipline both their members' professional behavior and their actions as private citizens. Doctors in Prussia, by contrast, fearing "political control," managed to insert a clause that excluded from the disciplinary purview of their honor courts members' "political, scientific, and religious views."[87] But much of members' private lives did remain subject to disciplinary action, given that, according to professional regulations, every member was required to "show himself worthy of the respect that his profession demanded, in his conduct both during and outside medical practice."[88]

---

[84] Andreas-Holger Maehle, "Professional Ethics and Discipline: The Prussian Medical Courts of Honour, 1899–1920," *Medizinhistorisches Journal* 34 (1999), 314 ff. The Rechtsanwaltsordnung empowered panels of judges and lawyers with the right to reprimand and even expel members for infractions, and established an appeals court (Ehrengerichtshof) in Leipzig at Germany's Supreme Court. Likewise, medical honor courts at the state level, many modeled after the Rechtsanwaltsordnung, were forming in the latter part of the century: e.g., Braunschweig in 1865; Baden, 1883; Bavaria 1895; Prussia, 1899 (idem, p. 321). Both Maehle and Barbara Rabi, *Aerztliche Ethik – Eine Frage der Ehre?* (Frankfurt, 2002), make similar arguments about the role of honor in the professionalization of German medicine.

[85] Maehle, "Professional Ethics," p. 313.

[86] Karl Thiess, *Der Verband deutscher Journalisten- und Schriftstellervereine und die Beschlüsse seiner Delegiertentage, 1895 bis 1904* (Hamburg, 1905).

[87] Ibid., p. 319.   [88] Ibid., p. 320.

The regulation of both professional and personal conduct was meant to enforce a corporate "lifestyle" in the Weberian sense of the term. Its behavioral code and ethics, those of the bourgeois gentleman, were not unique to Germany. Nye discusses in his study the honorable characteristics of nineteenth-century French physicians: courtesy, generosity, honesty, loyalty, discretion, disinterestedness, "chivalrous sentiment" – values, he argues, that were an adopted mix of "aristocratic chivalry" and traditions and practices from the bourgeois social "circle."[89] Something very similar was occurring in Germany, where bourgeois honor norms, having assimilated elements of both aristocratic court culture and guild traditions, undergirded professional identity. Accordingly, the model of gentlemanly professional behavior involved intense efforts to distance the professions from anything smacking of business and money-making.[90] In Prussia, the regulations and honor-court rulings of physicians after 1899 (when the courts were established) enforced strong taboos against doctors advertising their practices or engaging in any behavior that hinted of the pollution of capitalist enterprise. Acting like a "businessman," as one verdict scoffed in announcing the punishment of a doctor who had too liberally distributed his calling card to potential patients, was "unworthy of the medical profession."[91]

Notwithstanding, corporate honor was deeply linked to material interests. No better example of the intertwining of the two is that of the "border disputes" between university-trained physicians and advocates of natural healing (*Naturheilkunde*), a popular alternative medicine movement. Here, offended honor and the *Privatklage* were tools doctors transparently employed to police the borders of their profession against outsiders and "quacks." At a meeting of Berlin's Magnetism Society, to give one instance, Reinhold Gerling, a

---

[89] Robert Nye, "Honor Codes and Medical Ethics in Modern France," *Bulletin of the History of Medicine* 69 (1995), 92, 108, and 99ff.

[90] More broadly, on the "discomfort with the financial sphere in German political culture" (p. 186), see E. J. Carter, "Breaking the Bank: Gambling Casinos, Finance Capitalism, and German Unification," *Central European History* 39 (2006), 185–213.

[91] October 12, 1903 decision. *Entscheidungen des preussischen Ehrengerichtshofes für Aerzte*, I (Berlin, 1908), p. 4.

natural-healing leader, gave a speech in which he attacked academic physicians with: "the majority of doctors is so gone to the dogs ... that it no longer has any morals," and "I have come to know them, the doctors, and for my part I believe the majority of them capable of every crime, every perjury, every misdeed." Several of those physicians happened to be in the audience that night, and one sued for insult. The court agreed with him, finding a clear instance of words uttered by Gerling that were "inconsistent [*unvereinbar*] with the professional honor" of the physicians present that evening, and a collective insult against all doctors – a "disrespect of the personality of the majority of physicians." It declared Gerling guilty, sentencing him to one month in jail.[92]

Professional honor concerns, in turn, could translate into collective political actions. Journalists, for example, fought restrictive press laws in the name of free speech and civil rights while closely attending to the defense of their corporate honor. One sees this in their reaction at the turn of the century to recent court rulings in the Austrian Empire against the press's ability to file defamation lawsuits, a legal situation, as the Berlin Delegiertentag of 1902 resolved, that left the Austrian press vulnerable to "frivolous defamation lawsuits" and unable to protect its reputation and honor (with implications as well for non-Austrian, German-language authors publishing in the Empire):

The honor of the press is the honor of all those involved in the determination and maintenance of trends [*Tendenz*] and spirit ... Insults, libels, inciting contempt of the press strikes at its spiritual creators, and the judicial system must enable them to protect themselves.[93]

---

[92] 1903 court verdict of Berlin's Strafkammer, Landgericht I. GStPK, Rep. 85a, no. 58201. To be sure, as the court acknowledged, the physician plaintiff and prosecution witnesses had intentionally attended the meeting to collect incriminating material against their natural-healing enemies. But, it argued, the meeting had been advertised as free and open to the public, hence any legally-defined insulting statements made therein were actionable as public libel.

[93] Thiess, *Verband deutscher Journalisten- und Schriftstellervereine*, p. 36.

GENDER

While most public and especially overtly political libel trials were about male honor, a substantial portion of honor litigants were women. In the Reich statistics, which lumped together all forms of defamation actions, women generally appear as one-third of convicted defendants.[94] If one were able to break down by gender the figures for only simple insult tried as *Privatklage*, the ratio of women to men would probably be higher. One contemporary estimated that at least two-thirds of honor cases involved women.[95]

The norms of male and female honor differed substantially, and these manifested themselves in important ways in honor disputes. Notions of male and female honor were largely determined by the different social roles ascribed to the sexes, namely, that of male breadwinner in the public sphere and female caregiver in the private sphere of the home. Thus, as one legal expert put it, men's honor related to their orientation toward the "outside world" of work and public life, making of paramount importance the characteristics of "courage" and "reliability." To be sure, these qualities differed by class and profession: a judge's honor, for example, meant that he displayed reliability in his adherence to the law and his independence from outside influences; a merchant's reliability manifested itself in his honest and fair business relations. By contrast, women's honor consisted of their "purity in an interior life" – their kindheartedness and charity.[96] Above all, a woman's honor was composed of her sexual chastity and modesty.

---

[94] In 1899, for example, the ratio of women and men convicted of *Beleidigung* was 36:100: Aschaffenburg, *Das Verbrechen und seine Bekämpfung* (Heidelberg, 1903), p. 128. In 1909, the figure was 16,403 women to 43,270 men: *Statistisches Jahrbuch für das deutsche Reich* (Berlin, 1911), p. 341.

[95] Rudolf Beinert, *Die Ausdehnung der Privatklage* (Halle, 1906), p. 35, fn. 1, citing Kroeneker. The high number of female litigants continued for decades into the post-WWII era. Koewius's study of Bielefeld-area *Privatklagen* in the late 1960s gives the figure of 43.8% female to 56.2% male litigants: *Die Rechtswirklichkeit der Privatklage* (Berlin, 1974), p. 84.

[96] Liepmann, "Die Beleidigung," in Mittermaier et al. (eds.), *Vergleichende Darstellung des deutschen und ausländischen Strafrechts: Besonderer Teil* vol. 4 (Berlin, 1906), p. 13. For a recent historical study of the topic, see Frevert, "Ehre – männlich/weiblich."

Honor, defined as chastity, was a double-edged sword for women. On the one hand, it presupposed and helped maintain the subordination of women in the family. For centuries, patriarchy had been upheld through the control of women's sexuality, both for practical purposes related to the transmission of inherited property through the male line, and for ideological reasons (religion, science) related to notions of woman's weakness and her need of male protection. On the other hand, chastity was an exalted state, equated in the Christian tradition with purity, a notion, by the nineteenth century, still very much alive but secularized and inscribed in bourgeois culture. One spoke of women's spirituality, morality, and their special capacity for love and nurturance. Women in turn seized on these female virtues to claim social roles outside the home – in social welfare and reform movements – and, by the late nineteenth century, to demand equal or special rights in education, work, the family, and the political sphere.[97]

Both aspects of the chastity issue can be seen in the Kaiserreich's honor laws and litigation. On the one hand, legally women were second-class citizens. Married women were the legal dependants of their husbands (and before this, of their fathers). This gave husbands rights over their wives in many areas of life, including that of bringing lawsuits.[98] Technically, when a married woman filed a *Privatklage*, the person who controlled events and pursued the case was her legal guardian, the husband. She could testify in court but she was not formally the "plaintiff"; this designation belonged to her husband. And his control over the litigation was such that §195 of the StGB gave him the right to file a defamation suit in her (or his children's) name. There were no provisions denying him this right even when the wife was ignorant of the lawsuit or actively opposed it. Even after a divorce, the husband could pursue an honor lawsuit in his wife's name if it had been filed before the breakup. Thus, it was possible to imagine, as *Vorwärts* did, the bizarre situation where a husband files suit against a man for defaming his wife, subsequently the couple divorces and the

---

[97] For a general overview, see Ute Frevert, *Women in German History* (New York, 1993).
[98] On libel litigation, the key section of the Criminal Code was §195.

ex-wife marries the defendant in her husband's original honor suit. "The ex-husband then peacefully continues his suit 'for his wife' against her second husband."[99] Husbands had claims of their own to their wives' honor, and thus it was still possible in the early twentieth century for a cuckolded husband to bring a criminal libel suit against his wife's lover and have the man imprisoned. This happened in a 1911 Berlin court, which sentenced the male lover to one month's incarceration, because the love affair defamed the husband. Yet, by this time, such judgments were controversial indeed. The *Berliner Tageblatt* called it a reactionary throwback to "feudal" relations and "oriental" patriarchy, where the "wife is the property of the man."[100]

Yet, the norm of female chastity could also be empowering. Interestingly enough, anecdotal evidence suggests that women pursued sexual harassment offenses through libel actions. When her laundryman made advances to a young pregnant wife of a businessman (*Kaufmann*), she pushed him away, called out for help, and later, in consultation with her husband, filed a defamation lawsuit, the court meting out the very harsh sentence of two months' jail time because the victim was a "respectable" woman.[101] The couple's response – not charging the perpetrator with sexual harassment, which did not exist, or assault, but with defamation – flowed naturally from the historically specific concept of female sexual honor, i.e. that chastity was the essence of her honor, which made sexual violations a form of defamation to be prosecuted under the Empire's defamation statutes. This was empowering, in its own way. When, in 1911, a Hanover factory owner sexually molested his family servant, she sued for defamation and won (he received a fine of 1500M), a suit that inverted the prevailing power dynamics of both gender and class.[102]

---

99 "Aus der Frauenbewegung," *Vorwärts*, April 16, 1911.
100 "Gattenbeleidigung," *Berliner Tageblatt*, March 9, 1911.
101 "Beleidigung einer Kundin," *Vorwärts*, March 18, 1911.
102 "Beleidigung eines Dienstmädchens," *Vorwärts*, February 22, 1911. Granted, this
    was an unusual case. As the article said, if only "in all of Germany, defamations of
    servants by their employers would be pursued in similar manner, that would soon
    have an educational effect on employers."

One sexually abused woman, Elise Hessels, went on to publish a pamphlet about her nightmarish quest for justice after Berlin's police chief, she alleged, sexually assaulted her and then tried to silence her with a defamation suit.[103] Her pamphlet is eloquent testimony to the way honor ideas mediated her experience and actions. In 1870/71, Hessels, a middle-class woman from a Westphalian civil servant home, was working in Paris as a governess for an aristocratic family when the Franco-Prussian war forced her flight. Back in Germany, she sought help for her dire economic circumstances from the "Comité zum Schutze der aus Paris Vertriebenen," whose chairman was Police President (later Regierungspräsident) von Wurmb. According to Hessels, at their meeting in his office, he first tried to seduce her and, when she rejected him, tried to rape her – unsuccessfully because of her chastity belt. The assault was only the beginning of her problems. A determined fighter,[104] she denounced Wurmb to the state prosecutor's office, and, when it refused to press charges, appealed to the Prussian Landtag. But instead of seeing her perpetrator punished, the opposite occurred: to shut her up, Wurmb filed charges of "false accusation" and "calumny." She was tried and convicted. Hessels, the victim, thus found herself incarcerated in prison while her perpetrator – a sexual predator responsible, if the testimony cited in her pamphlet was true, for numerous rapes – stood vindicated. At this point, Hessels became a driven women, waging a decade-long public campaign for her own justice and for legal reform in general, filing court motions, appealing to the authorities, sending petitions to parliamentary bodies (the Prussian Landtag and the Reichstag), and facing stonewalling, rejection, humiliation, and a court diagnosis of mental unfitness.

What drove this astounding woman were her religious faith, her sense of justice,[105] and her feelings about female honor and dignity. It is the close links between the latter two that are most striking. Rape is both

---

[103] Elise Hessels, *Frauenloos in Preussen*.

[104] She also, to use psychological parlance, internalized the experience, falling ill and taking to bed for a long time.

[105] The front page of *Frauenloos* declared "Gott und mein Recht."

a physical event and, as scholars have shown, a historically contingent experience, shaped (in both victims and perpetrators) by the surrounding society and culture.[106] In Elise Hessels' case – a pious, respectable woman of the nineteenth-century bourgeoisie – rape meant, above all, dishonor, an existential and social violation as much as a physical one. The value she placed on female honor (as sexual chastity) profoundly colored both her experience (she literally called the attack an attempt at "dishonoring" her [*entehren*])[107] and her subsequent actions. It drove her anger and "outrage," just as it made her do things that seem very strange today, like returning to the scene of the crime (Wurmb's office) to demand an apology from her would-be rapist (!), believing that "a man of honor and feeling" would do so if confronted with "the results of his indecent behavior [*unziemendes Betragen*]."[108] (Instead, he allegedly assaulted her again.) Her later petition to the parliamentary authorities, she said, was not about revenge; it was about protecting other "honorable ladies from insults and abuse."[109]

In other cases, the legal defense of female honor merged with and reinforced repressive moral purity campaigns.[110] The wife of a *Kaufmann*, responding to an advertisement offering part-time work for young women, received in the mail an explanation from her would-be employer, a small business owner manufacturing women's underwear ("hygenic articles"), that, because he was unmarried, he needed to hire a lady to model articles of clothing, that the work was for women under thirty who were "not prudes," that fittings would take place either in his home or factory and would be paid tenfold what other "light work" paid. The *Kaufmann*'s wife, offended by the letter's "impudences," denounced him, and since the case had

---

[106] For a nuanced recent analysis of rape in Germany by Soviet soldiers during and after World War Two, see Atina Grossmann, *Jews, Germans, and Allies: Close Encounters in Occupied Germany* (Princeton, NJ, 2007).

[107] She also wanted her readers to know that a medical doctor had examined her and declared her "still in the possession of my female honor": ibid., p. 44.

[108] Ibid., p. 45.   [109] Ibid., pp. 56–57.

[110] On these campaigns, see, e.g. John Fout, "Sexual Politics in Wilhelmine Germany: The Male Gender Crisis, Moral Purity, and Homophobia," *Journal of the History of Sexuality* 2/3 (1992), 388–421.

implications for public morality, it was tried as a state lawsuit. The benighted businessman was convicted and fined 30M.[111]

Women turned the idea of female honor to their advantage in court.[112] Frau von Gerlach, the wife of the leader of the "Demokratische Vereinigung," did so when she was put on trial in 1911 for insulting a police official. The case stemmed from an angry confrontation on a Berlin street after Gerlach, on leaving a political meeting with husband and friends, was forcibly blocked from passing through a police street barricade and, during the ensuing scuffle with a police lieutenant, let forth with: "How can you be so shameless! You think you're an officer? This is impudence!" and, later, "Why do you involve yourself in such a dirty trade? Don't touch me, you make me dirty!"[113] At her trial (for insulting a civil servant, resistance, and gross misconduct), Frau Gerlach, who made sure the court understood that she suffered from an ongoing "medical condition," played to perfection the outraged lady, declaring that "Still to this day, I experience as the greatest disgrace [*Schmach*] of my life that I was dragged about by policemen as if I were a drunkard." The court did convict her – there were simply too many witnesses testifying to the truth of the police's version of events – but reduced her sentence (a fine), taking into account her probable upset from the "disgrace" and weighing this fact against the appalling nature of insults against the police coming from an "educated woman."

The historian Laura Gowing writes of a female culture of insult in seventeenth-century London, where women, shut out of formal institutions and avenues of complaint, used instead a language and practice of slander in daily conflicts.[114] This was a language, moreover, that was highly gendered, sexualizing abuse of women, but not of men, and doing

[111] "Gerichts-Zeitung: Scheineinserate," *Vorwärts*, 4. Beilage, March 12, 1911.

[112] For a striking example of this in France, see Edward Berenson, *The Trial of Madame Caillaux* (Berkeley, 1992).

[113] "Polizeibeleidigung durch Frau v. Gerlach," *Vorwärts*, February 18, 1911.

[114] Laura Gowing, *Domestic Dangers: Women, Words, and Sex in Early Modern London* (Oxford, 1996). Gowing's work is among the best of a particularly rich scholarship on late-medieval and early-modern gender, honor, and slander in Europe and America. Other examples include Pieter Spierenburg (ed.), *Men and Violence: Gender, Honor, and Rituals in Early Modern Europe and America* (1998); Susanna Burghartz, *Leib, Ehre, Gut: Delinquenz in Zürich Ende des 14. Jahrhunderts*

so because the culture as a whole "perceived women's virtue, honour, and reputation through their sexuality, men's through a much wider range of values."[115] One senses a similar, sexualized rhetoric of abuse in daily life among the small-town and city working-class and petit bourgeois women who made up the bulk of women's honor suits in the Kaiserreich. Epithets like "whore" were perhaps just as common in turn-of-the century Germany as they were in early-modern London or Saxony. Yet, most of their suits probably had little or nothing to do with the defense of sexual honor per se.[116] The typical trigger of such lawsuits was gossip or direct slander in the female spaces and relations of daily life: among neighbors and housemates, in the worker barracks of factory towns, at stores, and on the streets. Whereas bourgeois and upper-class women were more sheltered in the home and subject to norms of propriety that frowned upon verbal aggression (and the airing of female private matters in the courts), working-class women yelled, gossiped, reviled, and sued their opponents over the disputes of daily life. This pattern of female litigiousness in Germany goes back at least to the seventeenth century, when, as Eileen Crosby's study of Saxon defamation lawsuits shows, large numbers of women "from every level of the social hierarchy"[117] who brought honor suits, did so "independently of male claims,"[118] and for a range of reasons not confined to sexual matters. Even sexual epithets – "whore" being perhaps the most typical slander employed against and by working-class women – did not necessarily refer to sexual conduct. Rather, such words need to be seen as "provocative verbal shorthand for dishonorable behavior" in women.[119]

(Zurich, 1990); Lyndal Roper, "Will and Honor: Sex, Words, and Power in Augsburg Criminal Trials," in idem (ed.), *Oedipus and the Devil: Witchcraft, Sexuality, and Religion in Early Modern Europe* (London and New York, 1994), pp. 53–78; Rainer Walz, "Schimpfende Weiber: Frauen in lippischen Beleidigungsprozessen des 17. Jahrhunderts," in Heide Wunder and Christina Vanja (eds.), *Weiber, Menscher, Frauenzimmer: Frauen in der ländlichen Gesellschaft, 1500–1800* (Göttingen, 1996).

[115] Gowing, *Domestic Dangers*, p. 2.
[116] This I base on anecdotal evidence from surviving court records, *Schiedsmann* books, and the statements of judges with experience adjudicating *Privatklagen*.
[117] Crosby, "Claiming Honor," p. 132.   [118] Ibid., p. 130.
[119] Ibid., p. 131. Indeed, Gowing, *Domestic Dangers*, also shows that "whore" and other sexual expletives had a range of meanings and functions beyond the strictly sexual.

Men could be the plaintiffs in insult suits against women. Like the suit against Frau Schäfer, the wife of a smallholding peasant, these suits typically stemmed from the gossip of a woman. Schäfer told a joiner's wife that she should not let her son go to the farmer Bauer's house because bad things happened there: a local boy (Monz), she knew, engaged in lecherous behavior there with the wife and a maid; he also did it with his own sister. The boy's father (unsuccessfully) filed suit.[120] Similarly, the wife of a railway worker was sued by a master shoemaker for gossiping at a store about his alleged adultery. She was convicted and fined 10M.[121] In a further case, a schoolteacher filed suit against a grandmother, after being insulted by her critical remarks about his teaching methods.[122] Even some "respectable" educated women were hauled to court to answer for their foul mouths. The bookkeeper Martha Blume was tried and convicted for her behavior in an angry exchange with a male stranger on a Berlin streetcar. While she was disembarking at Friedrichstrasse, the long pins in her hat accidentally brushed against the face of one Karl Ladewig, master butcher. He cursed her, she called him an "old fart" (*Griesekel*). He sued and won.[123] Among the bourgeoisie, one also finds women in the courts implicitly defending a non-sexual view of their honor. In one case that reached the Reichsgericht, a wife sued her own husband for libel after he placed ads in the local (Alsace) newspapers warning shopowners that he would no longer cover her debts.[124] The wife's suit (a civil case brought under §823 of the BGB) demanded a public retraction of the ads.[125]

---

[120] Kurz, *§193*, p. 5

[121] Court judgment of February 18, 1914. Rep. 5E, Nr. 257, Brandenburgisches Landeshauptarchiv (BLA), pp. 84–86.

[122] At a public meeting, she criticized the way the teacher called her grandchildren and their classmates by "ugly animal names." "Wegen Lehrerbeleidigung," *Vorwärts*, September 12, 1902. She was convicted and fined 30M.

[123] She was fined the enormous sum, given the charge, of 75M. "Die langen Hutnadeln," *Vorwärts*, February 18, 1911.

[124] Richard Schmidt, *Der Anspruch auf Widerruf einer Beleidigung* (Göttingen, 1913).

[125] The court rejected her argument.

POLITICS

Minor business usually topped the day's agenda at the Reichstag, and Wednesday, March 31, 1909 was no different. Before the budget debate resumed from the previous session, members were asked to consider the request of two deputies, Mugdan and Kopsch, who were in the middle of a *Privatklage* with the writer Franz Mehring (the latter, having been sued by them because of one of his articles, was now countersuing). Mugdan and Kopsch wanted permission – a requirement for deputies under the imperial constitution (*Reichsverfassung*) – to pursue their countersuit, a request that was dispatched with a quick, assenting vote.[126] This was the kind of moment – the pausing for consideration of a libel lawsuit – that typically punctuated parliamentary sessions of the era because so many deputies were involved in these suits. Just how common such litigation was among Germany's legislators is suggested by the fact that political careers without libel actions, like those of Eugen Richter and August Bebel,[127] were considered anomalous curiosities.

Libel lawsuits pervaded Germany's politics to such a degree that it may be time to place the courtroom alongside the parliament, the political meeting, the street demonstration, and the press, as a site of political action. It was not only the incessant way the government used defamation law to prosecute campaigns against its political opponents (chapter 3). The citizenry and its politicians were perpetually prone to fighting out political differences around symbolic contests over honor, battles that frequently ended in the courtroom. And they happened everywhere – in elections, the legislatures, around a wide spectrum of issues from religious to ethnic to labor politics (the latter discussed above). It is not merely the ubiquity of these lawsuits that make them so interesting. It is also that they suggest a method of doing politics, one cleverly adapted to the legal, political, and cultural environment of the Kaiserreich. This section

---

[126] *Stenographische Berichte über die Verhandlungen des deutschen Reichstags* [SBR] vol. 236 (Berlin, 1909), p. 7884.

[127] They were each known for never having filed a defamation suit, a well-known fact remarked upon in "Die Beleidigungsklage," *Der Tag*, February 19, 1914.

begins with a survey of the general ways that honor and libel litigation interacted with politics; it ends with a closer look at the libel lawsuit as a mode of politics.

Electoral politics was to an extraordinary degree conducted through the courts in the Kaiserreich. Political animosities played out as personal invective that ended in honor scandals and libel suits. Antisemitic writers and politicians were particularly prone to such lawsuits (see also chapter 5). In 1911 alone, the antisemite Wilhelm Bruhn was engaged simultaneously in no less than three *Privatklagen* with newspapers he accused of attacking his moral character.[128] Electoral campaigns in general were rife with libel lawsuits. One example taken from the Kaiserreich's religious politics is the bitter 1882 campaign between Protestant National Liberals and the Catholic Center party for the Prussian Diet's seat in Krefeld. Deputy Seyffardt, a liberal *Kulturkämpfer* and factory owner, had recently lost his seat to a Center politician, and Krefeld's liberals badly wanted it back. To this end, Seyffardt gave a rousing *kulturkämpferisch* speech against the Catholics, which was repaid in kind a couple of days later when, at a Catholic meeting, two Center activists (Titz and Urfey) called Seyffardt a "scoundrel" (*Bubenstück*) and declared that "it is a lesser sin to spit in one's mother's face than to vote for Herr Seyffardt." Liberals responded with, according to one Catholic account, a campaign of "defamation" against Catholics in the local National Liberal newspaper. The conflict then moved into the courts, Titz filing a defamation *Privatklage* against the newspaper and the National Liberal electoral committee, and Seyffardt countering with a suit against Titz and Urfey for "public persecution."[129]

Honor conflicts both reflected and exasperated conflicts between the parties. This was the case, for example, in Mecklenburg in 1914. Conservative party secretary Jordan published a pamphlet lampooning the progressive Reichstag deputy Hugo Wendorff, who had won his seat in 1912. Immediately afterwards, Jordan published a pamphlet,

---

[128] "Einige Bruhn-Prozesse," *Vorwärts*, April 7, 1911.
[129] N.a., *Process gegen die Herren Caplan Titz und Dr. Urfey* (Crefeld, 1883).

"Die Ursachen der Teuerung," in which he attacked Wendorff for acting not out of conviction but in the interests of speculators and big business to the ruin of the local agricultural economy. Wendorff sued for defamation. The district attorney initially rejected the case, arguing that the comment constituted legitimate political speech and attacked Wendorff not personally but as representative of a political party. It took the intervention of the state attorney's boss, the Oberstaatsanwalt, for the case to be prosecuted. Jordan was convicted, fined 500M and ordered to cease publication and distribution of his pamphlet. He ignored this order, continuing to distribute it in Wendorff's voting district, with the state attorney (who had initially refused to prosecute Jordan) suspiciously unwilling for months to intervene.

The lawsuit, in turn, turned into a wider ranging debate about the nature of politics and the legal system. The conservative *Mecklenburger Warte* weighed in with the charge that the state had no business prosecuting the case because the insult of Wendorff did not rise to the level of "public interest" (the criterion for state defamation prosecutions). Only "men and circles of people" who act in the "spirit of the organic forward development of state life" deserved such treatment, not politicians like Wendorff who ally themselves with the Social Democrats. The state's motives in prosecuting the case, the article implied, were political, since the prosecutor's office is inherently a "political organ." The left-liberal Halle paper *Saale-Zeitung* countered with a critique that analyzed the conservative position in terms of a broader troubling trend in German conservatism: its rejection of a state based on the rule of law (*Rechtsstaat*). The district attorney, it argued, is not a "political authority"; it is charged with applying the law equally, irrespective of the person's position or politics. The conservative position on Jordan–Wendorff, however, is typical. For conservatives, "whoever is conservative has the right to the full protection of the authorities, liberal men, to the contrary, are outlawed. That is nothing but the direct negation of the *Rechtsstaat*," and a disturbing development in an increasingly "demagogic" party.[130]

---

[130] "Staatsanwalt und konservativer Parteisekretär," *Saale-Zeitung*, March 6, 1914.

Honor disputes in the parliaments were likewise stand-ins for deeper political rifts and partisan passions. In 1908, such a conflict erupted in the Prussian Landtag when the Conservative deputy and reserve officer Hahn called the Progressive Party a patsy of "stock-market" men "on the Riviera." The statement was galling because it lumped the Progressives together with the rich at a time when that party was gearing up for an election on a platform of democratizing the Prussian franchise. But it was also distressing (and effective) because of the implicit xenophobia, antisemitism, and social snobbery of its imagery, the stock market, Riviera men standing in for a Jewish, French-loving *nouveau riche*. Angered, the Progressive deputy and Jew Goldschmidt called out: "that is a piece of impudence! [*Frechheit*]," choosing a phrase that, apparently, was beyond the pale of appropriate parliamentary speech. Conservatives immediately demanded an apology and retraction, but Goldschmidt refused, saying he would take back his comment only if Hahn retracted his own derogatory comment about the Progressives.[131] The argument now moved into the press, where commentary on both sides revealed its underlying class politics. The Progressive *Freisinnige Zeitung* related deputy Hahn's touchiness, with his reserve officer status and its accompanying military dueling ethos, accusing him of "flaunting his rank as first lieutenant of the reserves," and bemoaning how, as a result, parliamentary "differences that arise in debate are settled with the sabre or the whip."[132] The Conservative *Ostpreussische Zeitung* responded with a lecture on social etiquette, mocking Goldschmidt's lack of "understanding ... for the essence of honor affronts." Any person of the right social class, it said in so many words, knows that a personal insult [Goldschmidt's "*Frechheit*"] that is not a critique of a political party [Hahn's stock-market Progressives] is defamatory and requires satisfaction. Furthermore, Hahn responded as he did, not because he was an officer (in fact Hahn was against dueling), but because anyone in "respectable society" (*gute Gesellschaft*) would do so.[133]

---

[131] "Besseren Schutz der Ehre!" *Ostpreussische Zeitung*, March 19, 1908.
[132] Quoted ibid.   [133] Ibid.

Honor could be a cudgel used against social inferiors (e.g. upstart Jews like Goldschmidt) and the politically weaker (see chapter 3), but it could also function in the reverse way, directed from below at the powerful. One sees this in a lawsuit touching on the "Polish question" – clashes over Prussia's Germanization of its eastern provinces and its discriminatory policies against the Polish inhabitants. In 1904, one element of German-Polish tension was the attempt by some Polish-speaking doctors to have their German counterparts excluded from Posen's medical board. Prussia's Interior Minister, von Hammerstein, responded in a speech before the Prussian Landtag that ended with: "Gentlemen! I believe the word cannot be said enough: it is an *impudence* [*Unverschämtheit*] of Polish physicians to go to the medical board with such a proposal."[134] One of those (unnamed) Polish doctors, a Dr. Jerzykowski, promptly sued the minister for defamation. The lawsuit focused on a seeming triviality: the dishonoring slur "impudence." But behind the rhetoric of honor and the technicalities of the legal proceeding lay the bitter politics of German-Polish relations. Von Hammerstein's remark had come in defense of a bill before the House to extend German settlements in the east. The bill, strenuously opposed by Polish and Center representatives, was excoriated by representative Roeren for "its unbelievable harshness" and discriminatory policies that would alienate and economically devastate the Polish population.[135] It was at this point that von Hammerstein had risen to defend Germanhood against the Poles. Jerzykowski did, however, lose the case. Two courts ruled that, while "impudence" was indeed seriously insulting, the minister's statement, made in an official capacity and in defense of a government policy, came under §193 protection. It was, in other words, legitimate dishonoring speech.

The politicized libel lawsuit was not merely a question of honor-obsessed men acting out their emotions in politics by personalizing

---

[134] My emphasis. The statement was reproduced in a subsequent legal proceeding. I.HA Rep. 84a, Nr. 139, GStPK pp. 152–53.

[135] The quote and paraphrase of Roeren is taken from the appellate court judgment. Ibid., pp. 153ff.

their differences. The libel lawsuit was a *method* of doing politics – calculated, adaptive, and highly effective. It was a method that used the lawsuit as a form of political discourse to pursue goals we associate with politics: exposing opponents and public wrongdoing, educating the public, advocating for a cause. Its mechanics involved intentionally provoking an opponent to bring a libel lawsuit against oneself, thus creating a forum at trial to publicize and elaborate on one's agenda. The original libel thereby functioned as a pretext for a defense strategy of introducing into the court record with the *Wahrheitsbeweis* device reams of testimony and evidence about one's broader cause, which in turn, was aimed at catapulting it into the press and public debate.

A perfect example of this method comes from one of the higher-profile libel trials of the Kaiserreich: the *Bochumer Steuerprozess*, a legal proceeding in 1890/91 that rocked the public with its implications of large-scale public graft and its overtones of religious and class politics.[136] The main defendant, Johannes Fusangel, a Catholic newsman and editor of the *Westfälische Volkszeitung*, was no stranger to the political libel; since the *Kulturkampf* battles of the 1870s, he had twenty libel convictions and at least eleven months in jail under his belt. But "Bochum" was his masterpiece. In an unrelenting series of exposés written by his reporter co-defendant in 1890, the *Westfälische Volkszeitung* charged that, for religiously and politically partisan reasons, members of Bochum's tax commission knowingly and intentionally undervalued the taxes of their Protestant and National Liberal brethren among the city's elite. This was muckraking journalism and more, in the German context, since Fusangel knew very well that he was heading straight to court. At a certain point, in fact, exposing wrongdoing and goading the wrongdoers into a libel lawsuit probably merged in his intentions. And indeed, after six months, the result was a mammoth lawsuit filed by about thirty plaintiffs from Bochum's Protestant power elite: members of the tax commission, magistrates, mayors, councilmen, a legislator, an industrialist, an

---

[136] I. HA Rep. 84a, Nr. 49799, GStPK, contains the court judgment and other documents, including press articles, on the case.

engineer. Surely, these men did so with reluctance – suggested, among other things, by how long they waited to sue – dreading that a trial, while required for their honor, would simply give their Catholic enemies greater ammunition and a public platform to air their charges. This was exactly what happened: at trial, Fusangel invoked his right to present evidence supporting the truth of his libels (the *Wahrheitsbeweis*) with devastating effect on both plaintiffs and defense witnesses forced to testify. In the outraged description of the National Liberal *Kölnische Zeitung*,

> More than 150 citizens of the city, including a number of the most highly regarded men who held all manner of honorable positions, in wartime as officers and soldiers, in peacetime as civil servants and honorary officials … a court hearing in which they were forced without mercy not only to publicly reveal the most intimate matters regarding their finances and family affairs, but also stand by and watch while a personality like the defendant brings the credibility of innocent witnesses into question through all kinds of outrageous methods of interrogation evidence motions – this is intolerable![137]

Fusangel was eventually convicted and sentenced to one month in jail, but not before inflicting serious damage on his opponents. His strategy, which he shared with perhaps thousands of other libel defendants in the Kaiserreich, was perfectly calibrated to the conditions of culture, law, and politics prevailing in Germany, ones that set the parameters of speech, both limiting and channeling it into the courts. It assumed and used the collective knowledge that individuals with wounded reputations respond with lawsuits, and it worked a system stacked against effective challenges to power elites by turning legal limitations on speech (via defamation law) against those elites in the courtroom. Massive censorship of the press and of disrespectful attitudes toward the state, to which the following chapter turns, was a critical context for this kind of political action and, more generally, for the history of honor and libel in the Kaiserreich.

---

[137] "Ein Rückblick auf den Bochumer Steuerprocess," *Kölnische Zeitung*, June 20, 1891.

CHAPTER 3

The state

"Whether he is in a private office or a public bureau, the modern official always strives and usually enjoys a distinct social esteem as compared with the governed. His social position is guaranteed by the prescriptive rules of rank order and, for the political official, by special definitions of the *criminal code against 'insults of officials'* and 'contempt' of state and church authorities."[1]

That censorship in the Kaiserreich operated through defamation law is vaguely known but massively underappreciated and underresearched.[2] Honor and its defense through libel actions were fundamental to state power. This was true at every level, from the Kaiser, who was not above suing an erstwhile flower girl and "prostitute,"[3] down to the lowest village clerk and nightwatchman. The state

---

[1] My emphasis. Max Weber, from *Wirtschaft und Gesellschaft*, in Gerth and Mills (eds.), *From Max Weber: Essays in Sociology* (New York, 1981), p. 199.

[2] One typical and detailed example of the literature: Wolfram Siemann, "Verbote, Normierungen und Normierungsversuche," in Georg Jäger (ed.), *Geschichte des deutschen Buchhandels im 19. und 20. Jahrhundert: Bd. I Das Kaiserreich* (Frankfurt am Main, 2001), p. 95 and passim, which examines censorship in terms of the direct banning of certain printed material and offers only a passing mention of libel actions. Irene Fischer-Frauendienst, *Bismarcks Pressepolitik* (Münster, 1963), p. 17, mentions Bismarck's frequent use of the libel lawsuit against opponents, whose heyday, she argues, began in 1874 against Catholics during the *Kulturkampf,* and subsequently during the persecution of Socialists (*Sozialistenverfolgung*). Kurt Koszyk, *Deutsche Presse im 19. Jahrhundert: Geschichte der deutschen Presse Teil II* (Berlin, 1966), pp. 231–32. For an overview of the censorship of literary works, see Dieter Breuer, *Geschichte der literarischen Zensur in Deutschland* (Heidelberg, 1982); on the laws, see Konrad Dussel, *Deutsche Tagespresse im 19. und 20. Jahrhundert* (Münster, 2004), pp. 51ff. and passim.

[3] Now married into aristocracy, she claimed he had fathered her children as a result of an affair. I. HA Rep. 84a, Nr. 49812, GStPK, pp. 27ff.

wielded the defamation lawsuit unremittingly, harassing, disciplin-
ing, and silencing written and spoken, public and private speech.

Its most important tools were the *Beamtenbeleidigung*, §193, and
the lèse-majesté clauses of the penal code. Formally, as we have seen,
Beamtenbeleidigung no longer existed in the Criminal Code.[4] In
practice, it was ubiquitous. There was, it seems, a short period around
the years of the Reich's founding when some courts had taken the
new egalitarian direction in defamation law literally, refusing to grant
libeled officials special treatment in the courts. Thus, in one controversial Saxon case, a Leipzig lower court in 1872 had denied a state
prosecution of a newspaper (*Volksstaat*) that had allegedly libeled a
district court and state attorney, treating the plaintiffs instead like
regular citizens and directing them to the *Privatklage* and the (pre-
1877) civil courts. Outrage ensued at the top levels of government
with the Saxon justice minister moving to reaffirm the superior honor
status of officials in a directive ordering state criminal prosecutions
for libeled state officials (*Beamten*).[5] As a result of this kind of
pressure from on high, as early as the beginning of the 1870s special
protection of officialdom's honor was being reinstated by the courts
through rulings that came to treat all libels against officials (when the
defamation dealt with actions or statements done in their official
capacities) as matters of "public interest" meriting state prosecutions.[6] Such an interpretation of the law also encouraged the superiors of lower-level libeled officials to file criminal charges in the
latter's name (§196), irrespective of the libeled official's own wishes
or actions, since, as one Prussian court put it, what was at stake was
not just his own "integrity," but the "safeguarding of the honor of the
office."[7]

---

[4] For an excellent discussion of state repression and the law of lèse-majesté, see Alex
    Hall, "The Kaiser, the Wilhelmine State and Lèse-Majesté," *German Life and Letters*
    27 (1974), 101–15.
[5] I. HA Rep. 84a, Nr. 8138, GStPK, pp. 33ff.
[6] See the documents in I. HA Rep. 84a, Nr. 8138, GStPK, pp. 21ff.
[7] Verdict of the Königliches Ober-Tribunal, January 4, 1875. *Justiz-Ministerial-Blatt
    für die preussische Gesetzgebung und Rechtspflege*, 37. Jg., Nr. 12 (March 19, 1875).

Moreover, while §193 formally protected defamatory speech against officials and others if made for the purpose of "defending legitimate interests," the courts, led by a series of Reichsgericht (Supreme Court) decisions, came to define "legitimate interests" so narrowly as to essentially eliminate the protection of newspapers that criticized official actions.[8] Third were the lèse-majesté laws and their interpretation by the courts that equated insulting (or even critical) statements against the Kaiser, ruling royalty/princes, and their families as akin to acts of treason against the state itself, and that, accordingly, formed the basis for thousands of prosecutions.[9]

With the rise of a mass press and the democratization of politics, a kind of panic in government circles took hold about real and perceived attacks, and about the political and symbolic import of honor injuries against the state. This chapter begins at the top with meetings of the Prussian Ministry of State, whose minutes illuminate the government's strategic thinking about defamation prosecutions. They also offer insight into how the upper reaches of government, in thinking through the defamation problem, were grappling more broadly with the institutional exigencies of a constitutional state anchored by an independent judiciary and a vibrant, nominally free mass press. The chapter moves out from there to the daily honor encounters and lawsuits between the population and officialdom, with emphasis on the campaign of repression against the Left. It concludes with the courts – their role in the suppression of speech, most evident in the crippling anti-free press rulings of the high court, as well as divisions within the courts themselves.

Government policy in Prussia on prosecuting defamations against the top echelon of officialdom – the German Chancellor and members of the Ministry of State – shifted over the years. For Bismarck, the

---

[8] A good discussion of the issues for the 1870s can be found in the commentary on §193 in *Strafgesetzbuch für das deutsche Reich*, pp. 392ff.

[9] For an overview of German lèse-majesté laws in the nineteenth and twentieth centuries, see Andrea Hartmann, *Majestätsbeleidigung und Verunglimpfung des Staatsoberhauptes (§§94ff. RStGB, 90 StGB): Reformdiskussion und Gesetzgebung seit dem 19. Jahrhundert* (Berlin, 2006).

defamation lawsuit was a critical tool of rulership. During his three decades in power, he used it relentlessly and systematically against his enemies and against critics of the state in general. In the early 1860s, during the Prussian constitutional conflict, he directed it against liberal deputies in the Prussian Landtag, as in the notorious case against Karl Twesten (chapter 1). By the later 1860s, such suits were focusing on Welfisch critics of Prussia's annexation of Hanover. By the 1870s, Bismarck was suing everybody – Catholics, Poles,[10] leftists, and ultra-rightists. Among the latter were a series of libel trials (resulting in years-long jail sentences) against editors of the far-right *Reichsglocke* for articles condemning the famous treason trial of Bismarck's arch-conservative rival, the former diplomat Harry von Arnim, and for charging Bismarck and Bleichröder with corruption (part of a more general right-wing backlash against Bismarck's break with traditional Prussian conservatism).[11]

But it was the Social Democrats who would become the chief objects of Bismarck's litigious ire. After 1878, during the era of the anti-Socialist laws and Bismarck's war against social democracy, the SPD press was bombarded with libel lawsuits. Bismarck pressed for prosecutions of the Left at every opportunity, even against obscure socialist writers and newspapers. It was not uncommon for Reichstag sessions, for example, to begin with a vote on one of his motions to approve prosecution of a (usually leftist) critic of the Reichstag. He did so, it seems, not for sentimental personal reasons of honor, but as a matter of principle to block challenges to himself and the state in general.

Even the most trivial reproaches by anonymous, insignificant citizens were not below Bismarck's radar. In one documented case that ended up before the country's high court, a man in a pub in 1879 was heard disparaging a Reichstag speech of Bismarck's as no better than what a "chimney-sweep" could do. Convicted of defaming the Chancellor, the defendant appealed the decision, which was overruled at the

[10] Bismarck's enemies during the anti-Catholic *Kulturkampf* and as a result of repressive anti-Polish policies in Prussia's eastern territories.

[11] For a contemporary account, see Gustav Meyer, *Proƶess und Vertheidigungsrede des Legationsrathe a.d. Grafen Hermann von Arnim* (Berlin, 1878). See also Barnet Hartston, *Sensationaliƶing the Jewish Question* (Leiden, 2005), pp. 14–15.

second instance, *not* in the name of free speech but because, in the court's august opinion, a chimney-sweep was an honorable profession and thus comparisons between that profession and a man's oratorical abilities did not have the power to dishonor the latter. The Reichsgericht, agreeing with the court of first instance, overturned the ruling.[12] Two years later, Bismarck had drawn back a bit, refusing to press charges against an office clerk because, he explained, "that he only presses charges against a simple verbal insult directed against himself when, either because of the place, time or other circumstances, it has a political character."[13]

When he was not bringing lawsuits himself or encouraging government organs (e.g., the Reichstag) to do so, Bismarck could be found behind the scenes putting pressure on the courts. In 1883 he had the foreign office communicate to Friedberg, the Minister of Justice, his displeasure with the leniency of a lawsuit brought against a reporter at the *Berliner Tageblatt* for defaming the Russian Interior Minister, Count Tolstoy. Bismarck was irritated that the state attorney had requested only a fine of 150M, an insultingly low sum, in his judgment, given Tolstoy's high status. He feared the case could have legal and political repercussions, including defamatory reprisals against German officials in "foreign papers."[14] Friedberg promptly ordered an appeal of the case (which ultimately was rejected by the Reichsgericht), and made it known to his underlings, the offending state attorney and his boss, that "mild" punishments were unacceptable.[15]

Prosecutions for defamations of top Prussian officials fell off dramatically under Bismarck's successors, although they far from disappeared. Generally, after 1890, the policy was one of cautious avoidance of such actions except in the most egregious (and winnable) cases.

---

[12] "Beleidigung des Reichskanzlers Fürsten Bismarck," *Annalen des Reichsgerichts* (Leipzig, 1880), pp. 29–30.
[13] I. HA Rep. 84a, Nr. 8139, GStPK, p. 61. It could be that this had always been Bismarck's policy and that he had considered the earlier "chimney-sweep" comment "political."
[14] Busch to Friedberg, Berlin, October 11, 1883. I. HA Rep. 84a, Nr. 8139, GStPK, pp. 75–77.
[15] Friedberg to Foreign Minister Hatzfeldt-Wildenburg, March 14, 1884. I. HA Rep. 84a, Nr. 8139, GStPK, pp. 77–78.

Caprivi brought no libel suits in the first years of his rule, only to partially reverse course in 1893 in the case of anti-government statements made at antisemitic political gatherings.[16] Both Hohenlohe-Schillingsfürst and Bülow were "averse" to such lawsuits, resorting to them only in a few extreme cases.[17] Bethmann Hollweg continued this pattern, even against his own impulses (see below). In 1907 Bülow ordered all police officials *not* to immediately pursue defamation charges for statements or images against the chancellor, that is, to generally abstain from suing.[18]

Bülow's order coincided with a decree issued earlier that year by the Kaiser himself aimed at limiting and moderating prosecutions of lèse-majesté. Henceforth, according to the Kaiser, only those insults against the royal house done with "premeditation and malicious intent" would be subject to legal action, a move that, though not uncontroversial (the SPD was deeply disturbed by the language of "malicious intent" that was adopted into later draft legislation – see chapter 4), had the potential of significantly limiting prosecutions.[19] Equally encouraging, the decree, seeking to weed out the many bogus denunciations from the public stemming from private fights and animosities, decreased from five years to six months the statute of limitations within which charges for the offense could be brought. Much of the press greeted this with enthusiasim and hope. "The era of lèse-majesté trials is happily

---

[16] Documents for another set of defamation charges against antisemitic publicists under Caprivi can be found in I. HA Rep. 84a, Nr. 55747, GStPK.

[17] This is a summary of Bethmann Hollweg's summary of the history in a December 28, 1911 letter to the Justice Minister, I. HA Rep. 84a, Nr. 8139, GStPK, pp. 240–41. One example of Bülow refusing to prosecute: in 1907, a Socialist engineer and writer, Max Grempe, gave a series of public talks, illustrated with lantern slides, on the 1905 Russian revolution. A police spy reported that Grempe was showing caricatures of the chancellor accompanied by "insulting" commentary. A criminal investigation got under way, only to be halted by the chancellor. Bülow to Interior Minister, June 30, 1907. I. HA Rep. 84a, Nr. 8139, GStPK, p. 163.

[18] "Beleidigungen des Reichskanzlers," *Deutsche Tageszeitung*, August 1, 1907; "Ein kleiner Fortschritt," *Breslauer Zeitung*, August 6, 1907.

[19] Decree of January 27, 1907. *Gerichtssaal* 70 (1907), 115. For an example of the kind of defamation cases the royal house was inclined to pursue in an earlier frame of mind (i.e. in 1900), see the report of a Berlin district attorney to the Justice Minister, January 31, 1900, in I. HA Rep. 84a, Nr. 49820, GStPK, pp. 23ff.

over," proclaimed (prematurely) the *Breslauer Zeitung*. Bülow's order, in particular, while "small," was, according to the author, a step forward.[20]

Prosecutorial restraint in all but the worst cases came to be the default policy not because Bismarck's successors were more open-minded toward their critics. It was a question, rather, of pure tactics – the least bad choice in an increasingly out-of-control situation caused by the growth of an unruly press and the rising electoral fortunes of the SPD. In this situation, draconian prosecutions, as in the days of Bismarck, were a declining option: they easily backfired, potentially strengthening the hands of the enemy (i.e. government critics). Legal actions taken against insignificant newspapers and authors brought them inadvertent publicity.[21] Equally, if not more, troubling was the *Wahrheitsbeweis* – the right of defense counsel to introduce into a defamation trial evidence from the life and actions of the plaintiff (in this case, a high state official) in order to prove the truth of the defendant's alleged defamation. Trials were forms of unscripted public theatre. They gave government critics a public podium. They allowed undesirable new facts and assertions to come to light and the replaying of controversial events and government actions. Consequently, the ministry feared, they could potentially influence the outcome of elections, increasing support for the Left. But maintaining a hands-off position posed its own set of problems. Failing to prosecute serious defamations could undermine the state's authority. There was the constant worry about how state inaction appeared in the eyes of the people, about "legal confusion" and "misunderstanding"[22] aroused by the government's seeming tolerance of attacks against itself.

There was, moreover, the problem of the duel, a growing controversy the government faced and one closely bound up with

---

[20] "Ein kleiner Fortschritt," *Breslauer Zeitung*, August 6, 1907.

[21] State Ministry meeting, April 27, 1901. I. HA Rep. 90a, vol. 142, GStPK, pp. 164–65. As von Bülow put it: the State Ministry has no "set practice with respect to the question of the prosecution of insults … but generally speaking, seldom finds occasion for pressing charges, especially when it is a question of minor newspapers, for whom a criminal investigation would only serve as publicity …"

[22] State Ministry meeting, January 6, 1911. I. HA Rep. 90a, vol. 160, GStPK, p. 21.

defamation law. By the 1890s, public outrage was increasing over the fatal spread of dueling and the extremely lenient sentences and pardons meted out by the courts to duelists. The alarm over dueling in bourgeois and rightist circles was fed, in addition, by the political capital that Socialists were making of the issue as they waged "a campaign against duelling on the grounds that it was an illegal class privilege and which condemned the kid-gloved attitude of the state towards the phenomenon as a flagrant example of class justice."[23] The Ministry of State shared the belief with growing numbers in the center and right of the political spectrum that minimizing the duel required giving elite men (those capable of giving satisfaction) an appealing legal alternative and that this should be accomplished by strengthening defamation law in the form of stepped-up prosecutions, higher sentences, and the better protection of plaintiffs' privacy with a crackdown on the *Wahrheitsbeweis*. But a Reichstag deal to sharpen defamation laws, even one placating the Left with sharpened dueling penalities (a losing Reichstag proposition in the 1890s), was bound to falter on the opposition of the Socialists. Led by Bebel, Socialists were convinced that defamation law reform along these lines would only strengthen the government's prosecutorial hand against the leftist press (see chapter 4).[24]

The Ministry of State was caught in a bind. Hence, the about-face reversal of course by chancellors such as Caprivi in 1893 after he had initially wanted to steer clear of the libel lawsuit.[25] Hence, also, that decisions by the Ministry about whether or not to pursue defamation charges tended to be ad hoc and made on a case-by-case basis involving the careful weighing of such factors as the severity of the offense, the importance of the defamer, the chances of winning in court, and the potential for damaging information against the state

---

[23] Ute Frevert, *Men of Honour: A Social and Cultural History of the Duel* (Cambridge, MA, 1995); Kevin McAleer, *Dueling: The Cult of Honor in fin-de-siècle Germany* (Princeton, 1994), p. 193.

[24] State Ministry meeting, October 6, 1897, I. HA Rep. 90a, vol. 131, GStPK, pp. 78 ff.; *Justizministerialblatt* 43 (December 1897), 285–86; I. HA Rep. 84a, Nr. 8139, GStPK, p. 141.

[25] State Ministry meeting, April 10, 1893. I. HA Rep. 84a, Nr. 8139, GStPK, p. 126.

to arise in a trial. The *Berliner Montags-Zeitung*, edited by Max Wittenberg, certainly insulted the Minister of the Interior in 1901, but it was "only a paper of scant importance"; pressing charges would simply bring it publicity.[26] By contrast, legal action was needed in the more egregious case of a Polish newspaper, *Gazeta Grudziadzka*, whose 1906 article on the controversial language issue in Prussia's eastern territories threatened the government with resistance and a "flood of invective."[27] The same applied to a Social Democratic writer and activist, a Dr. Pönsgen, who, despite an earlier criminal charge, was repeatedly voicing the "crudest insults" against the government at meetings in and around Berlin. Prosecute and "shut his trap," offered the Justice Minister.[28] Meanwhile (1897), the Ministry was requesting that public prosecutors be instructed to strengthen defamation punishments and, in light of the dueling issue, make the process more palatable to plaintiffs by "not making all of the hidden points from the past of the defamed person a subject of the investigation."[29]

By 1910, a sense of crisis had set in. Libels against government officials appeared out of control and the terrible blast of the Eulenburg scandal (chapter 4) was still reverberating. But the immediate cause in 1910 was public outrage over the repression of a worker uprising in Moabit and its litigious aftermath. Moabit was an important event in the history of labor politics,[30] the name itself becoming synonymous among contemporaries with class conflict.[31] In the courts, Moabit was

---

[26] Ibid., April 27, 1901, vol. 142, pp. 164–65.
[27] Ibid., October 30, 1906, vol. 153, pp. 124–25.   [28] Ibid., April 22, 1904, vol. 148.
[29] Ibid., October 6, 1897, vol. 131, pp. 78ff.
[30] Helmut Bleiber, "Die Moabiter Unruhen 1910," *Zeitschrift für Geschichtswissenschaft* 3(2) (1955), 173–211, provides a detailed, archivally based Marxist-Leninist analysis of the uprising and its origins. A more recent work, Thomas Lindenberger, *Strassenpolitik: Zur Sozialgeschichte der öffentlichen Ordnung in Berlin, 1900 bis 1914* (Bonn, 1995), which rejects Bleiber's interpretation, contextualizes the events within the history of German street politics. Neither study explores Moabit's legal aspects and its spin-off libel litigation. For more general information on the repression of workers and the Left, see Gerhard A. Ritter and Klaus Tenfelde, *Arbeiter im deutschen Kaiserreich, 1871 bis 1914* (Bonn, 1992), pp. 679 ff.
[31] Lindenberger, *Strassenpolitik*, p. 241.

a public relations disaster of the first order for the government. Resounding at the highest levels of government, the uprising and its aftermath weighed heavily on the minds of ministers as they conferred on the direction of libel policy. The event thus merits closer examination.

The unrest in Moabit, a working-class district of Berlin, began on September 19, 1910, with the walkout of coal workers at the firm of Kupfer & Co. after the breakdown of union negotiations over a pay raise. By the next day, the strike had spread to other workers in the area and had turned violent. The violence (at first rock-throwing and other attacks on strikebreakers) rapidly escalated when units of sabre-wielding police moved in to restore order. What ensued was a week of violent clashes between "the insurgent population of an extremely homogenous worker's neighborhood and police troops organized in military fashion, whose command was to suppress the unrest."[32] The culmination was three days of outright "street battles,"[33] as in a war zone, at the end of which hundreds lay wounded and one worker was dead.

Like so many events, both serious and trivial, in the Kaiserreich, Moabit was soon playing itself out as honor litigation. This was the case, first of all, in the two mass criminal trials of sixty-six workers,[34] whose charges, along with breach of the peace and sedition, included libel (the worker epithet of choice against the police during the unrest was "bloodhounds" [*Bluthunde*]).[35] The danger of criminal prosecutions – the unpredictable way they were subverted by government opponents – was on full display at the first trial in the winter of 1910/11. Here, the prosecution's politicized agenda was not only punishing the workers involved but proving the existence of a revolutionary Socialist conspiracy behind the uprising.[36] As such, the trial was a disaster, offering

---

[32]   Ibid., p. 291.

[33]   Jagow to Chancellor Bethmann Hollweg, September 29, 1910. I. HA Rep. 77, Tit. 2515, Nr. 3 Fasz. 4, Bd. 1, GStPK, pp. 42–43.

[34]   One of the indicted committed suicide in prison before the trial.

[35]   Court judgment, January 11, 1911. Ibid., Bd. 2, pp. 84, 206 and passim. Other charges included duress (*Nötigung*), violation of the commercial code, and vandalism.

[36]   The government, however, knew early on that the SPD leadership bore no responsiblity for the uprising. See, Jagow to Dallwitz, October 25, 1910. Ibid., Bd. 1, pp. 156–59.

instead a parade of defense witnesses whose testimony opened to the public a disturbing window onto the behavior of an out-of-control police force. This testimony turned the trial on its head, making, as Berlin Police Chief von Jagow complained, "the Berlin police into the de facto defendants."[37]

December 6, 1910, typified the problems the government faced during the trial. Among the two defendants on trial that day was one Romanowski, who admitted to once, on the night of September 28, "shouting [the libelous] 'Bloodhounds'" as he stood with his neighbors at the entrance of an apartment building watching the events in the streets.[38] The subsequent witness testimony began well enough for the prosecution: Police Sergeant Koch spoke of how a crowd at the apartment building began shouting at (*schimpfen*) the police, and how the people were ordered back into the apartment house. The crowd threw stones at the police and shots were fired; despite this, he concluded, the police acted "peacefully and without the use of weapons to try to disperse the crowd." But when the defense subsequently called its witnesses, a quite different picture emerged, one of rampant police brutality. They described the police sabre beatings of innocent bystanders, including an old man "peacefully walking down the street." According to the apartment house porter, "two policemen [*Schutzleute*] went after him," beating him "like a piece of livestock." The prosecution of a minor libel violation ("Bloodhound") was dangerously becoming an anti-police political forum. Months of similar testimony turned the trial, in the eyes of a wary government, into a "site of agitation" with the subversive aim, "as always," of "disparaging state authority ... especially through the reviling of the police."[39] The verdict in January, 1911, was a Pyrrhic victory for the prosecution, bringing in convictions but only after months of

---

[37] "Tatsächlich ist in diesem Prozesse die Berliner Schutzmannschaft in die Rolle des Angeklagten hineingedrängt worden ..." Jagow to Interior Minister, November 28, 1910. Ibid., p. 255.

[38] "Die Moabiter Vorgänge vor Gericht," *Vorwärts*, December 7, 1910. All quotes from this trial day are taken from this article.

[39] Jagow report, January 6, 1911. I. HA Rep. 77, Tit. 2515, Nr. 3, Fasz. 4, Bd. 1, GStPK, p. 228.

testimony and reportage in the mass press had damaged the image of the Berlin police in public opinion.[40]

Furious, Police Chief von Jagow, referring to the "over 100 instances of the most insulting expressions used [by witnesses] about my [police] officials" at the trial, implored the minister of interior to prevent a repetition in the next trial.[41] Even before the first trial, Interior Minister Dallwitz was deeply worried about the way the SPD was exploiting the situation in the press and in the organization of mass demonstrations across Germany, by which the Socialists, in short, were using the Moabit "tumult to systematically incite the population of the entire country against officials of the police."[42]

Both Jagow's and Dallwitz's views were symptomatic of a "secondary politicization"[43] of Moabit, whose dynamic was spurring further honor confrontations. The historian Thomas Lindenberger rightly emphasizes that this politicization primarily pitted Police Chief Jagow, defending the reputation of his police force and himself, against the leadership of the SPD, who sought to exploit the events for political gain (the aim was a breakthrough in the upcoming elections to achieve a parliamentary majority) while, following their characteristically legalistic methods, distancing the party from any responsibility or involvement in the uprising.[44] This strategy on the part of the SPD, shaped as it was by Germany's political culture of honor litigation was, however, more extensive than understood by Lindenberger.

By November, 1910, Dallwitz was searching for legal pretexts to crack down on Socialist agitators, issuing a memo to all *Regierungspräsidenten* about how "urgently necessary" it was to bring criminal lawsuits against "the untrue representation of the [Moabit] events" and the "calumnies

---

[40] The court verdict itself was explicitly critical of the police. Nineteen of the convictions were for libel. Such statements as "Schmeisst doch die Bluthünde" and "Hilft Genossen gegen die Räuber," the verdict concluded, had a consciously, in the minds of the accused, "ehrenkränkenden Character": "Sie wollte die Schutzleute [police] in ihrer Ehre verletzen …" Ibid., Bd. 2, p. 84.

[41] Presumably, he had in mind the threat of libel lawsuits. Jagow to Dallwitz, January 12, 1911. Ibid., Bd. 1, p. 209.

[42] Dallwitz to the Regierungspräsidenten, November 9, 1910. Ibid., 4, Bd. 1, p. 175.

[43] Lindenberger, *Strassenpolitik*, p. 242.   [44] Ibid., pp. 242, 294–97 and passim.

against the police," and explaining that all state prosecutors had been instructed for this purpose to consider the potential criminal liability of statements made in Socialist newspapers and meetings.[45] Jagow, who was in close contact with Dallwitz, was thinking along similar lines. He soon found a promising case: a provocative front-page story in *Vorwärts* that managed to accomplish in one thesis both sides of the SPD strategy: agitation against Jagow and the police, on the one hand, and distancing itself from Moabit, on the other. The story alleged (improbably) that Moabit's violent unrest had been the intentional work of undercover police agents provocateurs acting behind the scenes to incite the crowds, and doing so, with the implied involvement of the police chief, in the interests of "reactionaries ... lusting" for a "pretext" to reinstate anti-socialist laws (*Ausnahmengesetze*).[46] Jagow filed suit the next day (against the paper's editor, Barth). Other spin-off libel suits followed in the next weeks and months, several against Socialist papers that had repeated the agent provocateur charge.[47] As late as fall 1911, Jagow could be found immersed in a libel suit against the Socialist *Harburger Parteiblatt* for criticizing a speech he had given back in January in Berlin's Zoologischer Garten, where he had heaped praise on his police force: "the badge of honor of the police force is pure, it held to irreproachable manly discipline and fulfilled its duty [at Moabit]."[48]

Honor was the public language; political strategizing was the reality behind the scenes. In a memo marked "secret!," we discover that libel litigation was being purposefully orchestrated in these trials to create a public forum to refute the "agent provocateur" charges from the Left.[49]

---

[45] Dallwitz was considering bringing charges under §§110, 130, 131. November 9, 1910. I. HA Rep. 77, Tit. 2515, Nr. 3, Fasz. 4, Bd. 1, GStPK, p. 175.

[46] "Die geheimen Führer und Leiter der Moabiter Revolution," *Vorwärts*, December 6, 1910.

[47] State attorney report, March 3, 1911. I. HA Rep. 77, Tit. 2515, Nr. 3, Fasz. 4, Bd. 2, GStPK, pp. 109 f.; Jagow report, September 9, 1911. Ibid., pp. 176–77. *Vorwärts*'s chief editor was convicted in March, 1911, of libeling the Berlin criminal police in an article using the term "Knüppelgardisten." "Die beleidigte Polizei und der abgeschnittene Wahrheitsbeweis," *Vorwärts*, March 28, 1911.

[48] "Gerichts-Zeitung," *Vorwärts*, October 31, 1911.

[49] Jagow, September 9, 1911. I. HA Rep. 77, Tit. 2515, Nr. 3, Fasz. 4, Bd. 2, GStPK, pp. 176–77.

One hears strong echoes of Moabit in internal communications of the State Ministry that strategized policy for bringing defamation charges. The "steadily increasing calumny of the Social Democratic press," explained Chancellor Bethmann Hollweg in an internal memo, had reached intolerable proportions.[50] Most recently, there were articles "grossly insult[ing]" himself for his public comments on Moabit.[51] It was time to reconsider the policy of restraint. He wanted the opinions of all ministers on the matter. Their written responses and the subsequent discussion at a 1911 State Ministry meeting did not ultimately alter libel policy.[52] But it is illuminating, providing a window onto an ongoing debate at the top about the politics of libel and dissent.

The ministers were appalled by speech coming from the Left, and all assumed that nothing less than the authority of the existing state was at stake. They differed, however, on tactics. There were those, like Dallwitz, wanting stepped-up prosecutions. Defamations, he wrote, "are becoming ever sharper, more shameless, and frequent, thus contributing to … weakening the sense of respect for authority in the population."[53] The Minister of Public Works warned that Socialist libels went beyond the Minister-President to all top administrators; the intention was "thereby to disparage the authority of the highest authorities in front of their numerous lower officials and workers." War Minister Von Heeringen wanted prosecutions of all "odious" cases, even beyond the Socialist press, not so much in order to punish particular offenders, but as a symbolic statement to counteract "the confusion of public opinion" (*Anschauungen*) that arises when the state's highest officials are "insulted and made suspect."[54]

Those ministers advocating greater caution were equally concerned with public opinion, but saw the matter somewhat differently.

[50] President of the State Ministry, December 28, 1910. I. HA Rep. 84a, Nr. 8139, GStPK, pp. 240–41.
[51] His explanation about Moabit came later at the Ministry's meeting of January 6, 1911. I. HA Rep. 90a, vol. 160, GStPK, p. 250.
[52] The discussion, below, where not indicated otherwise, is based on the report of that meeting: State Ministry meeting of January 6, 1911, ibid., pp. 21–26.
[53] Von Dallwitz memo, January 3, 1911. I. HA Rep. 84a, Nr. 8139, GStPK, p. 246.
[54] Von Heeringen memo, January 4, 1911. Ibid., p. 248.

For them, the danger of a politicized defamation trial like Moabit outweighed the necessity of warding off "confusion" and signaling the limits of dissent through libel prosecutions. Bethmann feared the defense's ability at trial "to extend without limit the hearing of evidence." "At all costs" a repeat of Moabit must be avoided, he warned. The Finance Minister spelled out in greater detail the danger of libel trials and the *Wahrheitsbeweis*: the law provides insufficient protections against the plaintiff being further libeled in court and the ability of defense counsel to widen the issues raised at trial. Indeed, there was no protection whatsover against the other side using the trial for "political, party interests."[55] Justice Minister Beseler concurred: yes, there were dangers in not prosecuting, but one had to keep in mind the "big political picture" (*die grossen politischen Gesichtspunkte*), and the fact that "unscrupulous" defense lawyers were turning plaintiffs into defendants in the courtroom and before the public. Von Tirpitz likewise recommended caution, reminding everyone of the upcoming elections.

The debate boiled down to this: was action or inaction more politically costly? Which was worse: trial revelations of an embarrassing, compromising, or incendiary nature, as in Moabit, or allowing the government to appear weak and vulnerable in the eyes of the people? For it was the latter fear that seemed to underlie talk of the public's "legal confusion" or, as Dallwitz put it, the "weakening" of their "sense of authority."[56] Naturally, there was solid political theory on which this authoritarian position rested, namely (to put it simply), the repression of dissent in the interest of order. But, given the deeply entrenched honor culture of the men running Prussia and Germany, the ministers' reasoning clearly also derived from their honor code. As discussed earlier, the failure to challenge an insult (by dueling or litigation) in their world made one into a dishonorable coward (in the case of the dueling upper classes) or implied that

---

[55] Memo, January 3, 1911. Ibid., p. 245.

[56] Delbrück, Minister for Trade and Commerce, argued for the opposite position – i.e. to maintain the present government position on libels – because a rash of libel lawsuits could be taken by the public as a sign of "government weakness." Delbrück memo, January 4, 1911. Ibid., p. 247.

the insult was true. This honor logic – by which a libel left unpro-
secuted by the government would signal its truth to the German
people and/or the weakness of the government – seems also to have
been at play in the political calculations of the State Ministry. In the
end, those calculations favored caution. Bethmann agreed to maintain his current approach of bringing suit only in the most serious
cases and only if "the public interest demands it ... or if the libel is
such that one can count on a serious [*empfindliche*] punishment without the endless examination of evidence." But it was left to the
individual ministers to proceed as they saw fit.

When, during World War One, the *Frankfurter Zeitung* exhorted "the
German people to legal peace," lamenting the continued deluge of
libel lawsuits, it focused on a particularly ubiquitous type of defamation suit: the kind where "people who hold any type of authoritative
position instantly sue [*zum Kadi liefen*] over trivial matters
[*Bagatellsachen*]."[57] Landrichter Eberhard, writing in a legal journal,
filled out the picture: "mostly, it is a question of jostlings, abusive
language in a drunken or tipsy state or in agitation over some sort of
official action."[58] Such cases were not unique to the war years. They
included a suit, some years before, against a tenant farmer (*Pächter*),
Ernst Glander, who rented on government land in the district of
Marienwerder run by the chief official forester. In a dispute with that
official, Glander appealed to the government, writing that the forester
had changed the land boundaries to favor the gamekeeper.
Unspecified language in his complaint prompted in return a lawsuit
by the forester. Glander was convicted and sentenced to two months
in jail for the phrasing in his letter.[59] This case, on the face of it –
purely personal, occurring in an obscure area among obscure people –
was trivial by any standards. The authorities thought otherwise. It
could set a "dangerous" precedent, warned Marienwerder officials in
a report to Berlin that detailed Glander's subsequent acquittal on

---

[57] "Eine Mahnung zum Rechtsfrieden," *Frankfurter Zeitung*, December 12, 1915.
[58] Quoted ibid.
[59] Government report of October 23, 1882. I. HA Rep. 84a, Nr. 8139, GStPK, pp. 55ff.

appeal.[60] The appellate court found Glander's statement dishonoring but granted him §193 protections because of the apparent lack of malice (i.e., Glander did not intentionally seek to dishonor the forester) and because of the "form" of his statements. In response, Marienwerder officials worried that this verdict "implicitly recognized the right to inflict gross honor injuries [against officials] with impunity." Cases like this one placed the "honor of Prussian officialdom in danger" and, the report implied, there could be "political motives" lurking behind it.[61]

Notwithstanding the policies on high for top Prussian officials (above), prosecutions of insolence and irreverence toward – not to mention defamatory attacks against – state officials, as in the Glander suit, remained a perpetual and ubiquitous aspect of everyday governance in the Kaiserreich. In villages and towns across Germany, the pattern was of mundane clashes between citizens and mostly petty officials exercising an autocratic power by invoking their special honor status as incarnations of the state. The imperious officer, the small-town bully, the autocratic policeman – these were types one encountered everywhere in daily life. One gets a sense of the petty terror they spread from a laconic newspaper notice on a verbal dispute over theatre seating between a businessman, a man "with an esteemed position and the best reputation," and three military lieutenants, a dispute that ended in the businessman sentenced to two weeks in jail. One evening, at the theatre,

> The condemned [businessman Martin Lissner] … got into a verbal dispute with [the] allegedly defamed officers when they erroneously claimed a seat which correctly belonged to Lissner. The conduct of the officers understandably brought Lissner into such an excited state that he allegedly addressed the officers with language which the court considered insulting to the officer corps and specifically to the three officers involved in the dispute.[62]

---

[60] A Landgericht acquitted him on appeal not because the judge found his statements in order (the judge deemed them dishonoring) but because the judge found that Glander did not intentionally mean to insult the forester.

[61] Marienwerder, October 23, 1882. Ibid., pp. 55–57. A subsequent report from Marienwerder's attorney general categorically dismissed the notion of a politically motivated verdict and downplayed the broader significance of the case (pp. 62–66).

[62] "Eine Nichtbegnadigung," *Königsberger Hartnungsche Zeitung*, May 4, 1902.

One can imagine the scene: Lissner sitting peacefully, perhaps with his wife, waiting for the performance to begin; the entrance of the officers demanding their seats; Lissner's chagrined refusal; the officers' bullying; flaring tempers, public embarrassment, Lissner holding onto his seat; the humiliated and angry officers retreating, their feelings morphing into outrage over violated honor; the lawsuit and the devastating jail sentence for an upright bourgeois citizen.

In this case, the officers themselves initiated the lawsuit and the state prosecuted as a matter of public interest, since, as the court stated, it was a question not only of the honor of the three lieutenants, but that of the entire "officer estate." In other cases, by contrast, formal state charges were imposed from above by the superiors of libeled officals, who themselves, for reasons (almost always obscure) seemingly linked to their social existences and personal relations within communities, wanted to avoid litigation. In still other cases, the lawsuits went forward as *Privatklage* as a result of conflicts indistinguishable from those producing the masses of *Privatklagen* in the Kaiserreich.

State officials and civil servants, as previously explained, were held to high standards of professional conduct, standards that formed the core of their sense of honor, rank, and status. An official held in violation of these standards faced dishonor, discipline, and the possible ruin of his career. Accusations to this effect made by brazen citizens were, more-over, typically considered by their victims to be impertinent affronts to the honor and authority of the state itself. They were thus vigorously resisted by the official in question and by his superiors in the libel courts.

The libels of favoritism and bribery, two of the most dishonorable charges against a state official, often figured in these suits. In a property-line dispute between a prosperous farmer [*Ökonom*] and a baker, the farmer sought out the judgment of the district's official geometer (*Bezirksgeometer*), who concluded in favor of the baker. Angry, the farmer's wife wrote to the geometer's superiors accusing him of having been bought off (*abgeschmiert*) by the baker. The wife was subsequently tried and convicted of "dishonoring" a state civil servant.[63] A fruit

---

[63] Ferdinand Kurz, *§193: Beleidigung und berechtigte Interessen* (Nuremberg, 1909), p. 13.

seller, who several times had been cited by a rural constable and convicted of violating street regulations, wrote to the authorities accusing the constable of preferential treatment, after a shopkeeper over drinks at the pub told him that he (the shopkeeper) had not been cited for a similar offense because he had spoken politely to the constable.[64]

Then there were the less subtle conflicts between state and citizen, like the worker sued for biting a night watchman in the leg and calling him a "shit head" (*Dreckkopf*).[65] Or, at the other end of the social scale, the angry exchange on a Berlin street between Frau von Gerlach and a police lieutenant forcefully blocking her way, which prompted her yelling: "How can you be so shameless! ... Why do you involve yourself in such a dirty trade? Don't touch me, you make me dirty!"[66]

Many other kinds of speech as well were subject to *Beamtenbeleidigung* prosecutions. The state regularly brought libel lawsuits for critical statements uttered at public meetings (political, professional, trade), for written petitions and complaints against official abuse, in the workplace between workers,[67] and even for attorney statements made in a court of law. The latter included witness testimony and the statements of lawyers when critical of the state. The lawyer Max Lichtenstein found this out in 1912, when he was convicted and fined 500M. for a withering courtroom indictment of police abuse in Zabrze (Silesia):

It is unfortunately a fact that the police very often allows itself infringement [of the law] and that there is no protection against most of it, rather the police constitute a danger to the public ... As a result, the injured person rather than the official becomes the defendant and the official, protected by his oath of office, testifies [against the defendant].[68]

---

[64] Ibid., p. 7. The official won the lawsuit because, as the verdict explained, the honor of state officials lay in their 'impartiality,' which had been challenged and damaged by the defendant's accusation.

[65] Verdict, Potsdam, August 24, 1911. Rep. 5E, Baruth, No. 379, BLA.

[66] "Polizeibeleidigung," *Vorwärts*, February 18, 1911.

[67] An example of this latter in a Supreme Court decision: *Königsberger Allgemeine Zeitung*, August 20, 1913.

[68] "Das Reichsgericht gegen die Rechte der Verteidigung," *Vorwärts*, June 16, 1912.

The court rejected the notion that his speech served a "legitimate interest" and was thus protected under §193. It did so because it deemed Lichtenstein to have a "hostile" position toward the police and to have intentionally used the courtroom to pursue this agenda. The conviction was upheld by the Reichsgericht on appeal.[69]

Even the unpolitically motivated airing of complaints against officials was subject to libel prosecution. The lack of a transparent, regularized administrative complaint system within the state bureaucracy made such suits all the more likely.[70] The case of Elise Hessels, the woman who complained about attempted rape by Berlin's police chief and was slapped with a lawsuit for libel and "false accusation," is one example.[71] Another is that of a low-level railway official, one Karl Friedrich Kräuse, fired from his job, who, wanting it back, tried appealing directly to Bismarck himself. Kräuse's petition made the case that he had been illegitimately fired by the arbitrary and improper actions of his superiors. Bismarck read this petition from within the language of honor, seeing thus not a lowly civil servant desperate for the return of his job, but a series of accusations that, if true, threatened the reputations and careers of the railway officials in question. The petition, in other words, was defamatory, and Bismarck referred it to the top official in the rail bureaucracy, the Labor Minister, who promptly filed a defamation lawsuit against Kräuse.[72]

Finally, there were the non-verbal forms of disrespect toward officialdom meriting honor lawsuits. A local official [*Amtsvorsteher*], for example, felt egregiously dishonored when an information bureau [*Auskunftsbureau*], writing to request some information from him, voluntarily included in the letter a small sum of 30 pfennig as fee for the information. The *Amtsvorsteher* saw the money as a bribe and

---

[69] Ibid.
[70] James Whitman, "Enforcing Civility and Respect: Three Societies," *Yale Law Journal* 109 (2000), 1297–398.
[71] For commentary on the general problem, see, e.g. "Der Beweis der Wahrheit bei Beschuldigung von Beamten," *National Zeitung*, August 20, 1887.
[72] I. HA Rep. 84a, Nr. 8139, GStPK, pp. 104–112. Kräuse, however, was acquitted on the basis of §193. The case was then appealed to the Reichsgericht, which upheld the lower court's verdict in December, 1890.

believed that even the mere implication that he would possibly be open to such a bribe dishonored him. Here was a case of bureaucratic probity taken to its mad but logical extreme. While similar lawsuits over extremely trivial and benign actions can not have been common,[73] it is telling that the district attorney took the case seriously enough to file suit (the court, however, acquitted).

But, by far, the most controversial, visible, and politically significant form of libel censorship was that directed at political opponents of the government, particularly against their newspapers. This included the far-right, antisemitic and left-liberal press, but overwhelmingly meant Socialist journalists and publishers, who could receive outlandishly draconian sentences of six months' incarceration.[74] Moabit was only the most dramatic case in an unrelenting campaign of libel litigation against the left, one that affected everyone from the top echelons of the SPD to obscure provincial newspapers and other leftist critics. *Vorwärts* reported that a Socialist editor was given a two-week jail sentence for an article calling an Aachen Catholic relic exhibition a "piece of mischief" (*Unfug*).[75] The *Essener Arbeiterzeitung* was sued, convicted, and fined 500M in 1911 for criticizing the behavior of police who arrested two youths at a Socialist public lecture (the lecture allegedly contained "political" content, thus it violated the associational law banning youths from political meetings).[76] Lèse-majesté prosecutions were overwhelmingly directed against the SPD. August Müller, editor of the *Magdeburger Volkstimme*, was sentenced to four years' prison for lèse-majesté for an 1898 article – a "small fable" – critical of the emperor and Prince "Eitel Fritz." Reichstag deputy Albert Schmidt, the actual editor responsible for the article and feeling guilty and hoping to engineer Müller's release, subsequently gave up his parliamentary immunity and presented himself to the court

---

[73] The extremity of the case comes through in the title of an article on it: "Wegen 30 Pf. Eine kaum glaubliche Anklage," *Vorwärts*, March 11, 1911.

[74] For example, "Polizeiliches, Gerichtliches usw.," *Vorwärts*, March 16, 1911. For an excellent and pathbreaking study of Social Democracy, press censorship, and politics in imperial Germany, see Alex Hall, *Scandal, Sensation, and Social Democracy* (Cambridge, 1977).

[75] *Vorwärts*, February 15, 1903.　[76] "Was alles 'politisch' ist," *Vorwärts*, March 7, 1911.

for prosecution. He was given three years and lost his Reichstag and city council mandates. The disproportionately harsh sentences in the two cases went too far even for the bourgeois parties.[77]

When lower-level officials abstained from filing suit, their superiors, invoking §196, regularly intervened. Indeed, §196 had become so routinized, so utterly integrated into the apparatus of state power, that questions about whether or not, in a libel case, the official in question had actually been dishonored were often irrelevant. The legal defense of officials in the name of upholding state honor had become merely a euphemism for censorship. A particularly crass instance of this can be seen in an 1892 Prussian Justice Ministry directive that, in anticipation of press attacks against justice officials in the wake of a controversial murder of a boy, ordered all attorneys general to stand ready to "energetically counter" with "confiscations [of publications] and the use of §196."[78] The linking of literary confiscations and §196 prosecutions, and the routine readying of these tools before any libel had even taken place, is what is so striking in this document.

The situation for the lower-level officials in whose name §196 actions were brought could be complex. A small newspaper notice on one such case suggests the difficult position of these officials, some of whom wanted only peaceful coexistence with the civilian population but found themselves trapped in the crossfire of a larger battle. In 1911, the state brought charges against Danzig's Socialist *Volkswacht* for an article accusing a chief communal administrator (*Gemeindevorsteher*) of participating in a land-grant scheme to funnel free land parcels to communal deputies (*Gemeindevertreter*), which the newspaper had discovered was taking place in a neighboring rural district. The official, who had received one of the land vouchers thinking that he needed to be a landowner in order to run for local office, said he was "forced" by his superiors to file suit. The court fined the paper's editor 100M.[79]

---

[77] "Partei-Nachrichten: Der Majestätsbeleidiger," *Vorwärts*, October 30, 1902.
[78] Justice Minister Schelling to attorneys general, February 17, 1892. I. HA Rep. 84a, Nr. 8139, GStPK, p. 121.
[79] "Aus Westpreussens Gefilden," *Vorwärts*, March 28, 1911.

The Socialist activist Karl Liebknecht may not have been exaggerating when, in a speech on the floor of the Prussian Landtag, he claimed that defamation prosecutions of Socialists, involving extraordinarily harsh sentences, are "a daily occurrence" and that the Socialist and labor press were "systematically" denied §193 protection by the courts.[80] He certainly knew this from personal experience, being himself a constant target of such lawsuits. One case, for Liebknecht's alleged insults of the Russian Czar and the Prussian and Saxon governments in a speech at an SPD party congress, shows the lengths the government went to silence him: when three separate state attorneys refused to prosecute the case, the government turned to the civil honor court of Berlin's lawyers' guild (*Anwaltskammer*), of which Liebknecht, a lawyer by profession, was a member. This body, citing the fact that Liebknecht's remarks were made in a political, not a professional, capacity, in turn refused the case. In early 1911, when *Vorwärts* wrote about these events, the government was still refusing defeat.[81]

Reichsgerichtsrat Mittelstadt gave a sense of how out-of-control the situation had become (not just for the left) when, in 1890, he compared the present unfavorably with the (notoriously harsh) Vormärz (1815–1848) censor, calling the latter "endlessly more comprehensible and tolerant[!]"[82] Just how incendiary *Beamtenbeleidigung* prosecutions became under the Kaiserreich is reflected in a judge's "warning" sent to jurists and upper-level civil servants during World War One to refrain from the practice in trivial cases in the interests of "social peace": one should try to avoid, he explained, inciting the wrath and discontent of the masses, who are only provoked by the flood of petty insult lawsuits by low-level *Beamten*.[83]

The widespread sense within public opinion that state prosecutors were applying the law inconsistently to punish and silence government opponents had a solid basis in fact. An 1884 Justice Ministry

---

[80] SBPA, February 22, 1912 (Berlin, 1912), p. 1451.
[81] "Ein echtpreussisches Meisterstück," *Vorwärts*, March 16, 1911.
[82] "§193," *Rheinischer Kurier*, July 20, 1894.
[83] "Eine Mahnung zum Rechtsfrieden," *Frankfurter Zeitung*, December 12, 1915.

directive to all state attorneys provides one piece of corroborating evidence. It ordered internal reports on such defamations to include not only facts about the case and the accused, which officials routinely needed to decide whether to press charges. Those facts, the directive instructed, must be available to defamed officials and should include the "reputations" [*Rufe*] and "political" behavior of the accused.[84] There was also a clear policy at the highest levels to target Socialist writers and activists. An 1891 Justice Ministry directive instructed state attorneys to accord special treatment to individuals defamed by Socialists. Normally, as explained above, private individuals who felt themselves defamed were left to their own devices, i.e. to the path of the *Privatklage*, since such cases were not deemed relevant to the "public interest." *Privatklage* plaintiffs were as a result at a distinct disadvantage, functioning as both plaintiff and prosecutor but lacking, among other things, the resources of state prosecutions. The 1891 directive, in effect, came to the rescue of plaintiffs defamed by Socialists or, what it called "that part of the periodical press which battles state and social institutions." Increasingly, it argued with alarm, assaults on the "established order" were taking the form of "personal attacks" against private citizens associated with that order. It followed that such defamations should be treated not as private cases and referred to the *Privatklage* path of litigation. Instead, prosecutors were ordered to treat such cases as attacks on the state and public order, and prosecuted accordingly.[85]

State policy also involved proactively searching out plaintiffs, inducing them to file suit against Socialists and labor activists. This was not always easy. During a labor strike in the Ruhr in 1911, for example, a group of striking workers insultingly cussed out a strikebreaker for being a "*Rausreisserdienste*." The problem, however, from the government's point of view, was that the worker – the supposed victim – did not himself feel insulted and thus had to be brought in to the prosecutor's office to be instructed about why he had been defamed. (The term "strikebreaker" itself had been

---

[84] Berlin, October 8, 1884. I. HA Rep. 84a, Nr. 8139, GStPK, p. 83.
[85] Justice Minister Schelling, Berlin, July 4, 1891, ibid., p. 118.

ruled by Germany's highest court as libelous and punishable by incarceration.)[86]

A double standard of justice against Socialists, workers, and labor activists can be seen in certain convoluted legal judgments and inconsistent applications of the law. The Socialist deputy Auer, for example, was convicted in 1913 for a speech he made at a meeting of the South German Railway Association where he accused the Munich railway director of giving preferential treatment and funding to "clerical" associations. The courts, Reichsgericht included, denied him the protection of §193 even though he was speaking in his capacity as a parliamentary deputy.[87] A legal double standard was also implicit in the numbers and frequency of prosecutions against Socialists, in the harsh sentences meted out, and in the pettiness of some of these cases, suggesting the lengths to which the government and courts were willing to go. One case had the Reichsgericht upholding the conviction of a Social Democratic book peddlar (*Kolporteur*) for sending a police sergeant a pamphlet urging *Beamten* to vote Socialist in the upcoming (1913) Prussian elections.[88] The courts considered this a legally prosecutable insult act because, since *Beamten* were forbidden to vote for anti-government parties, it involved asking a *Beamten* to violate his duty, a request, in this reasoning, that somehow inherently implied the police sergeant would engage in dishonorable behavior. This was justice as a form of harassment.

A double standard of justice carried over into the treatment of Socialist plaintiffs (the injured party), where there is evidence of reluctance and outright refusal on the part of the state to prosecute some of these cases. In 1914, the state attorney's office rejected an SPD suit against a Prussian officer, Lieutenant General Wrochem who, at the founding meeting of the Preussenbund, had made strongly defamatory remarks against the Reichstag with allusions

---

[86] "Die Ehre des Arbeitswilligen!" *Vorwärts*, March, 17, 1911.
[87] "Reichsgericht und Abgeordnete," *Münchener Post*, May 10, 1913, written with outrage and sarcasm, provided the reasoning of the Reichsgericht.
[88] "Beleidigung von Beamten durch die Zumutung, sozialdemokratisch zu wählen?" *Deutsche Tageszeitung*, March 8, 1913. This anti-socialist newspaper found the conviction, if not the precise reasoning of the court, fitting.

to the SPD, calling the Reichstag a "mixed society" and "rabble." The state rejected the case, arguing that Wrochem, as a military official, was under the jurisdiction of the military court system, not of the state attorney's office, and that, moreover, the Reichstag itself, as the defamed party, would have to inititate the lawsuit. Even *Germania*, a Center newspaper and no friend of the Socialists, was outraged by the decision. It pointed out that defamation cases were normally never intitated by the Reichstag; rather the reverse was standard practice, the state attorney requesting of the Reichstag an "authorization" to prosecute defamations against the institution. As to Wrochem's military status, the prosecutor's office could and should have referred it to the military authorities rather than washing its hands of such a serious defamation. *Vorwärts* commented with sarcasm and disgust on the double standard of justice and the violation of the basic principles of equality before the law in a Rechtsstaat:

a conservative general may insult the Reichstag as much as he wants. But if an opposition writer uses a hot-tempered word against the Crown Prince or the undemocratically elected lower house of the Prussian parliament [*Dreiklassenhaus*], then the state prosecutor is instantly ready to initiate a criminal proceeding. Prussia, namely, is a state based on the rule of law [*Rechsstaat*] where all are equal before the law.[89]

And yet, it must be said: if massive censorship of government critics occurred under libel (and other) laws in the Kaiserreich, it was an odd and ineffectual sort of censorship, one consistent with an evolved Rechtsstaat, that sent newspaper editors to jail for a wrong word or phrase but allowed those same editors to publish lengthy critiques of their convictions and of the legal system in general. So, for example, after *Vorwärts'* chief editor was convicted in the Moabit case for libeling the criminal police, the paper published a scathing commentary that began with: "the court proceeding is a gross violation of

---

[89] "Der beleidigte Reichstag und der schwerhörige Staatsanwalt," *Vorwärts*, March 9, 1914. How widespread such cases were is impossible to know. But troubling, in light of later history, is the willingness of state officials even before WWI to abandon (symbolic) protections of the Reichstag.

the legal rules that form the most important guarantees for defendants."[90] Here, in the environment of mass politics and the modern press, the antiquated honor codes underlying the censorship of speech in such litigation seem no longer up to their task.

The courts, dominated by pro-government, conservative jurists, were fundamental to government libel policies, but not entirely. Judges were formally independent and perfectly capable of ruling against the government. They acquitted defendants for lack of sufficient evidence; granted §193 protection of speech; and made other rulings unfavorable to the government and state prosecutors.[91] Such was the case, for example, when a lancer (*Ulan*) killed himself, and his mother denounced to the military authorities the sergeant in charge of her son's military unit, whom she accused of abusive treatment, which, she believed, had driven him to suicide. The sergeant turned around and successfully sued her for *Beamtenbeleidigung*. But on appeal, her conviction was overturned when a court granted her slander the status of "legitimate interest" (i.e. §193 protection).[92] The case was not untypical. Prussia's Minister of Justice complained in 1887 that fully 41.1 percent of government cases failed on appeal.[93]

The justice system, furthermore, was far from a monolith. There were numerous differences of opinion and interpretation of the law among the courts (see below). Yet, their role in the suppression of speech during the Kaiserreich and beyond can not be overemphasized. Led by a stream of draconian Reichsgericht rulings, the courts

[90] "Die beleidigte Polizei und der abgeschnittene Wahrheitsbeweis," *Vorwärts*, March 28, 1911.
[91] This occurred, for example, in the case of a writer whom the government prosecuted for having sent a petition to Bismarck that included a denunciation of the railway authorities, and who was acquitted by a Cologne court in 1890 (later upheld by the Reichsgericht). GStPK, Rep. 84a, Nr. 8139, pp. 103–8. Another example is that of a high court reversing on appeal the libel conviction of a Socialist defendant. "Polizeiliches, Gerichtliches: Erfolgreiche Berufung," *Vorwärts*, August 24, 1902.
[92] "Der Beweis der Wahrheit bei Beschuldigung von Beamten," *National Zeitung*, August 20, 1887.
[93] Justice Minister to all attorneys general, May 10, 1887. I. HA Rep. 84a, Nr. 8139, GStPK, pp. 88–91.

were progressively tightening and broadening defamation laws in favor of plaintiffs and in the name of defending honor, with especially devastating consequences for press freedoms.[94]

The key Reichsgericht decision came in a ruling of December 16, 1881 in the case of an editor of a newspaper (*Berliner Zeitung*) convicted by a lower court for an article about a political meeting of antisemites.[95] Noting that the meeting, although very "agitated," failed to be dispersed by the police, the article went on to criticize an apparent double standard prevailing between police treatment of liberal and right-wing, antisemitic meetings. The police lieutenant in charge sued and won for defamation, claiming, with emphasis on his official status, that the "insulting charge" (*kränkender Vorwurf*) of "corruption and violation of his duties" harmed his "professional honor."[96] The court, in rejecting the editor's appeal, set out a broad and cripplingly limited view of press rights:

There exists no general right for the daily press to publicly criticise putative wrongdoing or to publicise every occurrence even when it harms the honor of others.[97]

The court's reasoning turned on a very narrow – and extremely controversial – interpretation of §193 of the Criminal Code. That clause set out what appeared to be wide protections for certain kinds of public speech:

Critical opinions about scientific, artistic or commercial achievements, as well as remarks that are made to realize or defend rights or *legitimate interests*, as well as criticism or reprimands by superiors of their subordinates, official reports or judgments on the part of officials, and similar cases are punishable

---

[94] This was happening in both criminal and civil law, in legal interpretations of both the criminal and civil codes.

[95] *Entscheidungen des Reichsgerichts in Strafsachen* 5 (1882), pp. 239–41. Like other Reichsgericht decisions, the ruling, unlike those of the American Supreme Court, established merely a guiding principle for the lower courts.

[96] For a general overview of §193 and its interpretation by the Reichsgericht, see Lilienthal, "Üble Nachrede und Verleumdung," in Mittermaier et al. (eds.), *Vergleichende Darstellung des deutschen und ausländischen Strafrechts: Besonderer Teil* vol. 4 (Berlin, 1906), p. 408ff.

[97] Ibid., p. 240.

only insofar as the presence of an insult proceeds from the kind of language used or the circumstances under which it occured.[98]

The trouble was that *berechtigte Interessen* (legitimate interests), left undefined by the statute, was open to alternative interpretations, and the one chosen by the Reichsgericht was extremely narrow indeed. Rejecting the notion of a special protected status for defamatory speech (of the press) in the public interest, the court argued that the statute protected only the defamatory speech of private individuals (and some professional groups). The press was therefore to be held to the same standards as private individuals. To be sure, a journalist or editor had speech rights and could successfully invoke §193 to defend himself against defamation charges. But he could only do so as a private citizen, in defense of his personal honor and reputation. The press, as the high court argued in this and subsequent rulings,[99] had, in other words, neither greater nor lesser rights than private citizens.

---

[98] My emphasis.

[99] Another enormously controversial high court ruling on §193 sparking a lot of commentary in the press came in 1894. See, e.g., "Die Parteipresse und der §193," *Vorwärts*, May 22, 1894. Two later examples in 1908 include rulings that limited the definition of "ähnliche Fälle" (similar cases) in that part of §193 giving protection in certain instances to defamations committed in the critique of "wissenschaftliche, gewerbliche und künstlerische Leistungen ... und ähnliche Fälle." In the case of a schoolteacher (*Provinzialschulrat*) who sued for a defamation regarding his profession, the Reichsgericht ruled against the defendant, denying that this was an "ähnlicher Fall" case and arguing that "it is not in the general interest for the free criticism of state officials to go so far as being able to harm their reputations [*Ansehen*]." Another case involved an author-defendant who had used the words "juridical child murder" to describe a one-year prison sentence given to a twelve- and thirteen-year-old for endangering a train transport. The suit was brought on behalf of the judges and prosecutors in the case, who were deemed to have been defamed by the sentence. A lower court initially exonerated the defendant because it judged the statement to be protected under §193 as a critique of "wissenschaftliche Leistung." The Reichsgericht later reversed this decision. Court rulings, it stated, are not "wissenschaftliche Leistungen"; they are, to paraphrase the *Vossische Zeitung*'s description of the ruling, acts of state. But neither do they fall in the protected category of "ähnliche Fälle" when the defamer's critique is in a form "mehr agitatorischer als sachlicher" and the defendant is in the role of an "ironisierenden und politisierenden Agitator." "Reichsgericht und Presse," *Vossische Zeitung*, March 23, 1908.

This logic had enormous implications, seriously undermining for decades freedom of the press by removing the press's ability to function as a public watchdog, leaving it instead vulnerable to prosecution for defamation when it sought to enlighten the citizenry about government corruption and other abuses in public life.[100] Bizarrely, as commented on in the deluge of newspaper coverage accompanying the high court's rulings on the issue, this interpretation of §193 effectively protected the private interests of individuals *at the expense* of the general interests of society (*Gesammtheit*). The *Vossische Zeitung* gave the example of police abuse: "if a newspaper censures police excess, according to present practice, it is only guaranteed the protection of §193 if the editor himself is attacked."[101] The Reichsgericht's personal interpretation of "legitimate interests" did not even make sense on its own terms. Is it not strange, noted the *Kölnische Volkszeitung*, that normally the "advocacy of naked self-interest is seen as something inferior," yet the high court has ruled exactly the opposite case when it comes to the press and §193?[102] To reject the notion of a special protected status for defamatory speech in the public interest "contradicts all other areas of accepted opinion."

Even within the court's own logic, there could have been ways to grant the press greater speech rights. For it had ruled elsewhere that certain small groups – those where each individual in the group was "recognizable" – could constitute a legal person (*Personenmehrheit*) with the individual's accompanying §193 rights.[103] In one case, the court displayed remarkable flexiblity in its definition of "small group," applying the concept to the entire Bavarian army (50,000 troops). Yet, at the same time, it consistently denied this same right to newspaper

---

[100] Later Reichsgericht decisions would restrict even further the conditions in which the press could claim a §193 defense.

[101] "Die Gefahren der Beschwerdeführung," *Vossische Zeitung*, October 8, 1898.

[102] "Presse und §193," *Kölnischer Volkszeitung*, February 18, 1911. The original statement in the article was not phrased as a question.

[103] Kronecker mentioned a Reichsgericht ruling that protected as a group under §193 the members of a Reichstag election committee that libeled certain state officials in the course of "excercising its voting rights." Aschrott and Liszt (eds.), *Die Reform des Reichstrafgesetzbuchs* (Berlin, 1910), p. 321.

editors and reporters, for whom "small group" would seem to have more legitimately applied.[104]

There were other instances over the years where the high court evinced a more lenient, pro-free speech attitude toward §193 rights. In 1887, for example, a Breslau newspaper reported that, in violation of the professional code, a (civil-servant) telegraph operator had communicated the contents of a telegraph message to a third party. The telegraph operator sued the paper for libel. After a lower court acquitted the newspaper, the district attorney appealed the ruling to the Reichsgericht, arguing that the proper way to pursue a public employee offense was to lodge a complaint with the authorities, not to publicize it in a newspaper. The court dismissed this argument, granting the newspaper §193 protection.[105] It offered a similar interpretation of the law in an 1890s case of a building contractor who, while running for local office, gave a speech at a gathering of the Democratic Party in which he criticized the municipal building administration for approving new building projects on a partisan basis. Sued and convicted of defamation (§186), the building contractor appealed his case all the way to the Reichsgericht, which sided with him and chastised the lower appellate court for having applied a "too narrow notion of legitimate interests in the sense of §193."[106]

What distinguished these and other scattered cases of leniency on the part of the Reichsgericht from its otherwise severe line against the press? It would take a systematic study of all of the many high court's rulings on §193 (an endeavor beyond the scope of this book) to answer this question with certainty and precision. But what one can say is that, in addition to technical legal considerations, a certain extra-judicial attitude toward honor, the state, and public order underpinned the court's rulings on §193. That attitude placed a premium on protecting the integrity of the state and the class order. This made obedience to

---

[104] "Büreaukratie und Presse," *Berliner Tageblatt*, May 6, 1894.
[105] "Oeffentliche Interessen," *Volks-Zeitung*, April 27, 1894.
[106] Ruling of May 23, 1892. *Entscheidungen des Reichsgerichts in Strafsachen* 23 (Berlin, 1893), p. 145.

officialdom, deference to superiors, and the integrity of honor – that symbolic quality underpinning the social and political hierarchy – into values that trumped freedom of speech. And the more important (whether literally or symbolically) the figure of authority, the more the tendency on the part of the court, it seems, to rule in favor of protecting honor against free-speech values. As the court phrased it in one 1892 ruling, "the more important the honor of [a particular] individual is to state order, the more sensitive the appraisal of it must be to what is permissible and impermissible [in speech toward that individual]."[107] The plaintiffs at issue in the above cases were, by contrast, inconsequential in the schema of state power, both practically and symbolically – the telegraph operator extremely so.

The Reichsgericht's narrow interpretation of §193 was extraordinarily controversial, sharply dividing both the public (chapter 4) and the courts. Some lower courts simply refused to heed its rulings. In 1911, a Hamburg court used §193 to acquit a newspaper that had been sued for exposing deplorable conditions in a bakery. Directly contradicting the Reichsgericht, the Hamburg court argued that "the press must point out abuses in order for the authorities to have the chance to take action against them."[108] Other courts resorted to eccentric reasoning in order to get around the high court's exclusion of the press from §193 protection: hence, for example, a 1910 ruling of the Leipzig Landgericht (appeals court) in the case of an author of a book on stock-exchange rates for devout (*gläubige*) Jews, who sued a newspaper for exposing his book as a swindle. Mindful of the fact that the Reichsgericht supported the right of small groups but not the press itself to the protection of §193, the Leipzig court, ruling in favor of the newspaper, argued the article was legal because it had been written at the behest and in the interests of representatives of the business class [*Handelsstand*].[109]

---

[107] Ibid., pp. 347–48.
[108] "Presse und §193," *Kölnischer Volkszeitung*, February 18, 1911. The quote is from the author of the article summarizing the court decision.
[109] Ibid.

Important cultural and philosophical differences regarding honor and speech rights underlay these divisions within the courts. The Reichsgericht's anti-press interpretations of §193 were based on a corporatist, primordial, and authoritarian notion of rights that privileged state power over free speech and that viewed rights as differential, hierarchical, and personalized. Its protection of libelous speech in defense of "personal" but not public interests may also have been a function of spillage into the courts of a privatized dueling ethos with which the judges, given their educational and class backgrounds, would have been familiar and at home. By contrast, at least some of the lower courts opposing the Reichsgericht used the reasoning of liberal principles, basing their decisions on a more abstract, universalist, and egalitarian notion of citizenship rights. These ideological splits are well illustrated in the reaction of the courts to the litigation (see chapter 2) between the two businessmen X and Y, where X, a military officer, had sued Y for writing him (X) a curt business letter that, seeking to break off any further dealings with X, "gifted" him the money Y felt was owed him. The courts split on the case, doing so along the competing models of honor and rights outlined above. Even though the lawsuit, deriving from an entirely private and trivial matter, was the stuff of a mere *Privatklage*, the state prosecutor decided to take up X's case thus elevating it to the status of a "public matter." He did so because, thinking about honor along corporatist and hierarchical lines, he ascribed importance to the defense of the principle of "difference[s] between *Standesehre* [here, that of an officer, X] and *bürgerliche Ehre*." X's military honor deserved special protection, which he received when the public prosecutor brought charges against Y for insulting an officer by offering him a "present" (!). An appellate court, however, later threw out the case, acquitting Y and rejecting the very basis of the initial trial, arguing instead along liberal lines that "all Prussians" are equal before the law.[110]

Yet, despite the opposition of some lower courts, by the early twentieth century the Reichsgericht's narrow interpretation of §193 and press rights had become the dominant position within the

[110] "Staatsanwalts-Anklagen," *Reichsfreund*, August 23, 1890.

judiciary.[111] This was politically explosive. It became a central point of contention in debates underway in the press and the legislatures about the broader implications of defamation law, honor, and state power – debates, discussed in the next chapter, that merged national politics and the personal politics of honor.

[111] It was, however, rejected by a large number of legal scholars. See, e.g., Aschrott and Liszt, *Reform*, p. 321.

CHAPTER 4

Politicization

> "Today's legal interpretation of §193 is nothing but a scare tactic against everything in the public interest [*jede öffentliche Wirksamkeit*]. Not only the woman, but the man is silenced under the Prussian state!"[1]
>
> "... our law courts almost completely fail in the task of protecting the honor of [our] citizens. Our system of justice has the ungermanic trait of protecting material property but not ideal goods [honor], which are contemptuously dismissed as merely conceited values."[2]

An impassioned debate over honor and the reform of libel law pervaded Germany's public square – in the press, the parliaments, the legal profession, and the courts – reaching a peak of intensity in the early years of the twentieth century. The debate was driven by two countervailing trends. On the one hand, state repression and press censorship were feeding tensions between Socialists and the government, while increasingly generating criticism beyond the Left. On the other hand, there were anxiety and anger about the perceived growth of threats to honor emanating most particularly from the "revolver press." The first trend led to outcries against *Beamtenbeleidigung* and §193, spurring demands for greater protections of free speech and legal equality. The latter trend led in the opposite direction to demands for a crackdown on trial publicity, the admissibility of evidence in court (*Wahrheitsbeweis*), and for strengthening defamation sentencing. The debates that ensued were bitter, intense, and raucous, profoundly dividing the German political class and entangling libel in some of

[1] "Das berechtigte Interesse," *Vorwärts*, October 28, 1904.
[2] "Der Kampf gegen das Duell," *Tägliche Rundschau*, October 30, 1901.

the key political debates of the day – on civil rights, class inequality, political power, and the state. In this environment, honor and its correlates – privacy and morality – were charged code terms reflecting broader political divisions and their agendas. This chapter follows the debates, placing particular emphasis on those accompanying the revised lèse-majesté bill of 1908 and the Eulenburg Affair, the national scandal surrounding trials between 1907 and 1909 involving members of the Kaiser's inner circle around charges of homosexuality, which led to the notorious "Lex Eulenburg" libel law brought before the Reichstag in 1909.

Even as the Reich Criminal Code was being signed into law, there were voices calling for its reform, and they grew stronger over time. By 1906, the government had committed to a general revision of the Criminal Code and put together a commission to this end whose first draft version (*Vorentwurf*) was presented for discussion to the public in a 1909 publication.[3] Extraordinarily wide-ranging and complex, this legislation was still under debate when World War One and the 1918/19 revolution intervened to temporarily halt it.[4] The ongoing preparation of the Criminal Code formed one context for the libel debates discussed below. Equally important was the enormity of what was taking place on the ground – the perceived attacks on personal and state honor, on the one hand; the incessant libel trials against the oppositional press, on the other – and the way these events fed into the broader political conflicts of the Kaiserreich.

Outrage and anger are the best terms to describe the reactions of a wide swath of public opinion to the stifling, inequitable effects of libel jurisprudence, sentiments that focused in particular on the incessant *Beamtenbeleidigung* prosecutions and the courts' narrow interpretation of §193. The liberalization of libel law in the nineteenth century, which had abolished corporate legal distinctions among litigants,

---

[3] *Vorentwurf zu einem deutschen Strafgesetzbuch* (Berlin, 1909). A number of the articles on the debates covered in this chapter can be found in I HA Rep. 84a, Nr. 8142, GStPK.

[4] It was taken up again in the Weimar Republic, but abandoned in the 1930s as a result of the constitutional crisis and the Nazi seizure of power. Eberhard Schmidt, *Einführung in die Geschichte der deutschen Strafrechtspflege* (Göttingen, 1983).

made the continued special treatment of officialdom all the more glaring and intolerable. For critics, these prosecutions, together with the refusal of the Reichsgericht to grant the press §193 protections, were enormously controversial, holding profound implications for free speech rights. Crushing the press's "legitimate freedom," they amounted to a regime of censorship.[5]

Public criticism of the Reichsgericht was fed not only by the draconian nature of its rulings against the press, but also by the legal uncertainties those rulings engendered given the statutes' lack of clarity and their inconsistent application in the courts. As a result, defendants and their attorneys searched for alternative defense methods and found one in the *Wahrheitsbeweis*: Germany's rule allowing libel defendants broad freedom to introduce into the court record evidence of the truth of the libelous statements for which he/she was standing trial. In effect, the *Wahrheitsbeweis* gave the defense substantial power — not only to prove the truth of their libels but, in doing so, to publicize the very information that plaintiffs or the state were trying to censor in bringing charges, and even in some cases, to turn trials on their head by introducing evidence that put the plaintiffs on the defense (e.g. the Moabit trial in chapter 3). As such, the *Wahrheitsbeweis*, along with the intertwined issues of §193 and *Beamtenbeleidigung*, also became a hot-button matter, lambasted by the Right and turning an otherwise arcane technical question of evidentiary courtroom rules into the stuff of heated political debate.

Socialists, focused on the ills of §193 and *Beamtenbeleidigung*, saw existing libel jurisprudence as an egregious tool of "class justice," a method for crushing socialism and defending the capitalist-Junker state — in short, as a form of class warfare. Many liberals saw in the same court rulings disturbing evidence of the fragility of civil rights and the constitutional state. But in both cases, the feeling was that basic citizen rights were under attack. What this disparate — and otherwise warring — group shared in common were certain liberal assumptions about civil rights and the rule of law: publicity, government accountability, equality of rights, freedom of expression.

---

[5] *Frankfurter Zeitung*, March 24, 1890.

Measured against such principles, libel law in the Kaiserreich was an outrage. Today's climate of denunciation [*Denunziantthum*] is so bad, wrote one National Liberal paper, that, had they been living today, Goethe, Schiller, and the other great writers would be in jail.[6] Other reporters compared Germany to "despotic Russia," arguing that, given the muzzling of the press, the constitutional state no longer actually existed. The *Berliner Tageblatt* described the ideal:

When public affairs are dealt with in a way that includes the participation of the entire nation, and all of its institutions ... are based on the principle of publicity [transparency] ..., then it is a given that public affairs are being subject to free criticism and that freedom of expression about those affairs must be unlimited.[7]

But this was far from the case in today's Germany, where, to the contrary, libel prosecutions and court rulings have made it no longer possible "to discuss public matters openly, creatively, and according to the truth, and without restraint."[8]

Legal inequities and the stifling of speech went hand in hand. *Das kleine Journal* warned of an ever-widening "chasm between the feelings of the people and the administration of justice" caused by the absurd lengths the courts were willing to go to defend the honor of state officials and civil servants.[9] Most recently, it noted, an Alsatian editor was sentenced to an eight-month jail term for publishing two satirical images, one showing an (unnamed, annonymous) arrogant, chauvinistic "Prussian officer" ordering a waiter around; the other image depicting a similar scene with the character of a teacher. "Insulting the officer and the teaching estates" read his conviction. "That a person should spend eight months in a small jail cell for such a petty matter," commented the paper, "in order to 'rescue' the honor of two of our most respected estates" – that smacked of the "Middle Ages." The *Berliner Zeitung* condemned the inequities of the law seen in the constant refusal of the courts to prosecute the right-wing Court Chaplain Stöcker and his incessant "meanest" libels, whereas the

---

[6] "Warnrufe," *Berliner Tageblatt*, February 15, 1896.
[7] "Wo ist Artikel 27 der Verfassung geblieben?" *Berliner Tageblatt*, August 1, 1883.
[8] Ibid.
[9] "Acht Monate Gefängnis," *Das kleine Journal*, May 11, 1908.

courts treated the other side, Stöcker's political enemies, very differently: "As soon as Herr Stöcker files suit and seeks the intervention of the state prosecutor, he finds a favourable hearing [of his case]."[10] And, indeed, with no deficit of other examples to draw from, the publicizing of such cases became a staple of leftist and liberal reportage in the Wilhelmine years.

These critical sentiments subjected judicial rulings and the finer points of the law to intense scrutiny and public discussion. Mass dailies published debates about whether the evidentiary rules for proving the truth of a libel should be construed broadly or narrowly (the Left was for keeping the law broad; the Right wanted to narrow it). There was much commentary on the legal basis of *Beamtenbeleidigung*. Leftists, for example, rejected its entire legal basis, pointing out that, while the courts were treating it as a serious honor offense, in fact neither the term nor a specified crime for it actually existed anymore in the Criminal Code. Citing liberal legal scholars like Professors Schulte (Bonn) and Bierkmeyer (Munich), they argued for rethinking this and other legal provisions along lines more favorable to the accused (and with an eye to decreasing libel litigation altogether).[11] There were debates about the "legitimate interests" clause of §193 and the role of motive in assessing guilt,[12] and about the need for a precise legal definition of honor, which rehearsed for a mass audience thorny questions long debated by legal scholars: is the thing being protected by defamation law "subjective honor" (i.e., the honor for which the complainant is demanding a legal remedy) or "objective honor" (the honor that the complainant in reality can assert)? If the latter, is it determined by the complainant's moral worth, social position, or rights of citizenship?[13]

Meanwhile, debates about *Beamtenbeleidigung* and §193 were becoming forums for discussions about fundamental questions of state power and citizenship rights. Exposés of specific trials went far beyond the

---

[10] "Die Beleidigungsprozesse in Deutschland," *Berliner Zeitung*, June 24, 1885.
[11] See, for example, "Die Strafsatzungen für Beleidigung," *Vossische Zeitung*, January 9, 1897; "Berlin, den 13. Juli 1894," *Volks-Zeitung*, July 13, 1894.
[12] For example, "Oeffentliche Interessen," *Volks-Zeitung*, April, 27, 1894; "Beleidigung oder Wahrung berechtigter Interessen," *Strassburger Post*, August 22, 1897.
[13] "Warnrufe," *Berliner Tageblatt*, February 15, 1896.

case at hand, or even libel law itself, to articulate visions of rights and the societal good. When, in 1898, a newspaper reported on the case of a private citizen who, having been abused by the police, lodged a complaint and was subsequently himself prosecuted for "false accusation,"[14] the point was to underline the broader nexus between official abuse and the repression of the press. For the answer to police abuse was nothing if not publicity – a risky legal proposition under present circumstances. How, wondered dozens of reporters, could the press do its job of enlightening the public and holding government accountable if investigative reporting in the public interest was not legally protected? Wasn't it the very function of the press in a constitutional state to "serve the newspaper profession, public opinion, and the general interest"? [15] How, moreover, could politicians and the citizenry rectify social problems if, as a result, they were ignorant of those problems? The plain answer was: they could not.

Socialists turned such questions into radical critiques of the political, economic, and legal systems, using exposés of libel law as agitation tools for raising consciousness and mobilizing supporters. Their newspapers[16] sustained readers on a regular diet of outrageous libel rulings against workers, the labour movement, and the SPD. *Vorwärts*, the SPD's main newspaper, also specialized in a kind of *Schadenfreude* reportage of bourgeois libel suits and officer dueling, all the more to show the stupidity of these characters. The newspaper related, for example, the farcical drama of factional fighting at the German Yacht Club that ended in a libel conviction of the Club's president, industrialist Adolf Steinberg.[17]

Socialists dismissed with contempt bourgeois and upper-class norms of honor, and actively agitated against the duel – that embodiment of

---

[14] "Die Gefahren der Beschwerdeführung," *Vossische Zeitung*, October 8, 1898.
[15] "Presse und §193," *Kölnische Volkszeitung*, February 18, 1911.
[16] After perusing editions of *Vorwärts* over a number of years, I randomly chose the articles from two years – 1902 and 1911 – to read and use in depth.
[17] "Vom Krawattenfabrikanten Adolf Steinberg," *Vorwärts*, April 5, 1911. But the paper also reported seriously and with sympathy on bourgeois libel defendants in order to critique state censorship. See, e.g., "Bewiesene Wahrheit – kein Wahrheitsbeweis," *Vorwärts*, October 25, 1902.

feudalist political power and German militarism.[18] They exulted accordingly in unmasking the hypocrisy and hollowness of the "gentleman's" honor code. In 1911, the Prussian Minister of Interior von Dallwitz gave an outraged speech before the Prussian Landtag accusing the SPD of having bribed a police official back in the days of Bismarck–Puttkamer to work as a Socialist Party spy, and in so doing dishonorably "luring him into disloyalty and violation of his oath of office."[19] SPD leader August Bebel responded with unrepentant glee, giving the Minister and his code of honor the verbal equivalent of the finger. Solemnly, Bebel was sorry to say that the situation had in fact been worse than Dallwitz imagined; the police official in question was actually the one who sought out the Socialists to offer his services, and did so requesting a *fee* – an alleged fact that made the man appear not only a political traitor but a thoroughly avaricious, and non-gentlemanly one. Further, Bebel clarified, the SPD would have been fools had they not accepted the official's services: his spying enabled the Party to "foil the devilish plans of the firm Bismarck-Puttkamer," revealed a whole "series of 'men of honor'" working against the Party as spies in the political police, and was an act of reprisal for all the spies recruited by the government from the Socialist ranks to work against their own comrades. So, Bebel concluded, you'll understand, Herr Minister, why "I can only smile and shrug my shoulders ... at your moral indignation."[20]

In the press and in the parliaments, there was no better way of exposing the inequities of class justice – the way "rank und class"[21] and political ideology influenced judicial rulings – than in narrating the stories of the discrepant outcomes of libel actions.[22] In a 1913 Reichstag speech, deputy Cohn let forth with an impressive litany of such cases:[23] the denial of §193 protections to the editor of the

---

[18] E.g., "Der Appell an die nationale Ehre," *Vorwärts*, March 23, 1911.
[19] A point of clarification: Dallwitz's speech referred to an article in which Bebel himself had revealed this information.
[20] "An den Herrn Minister des Innern v. Dallwitz," *Vorwärts*, February 19, 1911.
[21] Cohn speech, *SBR*, February 8, 1913, p. 3589.
[22] "Gibt es eine Klassenjustiz?" *Vorwärts*, March 14, 1911, provides one among many journalistic examples.
[23] *SBR*, February 8, 1913, pp. 3588f.

Rheinisch-Westfälische Zeitung whereas a court granted that very same protection to a Jena judge (an *Amtsgerichtsrat*), a defendant charged with calling a building contractor the "most insolent, mendacious, and money-obsessed [*händelwütigster*] scoundrel"; the inequality of class seen in a case arising from a carpenters' strike against construction-industry entrepreneurs, which led to boycott notices from both sides. For the same offense, a Hamburg court convicted the carpenters but refused to prosecute the entrepreneurs.[24] And so on.

Liberals, of course, rejected out of hand the Marxist critique and class analysis of Socialists. And there were other differences in rhetoric and approach among these critics. Both leftists and liberals, to be sure, articulated their outrage in terms of the violations of civil rights. National Liberal Eugen Schiffer, for example, bemoaning the "excessive growth of *Privatklagen*," called in a Reichstag speech for a civic and political "discourse of greater tolerance for free speech."[25] But right-leaning liberals tended also toward the rhetoric of nationalism and moral purity, as when Bonn professor and National Liberal Schulte emphasized the function of freedom of opinion for the health of the fatherland and the nation. Today's stifling of speech was instead only feeding discontent and the forces of revolution: "nothing is more dangerous for the fatherland than general discontent and griping ... within all levels of society about the feeling of being vulnerable to denunciations."[26] Liberals, moreover, tended to combine their critiques of state repression with vociferous calls for harsher penalties in *Privatklage* actions. Among other liberals, the rhetoric was more likely to revolve around the contrast between progress and backwardness – between a modern, free state, on the one hand, and the shameful, backward authoritarianism of the German Reich, which they compared to China, Japan, and despotic Russia.[27] When searching for the reasons for Germany's *Denunzianttum*, the *Berliner Tageblatt* felt

---

[24] Ibid., pp. 3590–91. The exact offense for which the carpenters were convicted is not clear.

[25] "Energieverschleuderung," *Berliner Morgenpost*, February 28, 1914.

[26] "Warnrufe," *Berliner Tageblatt*, February 15, 1896.

[27] "Die Rechtsstellung der Presse," *Breslauer Zeitung*, July 21, 1894. England for these and other commentators was often a reform model as well as a mirror used to

that the two deep-seated causes were the heritage of Bismarckean repression and "national character," namely, a "bureaucratism" that made the country value freedom of press less highly than England or France.[28] By contrast, a Socialist class analysis located the causes and injustices of libel law in capitalism and Prussian authoritarianism – in the protection of "personal profit," "egoistic interests" and power.[29]

Leftist and liberal critics were not rejecting honor per se. Far from it. They remained steeped in Germany's honor culture and made copious use of the *Privatklage* in their own lives, private and public. The Socialist editor of the *Potsdamer Nachrichten* filed a *Privatklage* against the editor of a rival newspaper, the *Potsdamer Tageszeitung*, for calling him a political slanderer (*politischer Brunnenvergifter*) and mole.[30] Even the Socialist leadership, while disdaining libel litigation against the "boorishness of political enemies,"[31] did not hesitate on occasion to file suit against those enemies.[32] General Lieutenant von Wrochem (pp. 105–06 above), at the founding meeting of the Preussenbund (Prussian league), called the Reichstag a "mixed society" and "rabble" (*Rotte*). The allusion to Social Democrats, the majority party in the Reichstag, was unmistakable, and, as the Center (no friend of the SPD) put it, such a comment was undoubtedly a defamation of the parliament, prompting a Social Democratic deputy to denounce Wrochem to the state attorney.[33] Farther to the right, liberals and Center Party members

---

critique problems in Germany. See, e.g., n.t., *Hannoverscher Courier*, April 17, 1895 on the Oscar Wilde case. But the liberal *Vossische Zeitung* ("Die Strafsatzungen für Beleidigung," January 9, 1897) argued, to the contrary, that England's libel laws were too harsh and unhealthy for free public debate.

[28] "Büreaukratie und Presse," *Berliner Tageblatt*, May 6, 1894.

[29] "Das berechtigte Interesse," *Vorwärts*, October 28, 1904. But most Socialist newspaper commentary did not provide causal analysis in this or any other vein.

[30] "Der Mandatsverzicht des Reichtagsabgeordneten Pauli," *Vorwärts*, March 18, 1911.

[31] "Ein Lümmel, der noch in den Dreckhosen steckt," *Vorwärts*, April 6, 1911.

[32] This goes back as far as Karl Marx himself. One example of a *Privatklage* brought by the Socialist leader Karl Liebknecht in defense of his professional reputation as a lawyer can be found in "Zurückgenommene Beleidigung," *Vorwärts*, April 12, 1911.

[33] "Der beleidigte Reichstag und die untätige Staatsanwaltschaften," *Germania*, March 9, 1914. Other examples of Socialist libel lawsuits can be found in *Vorwärts*, e.g., "Eine Episode im Kampf zur Erlangung von Versammlungslokalen," *Vorwärts*, March 16, 1911.

were particularly adamant about the defense of personal honor and privacy. At times they even sounded like conservatives when talk of citizenship rights included calls for harsher sentences in *Privatklage* lawsuits, or when it included attacking the "sensationalist" press for dragging people's private lives into the public arena.[34] Indeed, the commitment to personal honor created a quandary for many (and differences of opinion within the parties) when, as seen below in the Eulenburg Affair, the values of privacy and personal honor conflicted with those of publicity, free speech, and legal transparency.

Leftists and many liberals were advocating not the end of honor, but its redefinition along democratic lines. When, for example, the *Kölnische Zeitung* complained about low sentencing practices in *Privatklage* cases, it did so, unlike Conservatives, in a language that merged the idioms of honor and democracy, contrasting the low sentences imposed on defendants convicted of libeling ordinary citizens with the harsh ones meted out against the press for *Beamtenbeleidigung*. The inequality of the situation, the lack of proper respect for ordinary citizens, was what most disturbed: officials' honor, it opined, should not be valued and treated as something higher than the honor of "private people."[35] Calls to strengthen protections of personal honor, moreover, were carefully crafted so as not to infringe on the "rightful" rights of the press. Thus, the *Westfälischer Merkur* made clear that it was not the "political side of press freedom," but the "gossip press" – the element that mixed in "purely personal matters," sullying the "honor of daughter[s]" and their families – that needed to be reined in.[36]

Socialists, the most radical and the most affected by defamation prosecutions, articulated a thorough-going democratic-egalitarian

---

[34] May 11, 1908. For a specific instance, see the case of Kirchoff-Hairich, "Ist die Ehre genügend geschützt?" *Westfälischer Merkur*, October 11, 1893.

[35] "Beleidigungsprozesse," *Kölnische Zeitung*, November 7, 1902. Indeed, it argued that only when private people's honor is defended in courts with the same harsh sentences as those of government officials will the complaints about sentencing stop and, perhaps, people won't feel they have to resort to "extra-legal" measures (i.e. the duel).

[36] "Ist die Ehre genügend geschützt?" *Westfälischer Merkur*, October 11, 1893.

vision of defamation jurisprudence and the honor question. This can be seen, for example, in a Socialist commentary on a famous 1902 libel case bearing on the question of §193 and "legitimate interests." The case involved a libel lawsuit brought against the professor (later Prussian Minister of Trade and Reich Interior Minister) Clemens Delbrück by a Prussian senior tax inspector (Loehning) which was heard before two courts. The first, before a *Strafkammer* (criminal court), ruled in favor of Delbrück and free-speech rights. Its judgment was subsequently overturned in a second opinion issued by a higher appellate court (Berlin's *Kammergericht*). The initial *Strafkammer* ruling had acquitted Delbrück on the basis that, as a "higher state official" (*Staatsbeamte*), his alleged libel was protected by §193 (he had "the interests of the higher state officialdom to … safeguard"). The subsequent appellate ruling rejected that position, arguing that the higher state bureaucracy was too diverse a group to constitute a coherent "circle of people" recognizable by the law (the plaintiff, Loehning, was also a higher state official) and protected by §193. Socialist *Vorwärts* might have been expected to embrace the first Strafkammer ruling granting free-speech protection and to reject the *Kammergericht* opinion. But the newspaper in fact was critical of *both* rulings: the latter for its obvious anti-free-speech position; the former because of the *reasoning* it used to justify free-speech rights. To be sure, Delbrück's acquittal was a good thing, but the opinion justifying it provided a "far too narrow" legal basis for free-speech rights. Delbrück's libel, *Vorwärts* proclaimed, had a "legitimate interest" (and hence deserved acquittal) not because he was a professor (a higher state official) but because he was a citizen (*Staatsbürger*).[37] Freedom of speech, in other words, was not an end in itself – not if it was constituted on hierarchical and corporatist grounds. The goal, rather, was citizenship rights grounded on universalized principles of equality.

This meant narrowing and depoliticizing the definition of libel, circumscribing it to the sphere of private life and private morality. In a Reichstag speech, deputy Heine, referring to the "politics of insult" targeting Social Democrats and the growth, more generally, of a "dangerous denunciation-proneness and litigiousness" that had

---

[37] "Das berechtigte Interesse," *Vorwärts*, October 28, 1904.

overtaken German life, called for a definition of libel limited to false accusations aimed at "placing the moral character of a victim in a bad light."[38] A democratized honor, at the same time, required ridding honor of its corporatist past. *Vorwärts* succinctly articulated this democratized honor, appealing to its working-class base and referencing its socialist goals: "Personal honor," it declared, "is not a special right of a privileged personality. The proletariat possesses as great a right to respect of its personal honor as the capitalist, Junker, prince."[39] Socialists did not stand in opposition to "personal honor," it continued. Far from it. What they opposed was the hierarchical corporate-class state that underpinned the traditional ideology of honor:

> This honor of the personality, this pride in a spotless moral badge, this respect for personal honor, these we too hold as high as anyone else. But recognition of this honor of the socially lowest, which is not inferior to the honor of those who through accident or birth are superior, makes it also impossible for us to recognize another specially constituted honor for specific persons [the monarch]. We respect the honor of personalities, but we fail to understand reverence for rank or birth.

In terms of practical politics, a leftist position meant the championing of defendant rights and opposition to reforms that adversely affected freedom of speech and the press. Leftists (though not most National Liberals) opposed raising the penalties against defamation offenses. Joined by many liberals, they also wanted an end to *Beamtenbeleidigung* prosecutions and advocated a broad interpretation of §193 in order to protect critical and libelous speech and writing made in the public interest. To the same end, they called for changes in the way the courts treated the issue of motive. The defamatory intent of the accused, they argued, needed to be a central consideration in determinations of guilt. This would decrease verdicts against the press as well as mitigate the problem that defamation laws were too harsh against legitimate criticism while too weak against real, intentional defamation.[40]

---

[38] *SBR*, November 23, 1907, pp. 1741–42.
[39] "Majestätsbeleidigung," *Vorwärts*, January 29, 1907.
[40] "Warnrufe," *Berliner Tageblatt*, February 15, 1896; "Beleidigung oder Wahrung berechtigter Interessen," *Strassburger Post*, August 22, 1897.

Finally, many liberals and leftists emphasized the *Privatklage* as a reform tool. By the late nineteenth century, as we have seen, most jurists and legal scholars had come to loathe the *Privatklage* as a bottomless pit of trivial lawsuits, and advocated either its abolition or circumscription.[41] Many non-jurist liberals and leftists saw things differently. Within a continuing anti-state-prosecutor-monopoly rhetoric going back to mid-century (see chapter 1), they argued for expanding the *Privatklage* law. They spoke of its liberating benefits and the dangers, by contrast, of abuse of state power inherent in a system where the state monopolizes the filing of criminal charges. Some, like a commentator in the *Berliner Zeitung*, called for the wholesale elimination of state prosecutions in matters of defamation and their replacement by the *Privatklage*.[42] Referring to the unfair and politicized basis on which state prosecutors did or did not intervene in defamation conflicts (specifically, the Stöcker cases, above), the author argued there was "one simple method" to end the situation: "public charges in insult matters must be eradicated altogether," and ended with the chant: "Eradicate the 'public' official insult criminal lawsuit and eradicate the monopoly of the state prosecutor!" The *Privatklage* would protect personal honor while avoiding the ills of politicized libel suits.[43]

Philosophically, a leftist position on libel law involved a radical redefinition of honor, away from corporatist and hierarchical principles, and toward egalitarian and universalistic ones. It also meant a new relation of honor to the public sphere, namely, its depoliticization and removal to the realm of private conflict and the *Privatklage*. What the Left represented in the history of honor was not its elimination, in other words, but its dismantling as a tool of political repression. Yet, this anti-corporatist and anti-authoritarian vision of honor potentially clashed with the corporatist and status-conscious social and professional lives of many liberal voters and politicians (e.g. lawyers and

---

[41] See, for example, the discussion in *Die Reform des Reichsstrafgesetzbuchs* (Berlin, 1910), p. 310.

[42] "Die Beleidigungsprozesse in Deutschland," *Berliner Zeitung*, June 24, 1885.

[43] N.t., *Frankfurter Zeitung*, October 24, 1908.

civil servants – chapter 2). The result was division and ambivalence within the ranks of liberals and the Center (see pp. 148ff).

Right of center, the libel-honor debate looked very different. Far from worrying about restrictions on speech, conservatives condemned the personalized public attacks of a growing "revolver journalism" and pushed hard for strengthening laws that, in their view, inadequately protected citizens' honor. Like their leftist counterparts, conservative newspapers were filled with libel horror stories, only here the stories were of a very different kind. In 1911, for example, conservative commentators blasted a court decision that failed to convict a National Liberal Reichstag candidate from the district of Militisch-Trebnitz, who had been sued by the district commissioner (*Landrat*) for a campaign speech questioning the fairness of how district commissioners assessed taxes and accusing them of favoring the interests of large landowners. His exact phrasing went as follows:

The social position of district commissioners [*Landräte*] is subject to a certain degree of influence by the large landowners regarding tax assessments, which may lead to preferential treatment of the large landowners as compared to the small owners and to unjust assessments of taxes in the Militisch area.[44]

To be sure, the statement was "offensive," but the court ruled it protected speech, largely on the basis of an earlier Reichsgericht ruling that candidates' speeches delivered at electoral meetings to their party members were protected by §193. The court also noted that the candidate had never mentioned a specific name and that there was no evidence that he intentionally uttered a falsehood [about Militisch's Landrat].[45] The *Konservativer Korrespondent* was livid. That such "reprehensible" methods (the use of "lies" and dishonoring accusations) were granted §193 protection – this "surpasses the healthy moral feelings and conceptual abilities of the layman," it complained.[46]

[44] This version of the candidate's statements came from a quote in the *Konservativer Korrespondent* that was reprinted in "Konservative Unzufriedenheit mit der Rechtssprechung," *Leipziger Neueste Nachrichten*, September 12, 1911.

[45] "Berechtigte Interessen?" *Hamburger Nachrichten*, September 19, 1911.

[46] "Konservative," *Leipziger Neueste Nachrichten*, September 12, 1911.

In an election year, conservative anger and the party's exploitation of this mini-controversy was only to be expected. But the rhetoric chosen by the *Konservativer Korrespondent* had meaning far beyond the specific case and the newspaper's conservative readers. This was a rhetoric that took for granted that personal honor trumped political debate and that assumed, as a result, extensive restraints on speech. It was a rhetoric and a set of beliefs that could appeal to a broad constitutency, including many National Liberals. The National Liberal *Hamburger Nachrichten*, for example, weighed in on the case with an equally outraged reaction. Calling the candidate-defendant's behavior "political unrestraint," it warned of dire consequences if the principle underlying the court decision – the protection of political speeches involving assaults on honor with the use of "objectively untrue facts" – were to be generalized. It would "open the door to the most morally questionable unruliness [*Verwilderung*] in election campaigns," allowing candidates to drag the "honor" of their opponents "through the mud."[47]

Concerns over the inadequate protection of personal honor were widespread in the conservative and bourgeois press. A series of cause célèbre libel trials played an important role here as Germans were treated in the Wilhelmine years to the spectacle of the corrosive effects of libel on the lives and careers of high-standing public figures, including, most importantly, that of the Chancellor himself in the Eulenburg Affair (pp. 136–39).

The press was not the only cause of intolerable levels of libel. The courtroom itself was deeply problematic. Here, the country's flawed *Wahrheitsbeweis* wreaked its own kind of havoc, subjecting innocent plaintiffs and witnesses to the outrages of public exposure and humiliation. Almost two decades before Eulenburg that point was driven home in the most dramatic way in the Bochumer Steuerprozess (chapter 2), in which the defendant, Catholic editor Fusangel, defending the truth of his libels – the corruption of Bochum's tax commission – forced dozens of that city's elite Protestants and National Liberals to testify in mortification as plaintiffs or witnesses about private financial

---

[47] "Berechtigte Interessen?" *Hamburger Nachrichten*, September 19, 1911.

and family matters. The *Kölnische Zeitung* summed up the perniciousness of the *Wahrheitsbeweis* in the hands of libel defendants like Fusangel:

> In this way, the defamer succeeds in getting his grave accusations [the libels for which he is charged] out into the world unopposed and with people ready to believe them. Even though eventually, after months of investigation, the innocence of the defamed comes to light, on the one hand the damage can never be repaired and, on the other hand, in our fast-paced times, the mischief caused by the defamer will be long forgotten.[48]

Closer to home, anxiety about honor was fueled by everyday experiences – of plaintiffs, not defendants, and their search for security and justice. Many upstanding citizens were feeling personally victimized by a system that seemed to have so little sympathy for the plight of ordinary people and their struggles to defend their social positions and livelihoods. Generalsekretär St. (chapter 2) wrote in a tone of outrage about the kind of obstacles facing a man like himself – a "peaceful, orderly, good citizen" – who wanted nothing more than to redeem his honor in a court of law but who found instead a tangled, lax nightmare of a system.[49] This applied as well to civil servants and politicians attacked in the press, or to the businessman fearing the loss of credit sources.

Such experiences and sentiments help explain why those among the Right calling for legal crackdowns found a receptive audience beyond the conservative bastions of the East Elbian aristocracy, the officer corps, and the upper bureaucracy.[50] Building upon popular anxieties, conservatives, like their leftist counterparts, shaped them into an ideologically inflected legal agenda. For conservatives, honor was central to a worldview and a way of life that seemed under attack from all sides. Defined in corporatist and hierarchical terms, personal honor was code for the status and privileges of *Stand*, requiring

---

[48] "Ein Rückblick auf den Bochumer Steuerprozess," *Kölnische Zeitung*, June 20, 1891.
[49] "Wie es um den Rechtsschutz des Staatsbürgers als Beleidigten in Preussen und im Reiche steht," *Kölner Tageblatt*, August 20, 1910.
[50] Ibid.

elaborate codes of etiquette that anchored a world of clearly defined hierarchies and deference to established authorities (monarchy, the state, social superiors). But this world was being undone by social leveling, political challenges to authority, and the individualism and anonymity of mass society, one of whose symbols and symptoms was the mass press.

Conservative newspapers reinforced and fed back to their readers in alarmist terms their own experiences. There were the incessant attacks of the press, an institution riven by sensationalism, and the reason why "more and more a certain part of the public discussion degenerates into personal attack and defenses, insult and suspicion."[51] There was a judicial system stacked against a man's ability to protect himself and the sanctity and privacy of his family and home. And "when a man of honor is treated with dishonor," he might as well forget the law, given the outrageously low sentences and the other tribulations awaiting him in the courts. The Berlin daily, the *Tägliche Rundschau*, laid out the scenario of the "endless annoyances and unpleasantness" a plaintiff was forced to endure: first, he must pay a lawyer; then, as he waits a month or more for the hearing, he suffers "nervous tension." The day arrives, and if the court demands his personal appearance, it may require the expense of travel and leaving his business. If he thus withdraws his complaint, his opponent triumphs and he publicly demonstrates his inability to defend his rights. But if he goes forward with the proceeding, he risks public exposure of all kinds of private matters when his opponent, the defendant, uses the *Wahrheitsbeweis* to prove his innocence. Even if the plaintiff wins, what awaits him is the final insult of the "absurd fine," the "pitifully low" 10–20M. Eulenburg and other causes célèbres hovered (explicitly or implicitly) in the background as this and other writers anguished about the *Wahrheitsbeweis* and the potential of the trial itself to destroy a man's reputation. Not only did the courts fail to redeem a person's honor; they often increased the damage, since, with the *Wahrheitsbeweis* provision, the defendant could drag a plaintiff's private life into the courtroom in full public

---

[51] "Interimistisches Schweigen bei Beleidigungsprozessen," *Die Post*, August 20, 1892.

view, or, as in several well-known cases (e.g. the Bochumer tax trial, above), tarnish the reputations of innocent bystanders testifying as witnesses. Defamation trials, in short, made "a mockery of the natural feeling for law and honor."[52]

Conservative newspapers, in turn, merged objections to defamation law and the sensationalist press with a broader, antisemitically tinged social critique of modernity. Unprecedented press exposure and public discussion, often in the form of personal attack, left many people feeling exposed, vulnerable, undermined, and defenseless. The Right called this a decline of "civility" and contrasted it with an earlier time of propriety, when the press had a "feeling for affluence," "good morals," and "decency."[53] It lamented a world transformed by capitalism and social upstarts. A legal system that strongly protected "material property" (severe punishments for theft) but failed to protect "ideal property" (honor) was "un-german."[54] Civility had been replaced by "revolver journalism."[55] "Honor, law, and duty" had been replaced by "hedonism and the debased influence of money [*Mammondienst*]." If only the judiciary were made up of "irreproachable, impeccably brought up [men] with a Christian disposition and education," who moved in the right social circles, sighed *Das Volk*.[56]

The government's policy of singling out *Beamtenbeleidigungen* for prosecutions, in such a view, was absolutely correct and necessary. Insults against state officials had for centuries been treated more severely in German law,[57] and for good reason. The protection of state officials' honor was a crucial component of a society of order and "obedience." The conservative Berlin daily *Norddeutsche Allgemeine Zeitung* provided one such defense of *Beamtenbeleidigung* prosecutions: officialdom, essential to the entire functioning of the 'state organism'

---

[52] "Der Kampf gegen das Duell," *Tägliche Rundschau*, October 30, 1901.
[53] "Der Schutz der Ehre," *Kreuz-Zeitung*, March 28, 1908.   [54] Ibid.
[55] "Das Beleidigungs-Strafrecht," *Strassburger Post*, April 19, 1914.
[56] "Die Ehre und unsere Justiz," *Das Volk*, October 18, 1893. Also, for links between defamation, honor, and a critique of modernity, see "Verleumdung," *Leipziger Nachrichten*, November 20, 1913.
[57] For the early-modern era, see, e.g., Döhring, *Geschichte*, pp. 14–15. This was not unique to Germany.

and the values of duty and obedience, must be granted a special 'corporate-professional honor" status with special legal protections. And even though the Criminal Code incorporated *Beamtenbeleidigung* into the general defamation sections, it was entirely appropriate for the courts to treat these cases differently with state prosecutions and harsher sentences. The army, included as officials and "bearers of the monarchist principle in public life," was under attack from "oppositional and revolutionary elements." Therefore, the newspaper bemoaned the "light sentences" meted out in these cases and the fact that "only rarely" did convicted offenders receive the highest sentence of two years incarceration. Such laxness was producing a rise in defamatory statements against officialdom, encouraging a lack of obedience (*Gehorsamkeit*) in revolutionary elements, since offenders never faced the full brunt of the law; all they needed was people with money (*kapitalkräftige Leute*).[58]

Conservative angst over defamation litigation was of course in part purely rhetorical, since the dueling field, not the courtroom, was the quintessential space for the restitution of upper-class male honor. Indeed, the conservative press skillfully linked the duel and the defamation lawsuit in order to press its vision of legal reform. If critics on the Left wanted an end to dueling, they argued, then they had better do something about the laughably mild court sentences, the public exposure of respectable men's private lives, and other problems in the judicial system, which made dueling a positive necessity as the only way a man could properly protect his honor.[59] To be sure, commentators admitted, the aversion of the upper-class and officer corps to the defamation lawsuit was bound up with their honor codes, and to go against these constituted an "injury to class tradition [*Standesitte*]."[60] But many of these men could be enticed into the courtroom if drastic legal reforms made it worth their while. This was all the more necessary because, at a time when dueling – illegal but on the rise and a symbol of anachronistic aristocratic-military values – was under political attack, dueling excesses like the

[58] "Berlin, 4. Juni," *Norddeutsche Allgemeine Zeitung*, June 4, 1894.
[59] "Der Ehrenhandel," *Das Reich*, July 21, 1910.   [60] Ibid.

"rowdyism" and "honor terrorism" of university students were feeding revolutionary fervor in the masses. The *Tägliche Rundschau* worried that when prosecutors looked the other way in dueling cases, "it is heightening the pressure [*Gefühl*] for legal equality and is more grist for the Social Democratic mill."[61]

But in other ways, conservative worries about libel law were personal and real. Despite the assertions then and later, some members of the upper classes (not to mention conservative supporters farther down the social scale), as I have shown, did engage in honor lawsuits in the courts,[62] while many others who did not probably longed to, had it been more socially acceptable. The terrible burden that *satisfaktionsfähige* men lived with – the ever-present possibility of facing death in a duel over a personal insult – was most famously thematicized in Theodor Fontane's 1896 novel *Effi Briest*. In violation of her marriage vows and her sexual honor, the eponymous Effi, wife of a Prussian officer, engages in a brief love affair. When her husband, Innstetten, discovers this, he is deeply torn. He finds himself strangely indifferent to the affair itself and ill-inclined toward anger or revenge: the affair occurred years ago, he loves his wife, and, in truth, he feels no "hatred at all, or even thirst for vengeance."[63] Yet, as he confides to a friend, there is no doubt of acting on his feelings. He will duel (killing his opponent) and he will end his marriage (socially killing his wife), not because he wants to but because it is demanded of him by the honor code of his class. Fontane captured the rigidity and deadly coercion of that honor code in Innstetten's thought process: "I've turned this [dueling decision] over and over again in my mind," he tells his friend:

We're not isolated persons, we belong to a whole society and have constantly to consider that society, we're completely dependent on it ... we've become accustomed to judge everything, ourselves and others, according to its rules.

[61] "Der Kampf gegen das Duell," *Tägliche Rundschau*, October 30, 1901.

[62] It is certainly not hard to find cases of upper-class lawsuits against lower-ranked and *unsatisfaktionsfähige* people. Two examples: "Wegen Beleidigung des livländischen Barons von Rolcken," *Vorwärts*, March 16, 1911; a short, untitled notice on a libel suit brought by Landrat Freiherrn von Malzahn, ibid., October 30, 1902.

[63] Fontane, *Effi Briest*, trans. Douglas Parmée (London, 1967), p. 214.

And it's no good transgressing them, society will despise us and finally we will despise ourselves ... So once again, there's no hatred or anything of that sort and I don't want to have blood on my hands ... but that *something* which forms society – call it a tyrant if you like – is not concerned with charm or love, or even with how long ago a thing took place. I've no choice, I must do it.[64]

A man such as Innstetten who refused to duel faced ridicule, social ostracization, and possible penury. One example from the historical record is the Bismarck–Becker Affair of 1908. In an encounter between Becker, a journalist, and von Bismarck, a lieutenant officer, Becker, according to a press report, "behaved boorishly, refusing to offer [Bismarck] his calling card and giving him a fisticuff." A subsequent *Privatklage* trial (off-duty at the time of the incident, Bismarck had been dishonored as a private citizen) led to Becker's conviction, a jail sentence of 18 months, while the military authorities meted out their own punishment – of the plaintiff, Bismarck. For failing to challenge Becker to a duel, he had violated the honor code prescribed for his officer "estate" and was banished from the military.[65] Such men were caught in a terrible bind, torn between conflicting legal codes (dueling was outlawed by the state but required by the military honor code) and between the duel's physical violence, on the one hand, and the lax courts, on the other. No wonder that so many men, opined one journalist, were forced to passively tolerate unending *"Unannehmlichkeit"* in their daily lives.[66]

The anxiety caused by this predicament, strengthened by the enormous growth of libelous attacks in the chaotic world of mass politics, is palpable in conservative pleas for legal reform and in the kind of measures they advocated. Those measures, aimed at protecting personal honor and restoring "civility" to public life, focused on plaintiff rights and further restrictions on speech in the press and in the courtroom. Summing up the key aspects of this agenda in 1908, the *Kreuz-Zeitung* called for much harsher sentencing practices to deter libels and to make lawsuits worth the while of honorable men. It cited Chief Administrative Judge von Tzschoppe who suggested

---

[64] Ibid., p. 215. Emphasis in the original translation.

[65] N.t., *Frankfurter Zeitung*, October 24, 1908.

[66] "Interimistisches Schweigen bei Beleidigungsprozessen," *Die Post*, August 20, 1892.

raising the maximum penalties for simple insult (§185) from 600 to
1500M. For the more serious crime of public libels (§§186–187) –
offenses endangering a person's good name – he advocated in the
lesser and more serious cases of defamation raising penalties respectively to 2000M. and 5000M; those convicted of calumny should be
subject to a possible three-year sentence and loss of certain of their
civil rights (*bürgerliche Ehrenrechte*).[67] Second, and more importantly,
in light of recent events (below), the *Kreuz-Zeitung* and other conservatives wanted severe limitations placed on the kinds of evidentiary
facts a defendant was allowed to introduce into a trial in order to prove
the truth of his or her alleged libel (the *Wahrheitsbeweis* issue). Third,
the paper demanded the closing of certain sensitive defamation trials
from press coverage and the public square. Citing the Eulenburg
scandal and the general "desire for sensationalism" and immorality
of the modern press, it called for extending the rules governing marital
litigation in order to protect litigants' privacy, namely barring the
public and the press from the courtroom in libel trials.

These political divisions, developing over decades, partly reflected well-
defined ideological and philosophical differences, ones we have earlier
seen within the judiciary itself. In other ways, they evolved ad hoc in
reaction to events on the ground, especially to the mass of lawsuits in the
courts. Nowhere was this more apparent than at mobilizing moments of
great controversy over causes célèbres, moments that offer windows
onto the politics of honor in action. And there was no more important
event – in fame, political import, and sheer scandal – bearing on the
Kaiserreich's honor politics than that of the Eulenburg Affair.

The outlines of the Eulenburg Affair, as it came to be known, are
well known.[68] It began with articles penned by the journalist and

[67] "Der Schutz der Ehre," *Neue Preussiche Zeitung* (Kreuz-Zeitung) March 28, 1908.
The newspaper disagreed somewhat with the last point.
[68] For the events I have found particularly useful James Steakley, "Iconography of a
Scandal: Political Cartoons and the Eulenburg Affair in Wilhelmine Germany," in
Martin Duberman et al. (eds.), *Hidden From History* (New York, 1989), pp. 233–57,
and Isabel Hull, *The Entourage of Kaiser Wilhelm II* (Cambridge, 1982). For an
in-depth legal analysis of the case, see Karsten Hecht, *Die Harden-Prozesse:*

publisher Maximilian Harden accusing two members of the Kaiser's inner circle of homosexuality: diplomat Philipp Prince zu Eulenburg-Hertefeld and General Kuno Count von Moltke, military commandant of Berlin. These were explosive charges, not only because of the stature of the accused and the seriousness of the accusation (§175, Germany's anti-sodomy law), but because they came on the heels of an ongoing scandal over homosexuality in the army that had already led to the courts-martial and convictions of twenty officers.[69]

Harden's motive initially was purely political: to bring down Eulenburg, whose influence over the Kaiser Harden (and many others, including members of the military and Foreign Office) detested because of Eulenburg's "anti-imperialist outlook and willingness to seek an accomodation with the 'hereditary enemy,' France."[70] But, once set in motion, the charges took on their own dynamic, consistent with their scandalous nature, the logic of honor defenses, and the nature of German defamation law. Moltke promptly sued Harden for libel (Harden had refused a dueling challenge) and, after the state, to its later chagrin, refused to prosecute, the case went forward as a *Privatklage*.[71] At trial, Harden ought his defense with the tools available, skillfully using Germany's liberal evidentiary rules (*Wahrheitsbeweis*) to put on the stand witnesses who testified to Moltke's abnormal sexual proclivities. The result was a scandal. Moltke's former wife, Lili von Elbe, testified, in historian Steakley's words, that

Strafverfahren, Öffentlichkeit und Politik im Kaiserreich (Munich, 1997). For an analysis of the press and the monarchy, see Martin Kohlrausch, *Der Monarch im Skandal: Die Logik der Massenmedien und die Transformation der wilhelminischen Monarchie* (Berlin, 2005). On the case in terms of the history of masculinity, see Claudia Bruns, "Skandale im Beraterkreis um Kaiser Wilhelm II. Die homosexuelle 'Verbündelung' der 'Liebenberger Tafelrunde' als Politikum," in Susanne zur Nieden (ed.), *Homosexualität und Staatsräson* (Frankfurt, 2005), pp. 52–80; Martin Kohlrausch, "The Unmanly Emperor: Wilhelm II and the Fragility of the Royal Individual," in Regina Schulte (ed.), *The Body of the Queen* (New York, 2006), pp. 254–78. For a very detailed, first-hand account of the Moltke-Harden trial, see Hugo Friedlaender, *Interessante Kriminal-Prozesse* (Berlin, 1920), pp. 5–203.

[69] Steakley, "Iconography," p. 239.
[70] Ibid., p. 236.   [71] Many accounts incorrectly label the first trial a "civil" one.

in two years of marriage, conjugal relations had occurred only on the first two nights; on the few other nights they had shared a bed, Moltke had sometimes placed a pan of water between them to discourage her advances. She reported that her husband had once espied a handkerchief left behind by Eulenburg and had warmly pressed it to his lips, murmuring "Phili, my Phili!" Moltke had variously addressed Eulenburg as "my soulmate, my old boy, my once and only cuddly bear," and the two had referred to Wilhelm [II] as their "darling." They had behaved in such a blatant fashion that her ten-year-old son (by a previous marriage) had taken to imitating their "revolting" mannerisms with the servants.[72]

An equally devastating witness was the physician, sex reformer, and homosexual rights activist Magnus Hirschfeld, who opined on Moltke's "feminine side" and his "unconscious orientation [of] homosexuality" that allegedly existed irrespective of whether Moltke had ever actually engaged in such sex acts.[73] Harden was vindicated.

The disgrace of this trial – there was fear of the "undermin[ing] [of] public confidence in the regime" and the "respectability [of its] ruling class"[74] – made the state reverse course, taking up Moltke's case and prosecuting Harden in a second trial that found him guilty. Harden, seeking vindication, reacted by purposefully manufacturing a third (*Privatklage*) trial in April, 1908 that allowed him to introduce into the public record still more damning evidence – of past sexual relationships Eulenburg had had with a Munich milkman and a Starnberg farmer. This trial led to the overturning of Harden's earlier conviction for libel, as well as the filing of perjury charges against Eulenburg.[75] Meanwhile, a fifth libel trial – sending the public into "true paroxysms of rage" (*wahre Wutparoxysmen*)[76] – had seen the Chancellor himself (von Bülow) litigating against charges of homosexuality by the publicist Adolf Brand. Eulenburg himself, citing ill-health, managed to avoid his perjury trial over years of repeated attempts by the courts.

---

[72] Ibid., p. 241.   [73] Ibid., p. 242.   [74] Ibid.

[75] The perjury charge led to repeated but ultimately unsuccessful attempts over the years to try Eulenburg, who managed to sabotage all such attempts with claims of ill-health.

[76] Bruns's paraphrase of Hirschfeld's account (p. 54).

The Affair caught the government at a difficult time when the prestige and standing of the monarchy and the old elites were under pressure at home and abroad, and when the government, faced with the rising electoral fortunes of the SPD, was finding it increasingly difficult to put together legislative majorities in the Reichstag. Chancellor Bülow's *Sammlungspolitik* – governing with a coalition of non-Socialist parties to defeat the SPD – had faltered on the independent position of its linchpin, the Centre Party. Bülow's subsequent break with the Catholic Centre Party in 1907 and his formation of a new coalition – the nationalist, anti-socialist, and anti-Catholic "Bülow Bloc" – depended for legislative majorities on the impossible harmonizing of left-liberal and conservative interests. Any hope of this working was soon dispelled when the government, faced with the financial crisis of a mounting national debt, tried to cobble together support for a new tax bill. This required concessions to left liberals that deeply "alarmed" conservatives, united them with the Centre in opposition to the government, and helped bring about Bülow's fall in spring, 1909. At the same time, the government was facing serious setbacks in foreign affairs. Germany's defeat in the Moroccan Crisis of 1905/1906 underscored its mounting isolation in Europe as a result of the government's aggressive *Weltpolitik*.[77] The Emperor's political gaffes in his interview with London's *Daily Telegraph* in 1908 caused a domestic uproar and calls for his abdication, while further alienating Germany abroad. And now, the Eulenburg scandal.[78]

Harden-Molkte caused panic in some quarters of government. (It also, apparently, swamped the courts with copy-cat lawsuits.)[79] Prussian Justice Minister Beseler urged moving immediately on an amendment of

[77] These domestic and foreign policy developments are concisely summarized in Gordon Craig, *Germany, 1866–1945* (New York, 1978), pp. 251ff.

[78] On the political fallout of the Affair, some historians emphasize its contribution to a "shift in German [foreign] policy that heightened military aggressivenenss" and hence sped the outbreak of war in 1914; others have focused on its domestic implications and the role it may have played in undermining support at home for the Kaiser.

[79] "Acht Monate Gefängnis," *Das kleine Journal*, May 11, 1908.

the Reich Criminal Code to restrict the *Wahrheitsbeweis* and the publicity of sensitive trials.[80] Given a situation where the most "sensitive" aspects of plaintiffs' "private and family life" were being "exposed" and offered up for "public commentary," it was too "urgent" to wait for the completion of the more general Criminal Code revisions.[81] There were other reasons as well, among which loomed a foreign policy consideration: the potential damage to Germany's standing abroad caused by such scandals.[82] Furthermore, public opinion, whose pressure would be crucial for getting the bill passed, was at the moment intensely outraged, whereas waiting risked seeing such sentiment dissipate.[83]

Nieberding, State Secretary of the Reichs-Justizamt, the department overseeing the revision of the Criminal Code, did not buy Beseler's argument. He may have shared Beseler's feeling of urgency, but he was not letting it get the better of his political judgment, and that judgment told him that the votes in the Reichstag were not there for legislation in this form. That it was too late in the year to introduce such a bill was only the least of the government's problems. More important was the "political consideration" that doing so would contradict and thus undermine the strategy the government had long been using in its dealings with the Reichstag, namely denying the parliament's criminal law reform attempts via supplemental legislation with the argument that all reforms must wait upon the completion of the entire Criminal Code. If, in these circumstances, the government now presented its own supplemental bill, and one with distinct "political significance," the Reichstag would be sure to demand a trade-off with the inclusion of its own reform proposals. To prevent this from happening, Nieberding had an alternative plan: introduce the bill in the next legislative year and attach it to a host of other minor and non-partisan reforms like lowering the penalties for petty theft. This, he hoped, would make it harder for the Reichstag to demand "deeper" reforms like "sharpening dueling penalities."

---

[80] At this point, Beseler believed that raising the penalties for libel was not a realistic goal.

[81] Beseler, December 15, 1907. I HA Rep. 84a, Nr. 8405, GStPK, pp. 43–44.

[82] Beseler proposal to the Prussian Staatsministerium, January 17, 1908. Ibid., p. 3.

[83] Ibid., p. 7.

In other words, in order to get through parliament a conservative libel bill, the government would placate the Left by appearing conciliatory to parts of its legislative agenda while surrounding the bill with popular provisions that could not fail to pass.[84]

It was this plan of action that ultimately prevailed, as seen in the actual supplemental bill brought before the Reichstag in spring of 1909. This was a piece of legislation born of genuine moral disgust, fears about the prestige of the monarchy and social elites, as well as pragmatic political considerations. The bill, promptly dubbed the "Lex Eulenburg" by the SPD because of its clear link, despite government denials, to that scandal and the protection of upper-class honor interests, embodied aspects of the kind of libel reform conservatives had long been calling for. It proposed sharpening the maximum penalties for public defamation (§186 to 10,000M or two years prison; raising them from 900 to 3,000M for §187; from 6,000 to 20,000M for §188). Most controversially, in cases of public defamation[85] (§186) or when a libel was spread through writing or images, it declared that the truth of the alleged libel "need not be proven" when it concerned "private matters not in the public interest."[86] This was legalese for what, in such circumstances, would make the truth of a libel irrelevant to assessments of guilt and deny defendants the use of the *Wahrheitsbeweis*. In addition, it gave the plaintiff the power to decide on whether or not a hearing of the evidence would be allowed. Both were reforms that threatened to significantly shift the balance of power in the courtroom to the advantage of the plaintiff and both targeted the kinds of press libel litigation that were so controversial. The bill sought to lessen the sting of these libel provisions with, at the same time, a package of crowd-pleasers: decreased penalities for trespass, petty theft, and several other minor crimes; increased penalities for the abuse of animals and children; a more narrow and precise definition of blackmail.

[84] Nieberding, December 20, 1907 and January 6, 1908. Ibid., pp. 45, 48–50.
[85] Public defamation (*öffentliche Beleidigung*) meant defamations that reached a large number of people.
[86] Nr. 1262 "Entwurf eines Gesetzes," *SBR Anlagen*, vol. 253 (Berlin, 1909), pp. 7672ff.

Aware of the politically explosive nature of the bill (correspondence between Beseler and Nieberding was stamped "secret!"), the government tested the waters of public opinion by leaking its contents in advance to the National Liberal *Kölnische Zeitung*.[87] Having noted and assimilated the ensuing criticism, Nieberding rose in the Reichstag on April 23, 1909, to introduce the bill. His speech, seeking to assuage fears and placate the critics, was both defensive and disingenuous. From the outset, it sought to downplay the amendments' conservative bias and its association with the class politics surrounding the Eulenburg Affair, namely, the public perception of the special treatment accorded upper-class honor. Besides denial and outright falsehoods (it was simply untrue, Nieberding asserted, that the government was only interested in the libel section of the bill and that the rest of the legislation was intended for "wrapping the libel provisions in an acceptable mantle"),[88] the speech employed a tone of "objectivity," legalism,[89] and conciliation, with much being made of comparative law and, as planned, the other provisions of the bill. Nieberding divided the bill's amendments into material crimes (theft) and crimes against "the ideal [non-material] assets of the people," which enabled him to group together under the latter heading the crackdown on libelers with the crackdown on animal and child abusers. Pointing to the lower-class-friendly theft provision – which lessened penalties for crimes found "in the life of [the] poor"[90] – he set up a rhetorical parallel between helping the poor (theft) and helping the honor-challenged (libel). It was untrue that the government was trying to "conceal from the public morally damaging aspects of high-placed people's lives" (i.e. Eulenburg, Moltke, and Bülow). No, this bill was about ordinary people's needs:

[87] That it was an intentional government leak is my interpretation; the sources do not specifically say this.

[88] *SBR*, April 23, 1909 (Berlin, 1909), p. 8126. This was exactly what Nieberding's secret memo to Beseler had proposed doing.

[89] "... ich bitte Sie, uns zu glauben, dass wir ... bei dier Vorschrift ... von rein sachlichen Gesichtspunkten ausgegangen sind ..." ibid., p. 8128.

[90] Ibid., p. 8126.

The principal people who are protected by this bill are not those in high places or those who belong to distinguished circles, but rather people who, socially or governmentally, are not in a position whereby their situations are connected to the public interest [i.e. those using the *Privatklage*].

Gender seemed the perfect way to appeal on this point. Nieberding called up the example of a young, "blameless" woman (Olga Molitor), whose private life had been subjected to intense public scrutiny and (unfair) vilification as a result of her testimony in the famous 1907 murder trial of her brother-in-law Karl Hau.

In the political reactions to the Lex Eulenburg (and to the draft bill's similar libel clauses),[91] one can see how the experiences and ideologies outlined above merged, in the context of 1908/1909, to form the ways in which parliamentarians and the public reacted to and debated the issues,[92] and where such terms as honor, privacy, and morality functioned as codes for far-ranging political agendas. These reactions also suggest how polarized the libel debate had become in the wake of the Eulenburg Affair.[93]

---

[91] *Vorentwurf zu einem deutschen Strafgesetzbuch* (Berlin, 1909), pp. 51ff. The significant exception for the clauses that overlapped was that the *Vorentwurf* (draft bill) left out the provision that a hearing of evidence was dependent upon the plaintiff's agreeing to this. The *Vorentwurf*, in addition, regulated libel procedures that were not included in the Lex Eulenburg. Most importantly, §263 denied §193 protection for those charged with calumny (*Verleumdung*).

[92] The following discussion is taken from three Reichstag debates on the Novelle (Lex Eulenburg): the first occurred on January 18, 1909, after it was leaked by the National Liberal *Kölnische Zeitung*; the much lengthier second and third debates took place on April 23 and 24, 1909 when the government officially brought the measure before the Reichstag. I also cite several earlier debates on the Eulenburg Affair in the Prussian parliament.

[93] By contrast, the opinions of jurists and legal scholars on libel reform, while mixed, reflecting (and helping to shape) the political debates, were somewhat less polarized. For example, both Karl Binding and Franz von Liszt, who were the leaders, respectively, of the opposing positivist and materialist schools of legal thought in Germany, opposed the Reichsgericht's interpretation of §193. Aschrott and von Liszt (eds.), *Die Reform des Reichsstrafgesetzbuchs* (Berlin, 1910), pp. 321–22. For legal debates about libel reform, see ibid., pp. 309ff.; *Zusammenstellung der gutachtlichen Äusserungen über den Vorentwurf zu einem deutschen Strafgesetzbuch* (Berlin, 1911), p. 352ff.

The Affair channeled political passions into debates about privacy and the *Wahrheitsbeweis*, while highlighting the class inequalities of the legal system. In the 1880s, it was still possible for a paper like the *National Zeitung* to take a fairly nuanced and pro-defendant position on the *Wahrheitsbeweis*, calling, in effect, for the burden of proof about the truth or untruth of a libel in *Beamtenbeleidigung* trials to be shifted to the plaintiff (accordingly, the bar for proving the truth of a libel would be lowered so that acquittal would be possible if the defendant simply showed that the plaintiff had not proven the untruth of the defendant's defamatory words).[94] By 1909, it is hard to imagine any right-of-center newspaper taking such a stand, let alone trying to lower the admissibility of evidence bar. The Eulenburg Affair, more than anything, had made the Right obsessed with protecting the privacy of libel plaintiffs and putting limits on the press. In the Reichstag, they argued this in coded language supporting the bill in the name of protecting honor and the sanctity of privacy and family. "Honor," proclaimed deputy Varenhorst, is "the most precious possession of humans … and cannot be protected enough." Because of this, "the private life of the individual does not belong in public. One must draw a veil in front of private life." Limiting the *Wahrheitsbeweis* would thus help to protect individuals against "gossip in the press … which dwells on such things in order to satisfy the itch of curious people."[95] Indeed Varenhorst felt the bill did not even go far enough in limiting defense evidence.

Some within the Center and National Liberal Parties, horrified by the "sensationalism" of the press coverage of Harden–Moltke and its "dirty" contents (the trials had made known "vices and conditions to classes of the population who knew nothing hitherto of these matters"[96]), concurred. Von Campe, himself a jurist, called for limiting the *Wahrheitsbeweis* along the lines of English law.[97] Reichstag

---

[94] "Der Beweis der Wahrheit bei Beschuldigung von Beamten," *National Zeitung*, August 20, 1887.

[95] April 23, 1909 debate. *SBR* 236 (Berlin, 1909), p. 8132.

[96] January 18, 1909. *SBR* 234 (Berlin, 1909), p. 6339.

[97] January 28, 1908 debate. *SBPA*, 1 (Berlin, 1908), pp. 1226, 1231. To do so, Campe called not for expanding the *Privatklage* but its opposite: having the state afford the same gravitas to libels against private citizens by extending state prosecutions to these cases.

deputy Belzer, in January 1909, declared the Center ready to "help ... the government" despite the party's concerns for protecting the "principle of publicity."[98] And, very few people supported the defense's use of the *Wahrheitsbeweis* when the libel at issue involved the "dishonorable facts of [the plaintiff's] private life."[99]

But for many moderates and leftists, Eulenburg confirmed and intensified suspicions about the true nature of libel prosecutions in the Kaiserreich. On the Left, Socialist attorney and Reichstag deputy Wolfgang Heine proclaimed:

Today the charge of 'insult' is the means by which the bureaucracy, militarism and the ruling classes try to suppress any fearless criticism of public wrongs, and, unfortunately, often not without success. There is not much of the free German word to detect anymore in Germany.[100]

In fact, by European standards Germany had unusually liberal rules for the admissibility of evidence in court, and to tighten these would have done no more, essentially, than bring the country in line with its neighbors.[101] But most politicians outside the Right did not see it this way and refused to support this section of the bill. The *Wahrheitsbeweis* had been utterly politicized by decades-long battles over libel law and state censorship (in turn linked to the Kaiserreich's broader political divisions), as well as by the more recent Eulenburg Affair. It was in this context that this obscure technical feature of German law came to be a focal point for what many critics saw as a battle between the principles of the liberal Rechtsstaat and those of arbitrary absolutist and aristocratic power.

National Liberals, Center, Progressives, and Socialists were (rightly) suspicious of the circumstances of the bill, convinced that it was motivated by the Eulenburg scandal and thus about an upper

---

[98] *SBR*, January 18, 1909, pp. 6339–40.
[99] Liepmann, "Die Beleidigung," in Mittermaier et al. (eds.), *Vergleichende Darstellung des deutschen und ausländischen Strafrechts: Besonderer Teil* vol. 4 (Berlin, 1906), p. 107.
[100] Heine, "Lex Eulenburg," *März* 2 (April 1, 1909), p. 31.
[101] Lilienthal, "Üble Nachrede und Verleumdung," in Mittermaier et al. (eds.), *Vergleichende Darstellung des deutschen und ausländischen Strafrechts: Besonderer Teil* vol. 4 (Berlin, 1906), p. 413 ff.

class acting to protect its own interests and reputations. They were skeptical of the claim that the bill was aimed solely at the "Revolverpresse," fearing it would adversely affect the entire press.[102] Repeatedly (and accurately), they pointed out that the law already gave jurists the right to exclude from trial irrelevant facts that the defense sought to introduce to prove the truth of the alleged libel, and warned therefore about acting precipitously based on a case (Harden–Moltke) whose worst features should be blamed not on the law but on the mistaken application of the law by individual prosecutors and judges. And they worried about the indefinite terms "public interest" and "private life" in the bill, with their potential for arbitrary definitions by the courts to repress speech and accord special treatment to officially connected and high-placed plaintiffs.[103]

In the two-day Reichstag debate of the original Lex Eulenburg, only one deputy (the Progressive Heckscher) outside of the conservatives expressed support for its libel provisions.[104] There was a range of practical, juridical, and political objections raised against the Lex Eulenburg, including those made in the name of honor, namely that it would backfire and actually worsen the situation of plaintiffs. But what is also striking is the role that liberal notions of law – of publicity, transparency, and accountability – played in one form or another in making the (Prussian and Reich) government's reform agenda a hard sell beyond the Right. Roeren, Center deputy in the Prussian Landtag, was as appalled as any by the exposure of youth to the "dirt and most intimate sexual operations" in the press coverage of Harden–Moltke. But, he went on, there were other factors to consider:

One must after all consider that, as a basic principle, the judicial proceedings should be open to the public and that this principle has just been demanded by the representatives of the people, first, in order that the public be given the opportunity to keep an oversight [*kontrollieren*] of the administration of justice,

---

[102] Engelen speech, *SBR* April 23, 1909, p. 8131.
[103] Osann speech, *SBR* April 23, 1909, p. 8137.
[104] *SBR* , April 24, 1909 (vol. 236), pp. 8155–56. As the government expected and planned for, the amendment's other provisions were widely popular.

then also in order to further the universally approved ideal aim of promoting in the people the notion of the objectivity and independence of the justice system. Only in exceptional cases should the public be excluded; indeed, when decency and order demand it.[105]

Wladyslaw Seyda of the Polish party put it most succinctly: "In our view, the right to free speech is at least as in need of protection as personal honor."[106]

On the far Left, Socialists were equally or more concerned about civil liberties, but saw the matter of libel reform through the lens of class politics and years of government persecution. The Lex Eulenburg's attempts to raise libel penalties were really aimed at "financially ruining oppositional newspapers."[107] Reichstag deputy Frohme welcomed certain parts of the 1909 bill, given the "backwardness, injustice, and inhumanity" of the present criminal code. But he rejected out of hand the libel sections, labeling them "a type of exceptional law against the press" and "a new piece of class justice." The bill was not about honor; it was about protecting the upper class and "raping the right to truth – to free, public dissemination of information [*Kundgebung*]."[108] In an earlier Reichstag debate, deputy Heine took a less confrontational but cleverer tack, casting himself (and the SPD) as a defender of honor in order to make the argument that even on its own terms (i.e. those of honor), the bill was deeply flawed and unacceptable.[109] Socialist deputy Frank, as the government feared, demanded that any reform of libel laws take place in conjunction with reforms strengthening

---

[105] *SBPA*, January 28, 1908 (Berlin, 1908), p. 1213.   [106] *SBR* (1909), p. 8163.

[107] This is a paraphrase of a 1910 *Vorwärts* article. *Zusammenstellung der gutachtlichen Äusserungen*, p. 258.

[108] *SBR*, April 23, 1909, pp. 8141–42.

[109] *SBR*, January 18, 1909, pp. 6348ff. For example, he argued that the massive number of trivial libel lawsuits against the press was responsible for lessening the "feeling of responsibility" in the press toward respecting individuals' privacy and honor. In other words, if the government wanted to protect honor, it should stop persecuting the press. See also his article "Strafrechtsreform und politische Reaktion," *März* 4 (December 14, 1909), pp. 415–20.

punishments against dueling.[110] No legislative reform of the law was possible in such polarized political circumstances.[111]

In sum, these debates saw the articulation of widely differing notions of honor and libel law that were linked in turn to alternative visions of civil society and the state. Conservatives, on one side, defended a corporatist and hierarchical honor linked to the authoritarian state. Leftists and liberals, by contrast, generally sought the privatization and depoliticization of honor consistent with a more egalitarian society and liberal polity.

Yet, this Left/Right divide, though substantial, was far from simple or set. Politicians often held ambivalent views, were influenced by changing events, and might shift positions depending upon the context. Thus, while positions on honor and libel were in part predetermined, driven by political ideology and personal sensibility, there was also much blurring of political lines, complexity, ambiguity, and contradiction. Depending upon the political circumstances and the specific honor issue at hand, politicians could be pulled in different directions, buffeted between liberal and conservative positions, which found them at times siding with their erstwhile opponents. Germany's political culture of honor, in other words, was very much in play in these years, vacillating between the Left/Right poles described above.

This last section explores more closely the political dynamics shaping that culture. A number of forces interacted in complex ways: the Left/Right political divide; nationalism and the cult of the state; and notions of honor. In this context, national debates over libel legislation reflected the state of opinion. But they were also causal, the debates themselves occasioning shifts in the political dynamics. This was the case in 1907/08 during the Reichstag debates leading up to the passage of a bill revising the lèse-majesté laws – the provisions forbidding insults against the royal and princely houses.

---

[110]   *SBR* (1909), p. 8159.
[111]   As late as 1912, the government was still attempting in vain to get such a bill passed by the Reichstag. Bethmann Hollweg to the Kaiser, May 25, 1912. I. HA Rep. 89, Nr. 17726, GStPK, pp. 99–100.

These statutes, as explained earlier, had become enormously controversial. Not only were they draconian (minimum sentences, for example, of two months prison and loss of all public offices for insults against the Kaiser).[112] Over the years, they had been incessantly used to silence and intimidate critics of the state. Just as controversial was the indiscriminateness of the law, which required prosecution of all insults against the crown irrespective of the libeler's motive or context. This subjected to prosecution even statements lacking intent or consciousness to harm the crown. It also included statements uttered in private that became known subsequently to the state only through personal denunciations. The result, as Nieberding, State Secretary of the Imperial Department of Justice, put it, was the "growth of a base and hostile climate of denunciation [*Denunziationttum*]" in which "even members of the same family, indeed the best of friends, denounce each other for lèse-majesté the minute discord between them occurs."[113] Even denunciations brought years after the initial offense could lead to prosecution. All of this had made lèse-majesté law, in Nieberding's understatement, "not entirely reconcilable with the general sense of justice."[114]

By 1907, even the Kaiser understood how problematic this state of affairs was. On January 27 of that year, in a dramatic concession to public opinion, he issued an edict promising clemency to offenders whose insults against the Prussian monarchy stemmed "merely from lack of understanding, indiscretion, heedlessness [that do not involve] malicious design." Only insults made with "malicious intent" (*mit Vorbedacht und in böser Absicht*) would be prosecuted in the future.[115] Wilhelm's edict, which applied only to Prussia and Alsace-Lorraine, prompted the Reich government to bring before the

---

[112] For an overview of German lèse-majesté laws in the nineteenth and twentieth centuries, see Andrea Hartmann, *Majestätsbeleidigung und Verunglimpfung des Staatsoberhauptes (§§94ff. RStGB, 90 StGB): Reformdiskussion und Gesetzgebung seit dem 19. Jahrhundert* (Berlin, 2006).

[113] Speech at the November 23, 1907 session of the Reichstag. *SBR* 229 (Berlin, 1908), pp. 1729–31.

[114] Ibid., p. 1729.

[115] Reprinted in "Majestätsbeleidigung," *Vorwärts*, January 29, 1907.

Reichstag a bill extending the Kaiser's edict to include other sections of the lèse-majesté statutes and to apply to the entire nation.

The bill the government brought before the Reichstag in November 1907, which was debated in three readings in the winter of 1907/08, was presented as a significant concession to public opinion. In actuality, it sought to rid the system of abuses around private denunciations and apolitical prosecutions while preserving the state's ability to use lèse-majesté as a tool of political repression. Thus, on the one hand, it proposed softening prosecutions of non-public insults against the Emperor, the princes, and their families (StGB, §§95, 97, 99, 101) by requiring a prior judicial investigation. It also significantly lowered the statute of limitations (i.e. the period following the offense during which criminal charges could be brought) for prosecutions of lèse-majesté from five years to six months. Its third provision, on the other hand, which made the offense "punishable only in instances of malicious intent," also ostensibly aimed to reduce and soften prosecutions, but it did so with language – "malicious intent" – that controversially left the government wide prosecutorial latitude.[116]

The Reichstag's initial response was lukewarm at best. With the exception of the Right, all of the political parties had serious reservations about the malicious intent clause, perceiving it as a potentially dangerous loophole ripe for government exploition as justification for and possibly the intensification of political prosecutions and the repression of dissent. The SPD, predictably, was the most adamant. There was only one good thing about the bill, declared deputy Heine in a long speech redolent of bitter suspicion – the statute of limitation clause. Otherwise, the legislation had all of the "markings of its Prussian origins." Under the guise of tolerance, the law will only sharpen the partisan nature of the judiciary; in the hands of judges, the interpretation of "malicious intent" will be politicized to reward those "right-minded" people loyal to the regime and punish the "wrong-minded." Heine backed up his case with a litany of outrageous lèse-majesté rulings – one editor had been

---

[116] Bill no. 348, "Entwurf eines Gesetzes," *SBR. Anlagen* (Berlin, 1907), pp. 1959–60.

convicted for writing of the "slaughter" of wild animals at a royal hunt, because, unbeknownst to him, the Kaiser had been present at the event – all of them directed against Social Democratic defendants. But Heine went even further, rearticulating a radical policy move the SPD had been calling for since the 1890s: to treat the Kaiser and other royal personages like any other citizen and abolish the lèse-majesté laws altogether (according to Heine, they could perfectly well pursue defamation charges under the existing statutes of §§185ff). As *Vorwärts* put it, the SPD rejects the very notion of lèse-majesté because it is "based on the notion of the [unfree] 'subject,' of people with less honor vis-à-vis the honor of those who by chance and birth are the 'superiors'."[117]

The SPD's last proposal was far too extreme for the other political parties. But, from the Center-Left to the Center-Right, there was striking unanimity with the Socialists on the matter of free speech. All expressed in varying degrees the need to build into the wording of the bill greater protections against the politicization of lèse-majesté. National Liberal deputy Osann expressed concern that the bill lacked "objective criteria" for determining "malicious" statements.[118] Heckscher, speaking for the Progressive Party, put it in much stronger terms: use of the term "malicious" was "extraordinarily dangerous," practically demanding of judges that they consider a defendant's political views as a matter of course when seeking to clarify the motives behind a defendant. He gave the recent example of a judge who opened a court hearing with the question posed to the defendant: "Are you a Social Democrat?"[119]

Yet, just two months later, at the second reading of the bill, these concerns about protecting free speech had all but evaporated in the Center. The mood had perceptibly changed. Those who had earlier expressed reservations were now embracing the bill, leaving the Socialists isolated. National Liberals and Progressives were now suddenly convinced that the bill's wording sufficed to keep politicized prosecutions in check.[120] The Center, likewise, was ready to give the

---

[117] "Majestätsbeleidigung," *Vorwärts*, January 29, 1907.   [118] Ibid., p. 1735.
[119] Ibid., pp. 1746–47.   [120] *SBR*, January 21, 1908, pp. 2602–03, 2599.

bill its stamp of approval as an improvement, albeit flawed, over existing law.[121]

There had been a slight rewording in committee of the bill since its first reading, from "with malicious intent" to "with the deliberate purpose and the malicious intent to commit an injury to honor." But the new wording, invoked by deputies to justify their new-found support for the bill, was not much more than window dressing. What, more importantly, had changed since the last reading (besides any backroom deals, about which there is a lack of information) was the interjection into the debate of nationalism and anti-socialism. And what sparked this was an infamous lèse-majesté trial, ongoing during the Reichstag debates – the Königsberg lèse-majesté trial.

The trial stemmed from a critical and irreverent editorial of September 21, 1907, in the socialist *Königsberger Volkszeitung* on the upcoming dedication of a national monument in the east Prussian port town of Memel, the place in 1807 that became the seat of the Prussian government during the Napoleonic occupation, and where King Friedrich Wilhelm III had signed the October Edict abolishing serfdom and inaugurating the era of Prussian reform and renewal. The Memel monument, featuring a fresco of the King and his wife Queen Luise flanked by busts of important generals and statesmen, commemorated the 100th anniversary of those events.

Far from joining in the spirit of pious national commemoration, the *Volkszeitung* ridiculed the scene, calling the monument a *Schandsäule* (pillar of shame) and launching into an historical critique of the Prussian state under the hegemony of the Junkers and, since 1848, the bourgeoisie. For the article and its use in particular of the term *Schandsäule*, the paper's editor was tried and found guilty of insulting the monument and all the participants at its unveiling. Since one of those participants was the Kaiser, this made it into a lèse-majesté case. The editor was sentenced to a fifteen-month jail term.

On all sides, the case became a notorious cause célèbre: conservatives and National Liberals were outraged by the content of the article; Socialists were outraged by its repression in the courts. On

---

[121] Ibid., p. 2595.

the former side, nationalist outrage and anti-socialism, inflamed by the trial, generated a perceptible shift in the dynamics in the Reichstag as the deputies debated the new lèse-majesté bill, distinctly tipping the scales in favor of the government and the bill.

At the bill's first reading in November, 1907, the Königsberger case had not yet become the political vortex it would be two months later, sucking in and concentrating broader political debates. Only the far-right antisemite Bindewald, at this point, saw fit to mention it all, using it to scold the SPD in the name of the good German *Volk* and the protection of innocent children.[122] By the second reading, after the trial had inflamed opinion, that sort of rhetoric had migrated into the mainstream.

There was a correlation between nationalist outrage, anti-socialism, and the willingness, suddenly, on the part of deputies to reverse their earlier positions and support the government's bill. National Liberal deputy Osann, his pitch rising, suspected the SPD's "intention [in the *Volkszeitung* article] was to tear down — tear down Queen Luise, tear down those who participated in the monument and its unveiling (yes! Right and National Liberals) and who went [to Memel] with the conviction they would see not the unveiling of a pillar of shame but the erection of a national monument (tumultuous applause — shouting rejection from the SPD and opposition)."[123] At the same time, Osann now felt the need to make the case for the *importance* and *value* of lèse-majesté prosecutions as a kind of national duty: such trials were not about "the personality of the monarch"; they were about something much bigger — thwarting insults against the monarch as "representative of the state" itself.[124]

Even the Progressives were changing their tune. At the bill's first reading, deputy Heckscher characterized the proposed legislation as "extraordinarily dangerous."[125] By the second reading, his colleague Ernst Müller was backing away from this position. To be sure, he remained an opponent of "historical lèse-majesté prosecutions," calling them dangerous and smacking of judicial political partisanship.

---

[122] *SBR* 229 (Berlin, 1908), pp. 1747–49.   [123] *SBR*, January 21, 1908, p. 2601.
[124] Ibid., p. 2599.   [125] Ibid., November 23, 1907, p. 1746.

Müller preferred the British model: a monarchy that, in maintaining a policy of non-interference in public debates (according to Müller, there had been no lèse-majesté cases in Britain since 1823), incurs the respect of its citizenry. The British support their monarchy not because of "humiliating police surveillance" (à la Germany), but because the people are "trusted" and given free speech.[126] Müller, however, was now convinced that the revised wording of the bill sufficed to protect against future abuses.[127] Two days later, at the bill's third reading, the Progressives had thrown in the towel altogether. Deputy Gyssling, joining the nationalist chorus, attacked the *Volkszeitung* article as an "outrage" that has provoked the "indignation" of the "broadest circles in the entire German fatherland."[128]

Nationalism and anti-Socialism here were closely intertwined with honor and chivalry. What really upset someone like National Liberal Osann was the article's slanderous treatment of Queen Luise (1776–1810), the only part of the article about which he specifically spoke and doing so at length. He was incensed by the article's quote of Alexander von Humboldt calling the Queen "selfish, cunning, and underhanded" and of its picture of her, quoting from her letters, at the time of the Jena defeat, when starvation was rampant, enjoying leisurely strolls and squandering public money.[129]

Such talk was dishonoring to the point of sacrilege for Osann and other Protestant nationalists. Queen Luise had become a legend and cult figure of Prussocentric national memory in the course of the nineteenth century. Historians had turned her into the essence of virtuous, bourgeois femininity: pious, modest, devoted to husband and children, compassionate benefactress of the common people. As such, she became a perfect vessel for a historical narrative about Prussia's suffering and redemption in the era of the Napoleonic wars. In Droysen, she was an "emblem of hope – her purity and innocence reflect[ed] the uncorrupted freshness of the state reawakening from its deepest misery, and the birth of the constitutional

---

[126] Ibid., January 21, 1908, p. 2604.   [127] Ibid., p. 2602.
[128] Ibid., January 23, 1908, p. 2669.   [129] Ibid., January 21, 1908, p. 2600.

monarchy."[130] In Treitschke, she was the "violated and 'abused' victim of ... Napoleon" who spurred the "avenging spirit of the War of Liberation."[131] In short, she had become a maternal national icon, and to dishonor her, as the Socialists had done, stirred political passions capable of affecting (though, certainly, not entirely determining) the outcome of a Reichstag vote. As Osann put it, differences of opinion about the events and royal personages of the Napoleonic era were perfectly in order. But not when they crossed the line from "critique" to "insults," and this is what happened to Queen Luise.[132]

It is not that the political center had suddenly abandoned its concerns with civil liberties. Far from it. While conservative Edward Wagner worried only that the bill did not go far enough in protecting the "authority of the crown," progressives and even National Liberals remained worried about free speech issues. Osann's uneasiness was evident in the qualifications that hedged his criticism of the Socialists.[133] Yet, another, more emotional side of him – the part passionate about nation, honor, and chivalry – intervened to shift his vote towards the right. The point is not the authoritarianism of German honor politics, but its complexity and tensions – the fact that such politics were in play and the sorts of ideas and passions that drove its dynamics.

Meanwhile, as we will see in the following chapter, grass-roots movements outside the formal political institutions were forming pressure groups and a new style of politics that utilized a hybrid honor drawn from elements of both Left and Right.

---

[130] Regina Schulte, "The Queen – A Middle-Class Tragedy: The Writing of History and the Creation of Myths in Nineteenth-Century France and Germany," *Gender and History* 14 (2002), 281; Philipp Demandt, *Luisenkult: Die Unsterblichkeit der Königin von Preussen* (Cologne, 2003).

[131] Schulte, "Queen," p. 284.

[132] *SBR* January 21, 1908, p. 2600. Not that gendered language was not the exclusive monopoly of conservatives and moderates. The Socialists employed similar ideas but towards opposite political ends. Heine, for example, spoke of Germany's lèse-majesté laws as "circumscribing" the right of criticism and posing a danger to the "masculine openness of the nation." *SBR*, Nov. 23, 1907, p. 1742.

[133] January 21, 1908, SBR, pp. 2604, 2600.

CHAPTER 5

Popular mobiliζations: Jews and lunatics

In the early twentieth century, in the tiny town of Reppen near Frankfurt/Oder, a Jewish merchant from Berlin, Spiegel, was standing in a courtroom before a local magistrate when the latter, pointing at Spiegel, turned to his clerk and asked with disdain, "So what does this Jew want?" Mortified, Spiegel did what any self-respecting German would have done: he sued, rushing home to employ the services of the famous Berlin defense attorney Fritz Friedmann.[1] Spiegel got his insult trial, but in a place like Reppen it had the feel of a rigged Jim Crow courtroom. The antisemitic community was outraged at the affrontery of the suit, and Spiegel, probably sensing trouble, skipped the trial altogether, sending his lawyer in his stead. Entering the courtroom on the day of the trial, Friedmann had a portent of things to come when he found the defendant (the town's judge) socializing in a backroom with the judge-juror panel presiding over the case. The mood in the courtroom and in the town was so menacing that, after the case was dismissed, Friedmann, himself a Jew and fearing for his life, fled in the first train back to Berlin.

Spiegel's reaction to an insult made sense given the honor culture in which he lived. But the basis of his lawsuit was something new and, in a place like Reppen, controversial: antisemitism. Filing such a suit presupposed an inherent Jewish claim to dignity and the right to defend it in law. That Spiegel believed this suggests the sea-change underway in Germany as outsider groups were creatively seizing upon and transforming a juridical honor idiom to claim new rights.

[1] Fritz Friedmann, *Was ich erlebte* vol. 1 (Berlin, 1908), pp. 164 ff.

This chapter examines the way prejudice and injustice were experienced through the lens of honor, and how, in turn, new democratic ideas shaped the honor idiom into new political practices. It focuses on two groups: Jews and lunatics. Here, it was not only a question of individuals reasoning their way toward a more democratic vision of honor. Those individuals organized themselves into pressure groups that practiced a new style of grass-roots politics. Honor was central to that politics.

JEWS

Municipal statutes for centuries had classified Jews with other undesirables, such as criminals and vagrants, as "dishonorable" and unworthy of citizenship and guild membership. At the same time, there is also evidence of a tradition of Jewish-Gentile insult litigation going back centuries – a fact suggesting the de facto recognition in popular culture and law of a kind of honor status on the part of individual Jews. Most of these lawsuits, upheld in the courts, were seemingly indistinguishable from the kinds of suits brought within both the Jewish and Christian communities, revolving as they did around the typical insults of daily life, e.g. epithets like "whore" and "thief."[2] In one 1790s case, an angry exchange of words during a horse sale resulted in the buyer, a cavalry officer (*Rittmeister*), bringing an insult suit against the Jewish horse-dealer.[3] In another, a Jewish merchant actually brought a physical insult (*Realinjurie*) suit against a Prussian officer.[4] Jews, of course, also sued one another, as in the 1822 case of a kosher butcher who called the cantor a "cheat,"[5] or

---

[2]   By contrast, Jewish cases brought against Gentiles for "defamatory statements relating to allegedly Jewish characteristics or physical features" were rare. Robert Jütte, "Ehre und Ehrverlust im spätmittelalterlichen und frühneuzeitlichen Judentum," in Klaus Schreiner et al. (eds.), *Verletzte Ehre*, p. 152. Other examples can be found in Sabine Ullmann, *Nachbarschaft und Konkurrenz* (Göttingen, 1999), pp. 451–58.

[3]   II. HA Gen Dir. Frankisches Department, X, Nr. 394, GStPK.

[4]   The circumstances leading to the lawsuit are unclear. II Gen. Dir., X, Nr. 386, GStPK.

[5]   I, 75 A Sta 2, Nr. 52 (Ident.-Nr. 7812), Stiftung Neue Synagoge Berlin, Centrum Judaicum, Archiv (CJA).

the 1849 suit stemming from a confrontation outside a synagogue before the weekly services when a merchant and member of the Jewish community was physically prevented from entering and in the process "publicly slandered and insulted" because he had failed to pay his community dues.[6]

By the time of the Kaiserreich, a trickle of Jewish legal actions against Gentiles had become a flood, and the nature of these cases had changed as Jews directly confronted and resisted anti-Jewish prejudice. Whether it was the duel or the insult lawsuit, statistics show Jews disproportionately embroiled in honor disputes. In 1891, Jews were convicted of defamation at a rate of 181.8 for every 100,000 Jews in the population, whereas the figures for Protestants and Catholics were, respectively, 125.9 and 129.6.[7] The psychiatrist and criminologist Gustav Aschaffenburg was particularly struck by these figures because, as he said, most insult lawsuits involved alcohol, and Jews were not drinkers. Wagering a guess, he attributed the discrepancy to Jewish "racial" features, namely, the tendency of "southerners" for wild gesticulation, "shouting and easy excitability."[8]

In fact, Jews were litigating and dueling to defend their honor against antisemites. A Jewish soldier in 1905 brought a suit against a superior officer (a *Hauptmann*) for saying to him in front of the rest of the company, "well, you're from E.; I've heard that there are a lot of greasy cattle Jews [*Viehjuden*] there."[9] A Jewish merchant and employer brought a suit against the antisemitic *Deutscher Generalanzeiger*

---

[6] I, 75 A Dr 2, Nr. 24 (Ident.-Nr. 2161), CJA. The GStPK also has records of eighteenth- and early nineteenth-century litigation, both Jewish-Gentile and Jewish-Jewish. See, e.g. I HA Rep. 21, Nr. 206c3, Fasz. 1; ibid., Fasz. 25; II HA Gen Dir, Fränkisches Dept., X, Nr. 394.

[7] G. Aschaffenburg, *Das Verbrechen und seine Bekämpfung* (Heidelberg, 1903), p. 42. Jews were also overrepresented in dueling. Aschaffenburg, ibid., p. 43, cites a study of Baden university students in which Jewish students particpated in duels at a rate five times higher than the percentage of Jews in the population. See also Ute Frevert, *Men of Honor: A Social and Cultural History of the Duel* (Cambridge, MA, 1995), pp. 113ff on Jewish student dueling.

[8] Aschaffenburg, *Verbrechen*, p. 44.

[9] The court ruled in the plaintiff's favor. "Im Beschwerdewege," *Im deutschen Reich* (*IdR*) 8 (1905), p. 450.

for falsely accusing him of molesting a young female job applicant.[10] A group of Jewish lawyers and doctors in Karlsruhe sued the editor of another antisemitic paper (*Volkswacht*) for publishing an article calling on Gentiles to entrust "your legal affairs to no Jewish lawyer, your body to no Jewish doctor, your children to no Jewish teacher … in order that you are not harmed in your honor, body, and soul!"[11] The editor was convicted and given a two-week jail sentence. The great master of this kind of litigation was Hirsch Hildesheimer, the editor of the orthodox *Jüdische Presse*. One of his specialities was the intentional goading of antisemitic agitators into filing libel suits against him in order, as in the political method described above (chapter 4), to use the subsequent trials to publicly rake them over the coals.[12]

In other words, a discourse of honor that had originated in a premodern world of hierarchy and deference – a world that in important respects had classified all Jews as dishonorable – this discourse Jews were now adopting to make modern claims for dignity and equal treatment as citizens. When, precisely, such practices began is not entirely clear, but as early as the turn of the nineteenth century, one finds traces of a nascent new honor consciousness among Jews. It may have been present in Hirsch Wulff, whose lawsuit stemmed from an altercation in 1801 when, passing through an East Prussian town on business, he stopped in for some relaxation at a billiard room.[13] Another patron, a court clerk, yelled out to the room: "he [Wulff] doesn't know the rules; he's a son of a bitch [*Schweinehund*]." When Wulff took exception to these statements, the clerk lunged at him with a billiard cue, hitting him on the head; then two other patrons, the mayor and a merchant, allegedly joined in, beating him. Wulff sued for *Realinjurie* (physical defamation), an assault on a person's honor via the body, and the court ruled

---

[10] *IdR* 1 (1895), 109–10. The plaintiff in this case as well was successful at the first instance.
[11] Ibid., pp. 113–14.
[12] Barnet Hartston, *Sensationalizing the Jewish Question: Anti-Semitic Trials and the Press in the Early German Empire* (Leiden, 2005), pp. 87ff.
[13] I. HA Rep. 7A, Nr. 14D–Fasz. 4, GStPK.

in his favor, giving the clerk the minimum sentence of a 40 Thaler fine.[14] The court record made no mention of Wulff's Jewishness, but it seems implicit – in the hostility toward a Jew participating in a new space of bourgeois sociability (the court used the French term "the *Billard*") and thus the suggestive link to the ongoing struggles around Jewish efforts of inclusion in a new kind of bourgeois public sphere emerging outside the old corporate order.

The link between honor and struggles over Jewish emancipation was quite explicit in the contemporaneous Arnim–Itzig Affair, the famous 1811 incident in which a wealthy, well-connected Berlin Jew, Moritz Itzig, challenged to a duel one of the leading literary figures of the day, Achim von Arnim, only to be rebuffed as lacking (as a Jew) the requisite honor.[15] The Affair can be seen as a dialogue about Jewish emancipation within the symbolic language of honor. It started with Arnim giving an anti-Jewish public speech. Itzig's aunt, the salon hostess Sara Levy, responded by a reassertion of Jewish status in the one way she could: socially snubbing Arnim. She threw a party to which his wife Bettina but not Arnim was invited. Arnim retorted by showing up anyway, uninvited and dressed scandalously in street clothes, an intentional insult meant to put the Levy's back in their socially inferior place. It was at this point that Levy's nephew, Itzig, took over, challenging Arnim to a duel. Dueling was an upper-class affair between social equals. Thus, there could be no question of Arnim's acceptance, indeed the refusal of the challenge and a letter seeking an apology, which Arnim accomplished with the utmost disdain, offered the perfect avenue to ritually demonstrate Itzig's status as an inferior Jew. But given what was at stake (defense of his own dignity and the assertion, more generally, of Jewish honor), Itzig was determined to get his duel, setting out (with great courage) to literally pummel Arnim into it

---

[14] GStPK HA I, Rep. 7A, Nr. 14D – Fasz. 4.
[15] The following information is taken from Deborah Hertz, "Dueling for Emancipation: Jewish Masculinity in the Era of Napoleon," in Marion Kaplan et al. (eds.), *Jüdische Welten* (Göttingen, 2005), pp. 69–85. Hertz's analysis, which places the affair in the context of Jewish attempts to integrate into Gentile society, parallels and complements my own.

with the most provocatively insulting behavior. He physically accosted Arnim on the street and called him a scoundrel and a coward, the most heinous insults to an aristocratic man of honor. Arnim, however, had the last word, withholding to the end recognition of Itzig's honor by not only refusing to duel but by refraining from even a lower-level method of honor resolution, namely, the defamation lawsuit. Instead, Arnim chose to lodge assault charges, a form of litigation that implicitly refused Itzig any honor status at all.

Moritz Itzig was a Jew pushing the boundaries of honor with unusual boldness (or recklessness) for his time, and to this extent the affair was an extreme anomaly. This situation dramatically changed in the course of the nineteenth century. What drove that change was partly the spread of Enlightenment ideas about human equality, which were already making themselves felt in the Itzig and Wulff cases. Change also occurred because of the policies of the centralized state, which benefited Jews in the German lands both directly through emancipation laws and indirectly by the promotion of functional estates and an ethic of individual achievement as substitute for an older, more closed social order.[16]

The legal case of a Jewish merchant, Deutschmann, in 1840s Prussia exemplified this trend. Embroiled in a defamation suit against an innkeeper, Deutschmann adamantly wanted his case heard in a higher court (*fiskal*) befitting his sense of elevated honor in this era when libel law was still organized by estate. But this court was reserved for subjects belonging to higher estates (the upper bourgeoisie, aristocracy, etc.), and Deutschmann was only a draper and business agent (*Unterhändler*). A provincial court in Breslau accordingly dismissed his petition. Yes, it argued, Deutschmann did pay at a high tax rate, but he was really "only a Jewish shopkeeper and [small-time] trader" for whom no exception would be made. Berlin, however, subsequently reversed this decision, ruling in Deutschmann's

---

[16] Kathy Stuart, *Defiled Trades and Social Outcasts: Honor and Ritual Pollution in Early Modern Germany* (Cambridge, 1999), shows for an earlier period the way the central authorities sought to undermine the discriminatory honor categories against executioners and skinners of early-modern craft guilds.

favor by applying a much more flexible and generous standard of corporate status (and, thus, honor) that allowed his public service and high standing in his community to qualify him for exceptional treatment as a member of a higher estate.[17]

The Kaiserreich's Jewish litigation was driven by a structural contradiction inherent to Jewish life in that era. Jews since 1871 were legally emancipated and increasingly assimilating into a dynamic economy and civil society. At the same time, antisemitism remained and was now forming the basis of an organized political movement employing the tools of mass politics and newly minted racial notions of Jewish inferiority. As a result, just as their expectations for respect were growing, Jews were more than ever likely to experience the violation of those expectations, whether in their daily lives or in the press.

Like Spiegel and countless other Jews, they did so through the lens of honor, reacting with the duel or the libel suit. This could mean identification by elite Jews with the most reactionary aspects of Germany's honor culture, namely, aristocratic dueling traditions. One sees this, for example, in the popularity of dueling clubs among Jewish university students. The founder of modern Zionism, Theodor Herzl, was himself enamored with the duel. This embrace of aristocratic culture was particularly complex and vexed for Jews because of the way in which that culture was merging on the Right with a discourse of modern antisemitism. Fundamental to its ethic – where it appears in lawsuits, disciplinary hearings, and published sources – was a definition of male honorable behavior as disinterested, public-minded, and dedicated to a higher ideal (usually the state). Dishonorable people, by contrast, were motivated by personal gain. Over and over again in these sources, charges of greed, selfishness, and careerism appear as the insults triggering libel lawsuits. And these characteristics, all associated with modern capitalism, were in turn coded as Jewish. Some Jews themselves adopted this sort of thinking. Herzl's novel *Das neue Ghetto*, for example, has a Jewish mother counsel her son on his wedding day: "live according

---

[17] The documents can be found in I. HA Rep. 84a, Nr. 49527, GStPK, pp. 120–24.

to your means so you won't have to do anything unworthy. We have raised you to be a man of honor, and you also don't have the character that debases itself for money."[18]

But Jewish honor in the Kaiserreich also meant adapting older practices to a new post-emancipation environment, and this involved for many Jews linking honor with a discourse of democratic rights. In the 1870s and 1880s, Jewish defense, in particular the libel suit against antisemites, remained the province of individuals. By the 1890s, such lawsuits were being organized into a full-fledged Jewish defense movement with the founding of the Centralverein deutscher Staatsbürger jüdischen Glaubens (CV),[19] a group dedicated to defending German Jews against antisemites. Traditional Jewish authorities oversaw religious, welfare, and educational affairs of the community. This would be a new kind of Jewish organization: an activist interest group in the modern political sense, whose tasks were to monitor the progress of emancipation, intervening whenever Jewish "civil rights" appeared under attack.[20] This meant founding a news journal (*Im deutschen Reich*); lobbying legislatures for parity of the Jewish religion with other faith communities; agitating against the exclusion of Jews from trial juries or discrimination against Jewish job applicants in the health care profession.[21] And it meant unremitting litigation against the antisemitic press. In so doing, the CV hoped to "raise the social level of Jews so that they will be free, proud, and viewed with honor [*ihre Ehre bedacht zu sein*]."[22]

---

[18] Herzl, *Das neue Ghetto* (Vienna and Berlin, 1920), p. 26.

[19] For more on the CV and Jewish defense, see Arnold Paucker, "Der jüdische Abwehrkampf," in Werner Mosse (ed.), *Entscheidungsjahr 1932: Zur Judenfrage in der Endphase der Weimarer Republik* (Tübingen, 1966), pp. 405–99; Hartston, *Sensationalizing*; Sanford Ragins, *Jewish Responses to Anti-Semitism in Germany, 1870–1914* (Cincinnati, 1980); Marjorie Lamberti, *Jewish Activism in Imperial Germany* (New Haven, 1978); Richard Levy, *The Downfall of the Anti-Semitic Political Parties in Imperial Germany* (New Haven, 1975). For Weimar, see Douglas G. Morris, *Justice Imperiled: The Anti-Nazi Lawyer Max Hirschberg in Weimar Germany* (Ann Arbor, 2005).

[20] This discussion of the CV's aims and principles is taken primarily from a speech of Dr. Eugen Fuchs, deputy chairman of the CV, at the group's third Delegierten-Versammlung, "Vereinsnachrichten," *IdR* 3 (1896), 170–73.

[21] Ibid., pp. 171–72.   [22] Ibid., p. 172.

This was a new and hybrid form of activism, combining as it did modern political organizing and liberal notions of justice with the idiom and practices of honor. This is why, from the group's founding in 1893 until rising Nazi terror and other factors led to the end of its litigation in 1932, honor lawsuits were at the heart of its activities. Using both the defamation statutes and other sections of the Reich Criminal Code,[23] the CV systematically scoured the antisemitic press for litigatable libels, filing suit on behalf of countless individuals. More importantly, the organization pressed collective charges in the name of entire Jewish communities and the Jewish religion as a whole. In 1896, for example, for a Jewish ritual murder allegation stemming from a Hungarian case, it filed suit against the antisemite Karl Sedlatzek and his *Deutsche General-Anzeiger,* using §166 of the Criminal Code, which made it a crime to distribute literature attacking a religion, religious group, or secular creed in such a way as to disturb the peace.[24] In another group case from that year, this time on behalf of Jewish butchers, the CV, along with the state prosecutor, filed charges of *grober Unfug* (public nuisance) in a case stemming from an article accusing them of intentionally contaminating meat sold to Christians.[25] As articulated by the CV in another case against charges of Jewish ritual murder, "if German citizens of Jewish faith tolerate such an insult without utilizing all the available legal tools against the slanderer then they would in fact not be worthy of equality …"[26]

Litigation had a number of aims, not least of which was simple suppression – shutting down ("reining in") attacks from the antisemitic press. Centuries of pogroms were certainly in the minds of CV activists when they spoke of anti-Jewish hate speech posing a "grave danger." But an equally important goal of litigation was the publicity that court trials afforded. The CV worked with a deep belief, rooted in the Enlightenment tradition, in the power of knowledge and rationalist argument to defeat ignorance and hate. It thus

---

[23] Eg. §11 of the press laws; §166; and §130 of the Criminal Code.
[24] "Die Ritualmordlüge vor Gericht," *IdR* 11 (1896), 537 ff.
[25] "Fleischbefudelungs-Prozesse," *IdR* 10 (1896), 465 ff.
[26] "Ein zweifacher Rechtsirrthum," *IdR* 6 (1896), 294.

tended to treat trials as educational forums for exposing and refuting antisemites, hoping to sway the minds of Gentiles like those "scholars" who were "divided" on the question of Jewish ritual murder.[27] Implicitly, there was a final reason to expend so much energy on libel litigation: the requirements of honor. Had Jews and the CV not sued anti-Jewish statements, it would have been an admission either of the truth of the libels or a demonstration of their own cowardice. The mere fact of filing defamation suits, moreover, symbolically asserted Jewish honor, irrespective of the contents or outcomes of those trials.

A related benefit was the public shaming ritual of newspaper retractions that convicted libelers were often forced to publish. A good example is an 1885 *Privatklage* brought by one Alex Flechtheim against the author of a defamatory article, "Juda in der Sommerfrische," concerning himself and his family. A court convicted the author and sentenced him to two months in jail. It was at this point that Flechtheim, who had been friends with the defendant's father, offered the convicted man a deal he could not refuse: the prison sentence was dropped and in exchange, the libeler agreed to pay a sum of money to the town's needy (poor and sick) and to publish a public admission of guilt. This humiliating little public notice, which the CV gleefully reprinted in its journal, related the events of the case, including Flechtheim's generous offer, and concluded with the declaration that "everything derogatory that [my] article said about Herr Flechtheim and his family were libelous misrepresentations of the most shameful sort and my actions were all the more reprehensible because they lacked [reasonable] motive ..."[28] Flechtheim's justice was in the form of a shaming ritual that humiliated his opponent while restoring his own reputation.

Jewish honor litigation was either partially successful or mostly a failure, depending upon one's point of view. On the one hand were the numerous convictions of antisemites in individual cases, legal judgments that implicitly affirmed the dignity and equal citizenship of Jews in a Rechtsstaat. On the other hand, the more important

---

[27] Ibid., p. 295.   [28] *IdR* 3 (1896), 163.

collective lawsuits met with resistance at every turn and, seemingly, almost always failed. A key obstacle lay in a far-reaching 1881 Reichsgericht ruling that established the legal framework denying Jews the ability to bring collective defamation (*Kollektivbeleidigung*) lawsuits. The case involved several Jewish plaintiffs who had sued the author of a newspaper article for defamatory antisemitic statements. A lower court initially ruled in the plaintiffs' favor on the ground that, while the plaintiffs themselves had not personally been attacked, libels against Jews in general potentially targeted and harmed all Jews.[29] The Reichsgericht reversed this decision in a ruling with far-reaching implications that denied Jews as a group (unlike some other groups) the status of being a legal entity capable of suing in respect of defamatory speech. This decision in effect denied Jews protection as a persecuted group. It did so by arguing that proof of personal harm was required and that therefore to successfully bring a collective lawsuit, plaintiffs would have to meet the impossibly high bar of proving that *every Jew* was harmed by the libel being adjudicated.[30]

Thus, just as the modern politics of defamation law began, Jews were severed from what could have been a powerful legal tool. The Reichsgericht did, on the other hand, rule repeatedly that Jews qualified under §130 as a protected "population class." But many lower courts persisted in rejecting this interpretation of the law, ruling over and over again against Jewish plaintiffs.[31] Likewise, the courts were loath to interpret §166 (crimes of attacking a religion) as applying to Jewish libel plaintiffs when the libel did not directly target an individual. Thus, in the case of the butchers accused of contaminating meat, for example, the CV was forced to file charges

[29] Alfred Michaelis (ed.), *Die Rechtsverhältnisse der Juden in Preussen* (Berlin, 1910), p. 548–49.
[30] Ruling of October 6, 1881. *Rechtssprechung des deutschen Reichsgerichts in Strafsachen* 3 (Munich and Leipzig, 1881), p. 606. This ruling, which remained in effect for decades, had significant and long-lasting consequences, hampering Jewish resistance to the poisonous antisemitic attacks of the far Right in Weimar.
[31] "Korrespondenzen," *IdR* 8 (1900), 405 ff.

for "grober Unfug" instead of vilification of the Jewish religion (*Beschimpfung der jüdischen Religionsgesellschaft*).

LUNATICS[32]

In 1900, Elise Hegemann-Vorster, a devout Protestant, mother of ten, and widow of a wealthy Mannheim industrialist, took what can only be considered an extraordinary step: she published a pamphlet revealing her experiences, over many years, as an insane asylum inmate.[33] Strange as it might sound, Hegemann was not alone in her indiscretion. Between 1890 and 1914, dozens of "mad" people from the respectable bourgeoisie – businessmen, civil servants, pastors, academics, lawyers, doctors, writers – went public with the most intimate and stigmatizing details of their private lives.[34] The stories were frightening and desperate: healthy people branded as insane, deprived of their legal capacities, and incarcerated in insane asylums as a result of the machinations of doctors, police officials, judges, and family members. The pamphlets were also often didactic and enormously tedious, diatribes about corruption and malfeasance that took the reader through every twist and turn of events – family disputes, failed business partnerships, lawsuits, doctors' reports, and asylum experiences.

As the victims of grave injustices, the authors were now taking their cases to the "court of public opinion."[35] And the public readily

---

[32] The following chapter section was originally published in somewhat different form as Ann Goldberg, "A Reinvented Public: 'Lunatics' Rights' and Bourgeois Populism in the Kaiserreich," *German History* 21 (2003), 159–82.

[33] Elise Hegemann-Vorster, *Was ist Geisteskrankheit? Was ist Irrenanstaltsbedürftigkeit? Was ist Wahrheit? Selbsterlebtes in 7 deutschen Irrenanstalten* (n.d., self-published). The husband, whom Hegemann had previously divorced, died while she was writing the pamphlet. Her (living) uncles included a *Landesdirektor* and major, a captain, and an *Oberregierungsrat*.

[34] A good bibliography of this literature can be found in Bernhard Beyer, *Die Bestrebungen zur Reform des Irrenwesens* (Halle, 1912). Some of these pamphlets were written anonymously or under pseudonyms. Yet, given the detailed information that most pamphlets revealed, it would not have been difficult for an interested reader to find out their authors' identities.

[35] Fr. Kretzschmar, *Die Irrenfrage am Ausgange des 19. Jahrhunderts* (Großenhain, 1896), p. 253.

listened. These stories became the stuff of public scandal, debate, and politics. They were taken up by the press and debated in the parliaments.[36] They also became the basis of an organized "lunatics' rights" movement (*Irrenrechtsreform*), dubbed "antipsychiatry" by its opponents, that came to be centered in the Bund für Irrenrecht und Irrenfürsorge ("Bund") (1909–1922) – an extra-parliamentary pressure group founded and largely led by the "mad," whose journal (*Die Irrenrechts-Reform*), the organization claimed, had a circulation of 10,000.[37]

This was an extraordinary moment. The antipsychiatry movement after World War Two would be dominated by the discourse of experts and intellectuals – psychiatric, welfare, academic – especially by the philosophical tracts of Foucault, Szasz, and Laing.[38]

[36] For more on the parliamentary debates, see Ann Goldberg, "The Mellage Trial and the Politics of Insane Asylums in Wilhelmine Germany," *Journal of Modern History* 74/1 (March 2002), 1–32. Key parliamentary debates in Prussia and in the Reichstag on the insanity question can be found in: *SBR* 154. Sitzung, Jan. 16, 1897; 20. Sitzung, Jan. 28, 1899; 106. Sitzung, Feb. 20, 1908; 70. Sitzung, Nov. 26, 1912; Feb. 16, 1914; *SBPA*, March 16, 1892; 10 March, 1893; June, 1895; 18. Sitzung, Feb. 18, 1910; Feb. 14, 1914; *Stenographische Berichte über die Verhandlungen des Preußischen Herrenhauses*, April 1, 1892; May 26, 1893; May 29, 1894; July 9, 1895; April 29, 1913.

[37] For more on Wilhelmine lunatics' rights, see Goldberg, "A Reinvented Public"; Heinz-Peter Schmiedebach, "Eine 'anti-psychiatrische Bewegung' um die Jahrhundertwende," in Martin Dinges (ed.), *Medizinkritische Bewegungen im Deutschen Reich* (Stuttgart, 1996), pp. 127–59, provides an overview of many basic facts of the movement. Cornelia Brink, "'Nicht mehr normal und noch nicht geisteskrank ...' Über psychologische Grenzfälle im Kaiserreich," *WerkstattGeschichte* 33 (2002), 22–44. Several recent articles focus on the diagnosis of "Querulantenwahnsinn": Karen Nolte, "Querulantenwahnsinn – 'Eiginsinn' oder 'Irrsinn'?" in idem et al. (eds), *Moderne Anstaltspsychiatrie im 19. und 20. Jahrhundert – Legitimation und Kritik* (Stuttgart, 2006), pp. 395–410; Rebecca Schwoch and Heinz-Peter Schmiedebach, "'Querulantenwahnsinn,' Pschiatrikritik und Öffentlichkeit um 1900," *Medizin Historisches Journal* 42 (2007), 30–60. On a notorious asylum scandal: Goldberg, "Mellage Trial."

[38] Thomas Rechlin, *Antipsychiatrie, ihre Wurzeln und Voraussetzungen* (Bochum, 1987); Norman Dain, "Psychiatry and Anti-Psychiatry in the U.S.," in Mark Micale and Roy Porter (eds.), *Discovering the History of Psychiatry* (New York, 1994), pp. 415–44; Jaques Postel and David F. Allen, "History and Anti-Psychiatry in France," ibid., pp. 384–414; Gerald Grob, *From Asylum to Community* (Princeton, 1991).

Wilhelmine Germany's *Irrenrechtsreform* movement, by contrast, privileged the voices of the afflicted themselves (especially the bourgeois among them), who, in revolting against psychiatric abuses, seized on the tools of democracy, building a grass-roots social reform movement. As in the CV, the movement melded a litigious culture of honor with the tools of the pressure group – mass media, lobbying, citizen committees, petitions. However, it took this politics further, appealing much more broadly to a mass audience and self-consciously constructing a movement that transcended class and political ideology. In this sense, it was a quintessential, if largely unknown, example of the era's new populist politics.[39]

Irrenrechtsreform was a response to the massive expansion of the carceral system and the perception of psychiatrists as repressive, ignorant, and corrupt. In the early nineteenth century, psychiatry was a novelty, a barely recognized profession, and the modern insane asylum was identified among the educated bourgeoisie with humanitarian progress (freeing the mentally ill from the brutality of the early-modern madhouse and prison). By the end of the century, by contrast, asylums had become vast institutions warehousing an ever-expanding variety of social deviants and "degenerates." And psychiatry, fully professionalized with institutional bases in the universities, asylums, courts, and a network of professional organizations and journals, had established itself as a powerful arbiter of social norms. That professionalization, at the same time, entailed the shift from holistic and "anthropological" conceptions of mental illness toward biological determinism and degeneration theories.

---

[39] Its activists, in turn, were part of broader intellectual currents that included the popularization of anti-elitist and "holistic" scientific alternatives to the mechanism and materialism of the establishment sciences in the universities. More specifically, the *Irrenrechtsreformbewegung* had very close links to the natural healing movement (*Naturheilbewegung*), another, better-known popular movement against the medical establishment. Andreas Daum, *Wissenschaftspopularisierung im 19. Jahrhundert* (Munich, 1998); Paul Weindling, *Health, Race and German Politics* (Cambridge, 1989), pp. 3ff.

The lunatics' rights autobiographical pamphlet, on which part of this chapter section is based, derived from and spoke to this reality, one that encouraged the overuse and abuse of the insanity diagnosis. But that literature, written by the mad, who appealed to the public for justice and the recovery of their honor, can not be taken at face value as "true" in any simple or obvious sense of the term. Certainly many or most aspects of their asylum stories truly happened, but those stories were also (self-serving) constructed narratives whose original experiences they told were already mediated by bourgeois values and the political culture of the Kaiserreich. Even further, those stories did not simply uncover psychiatric abuse; they also helped in important ways to construct the figure of abuse and disenfranchisement (the wrongfully incarcerated and/or legally incapacitated, and the disenfranchised asylum inmate) who, as we shall see, then became the object of a whole new politics of extending rights to that group of people.

Bourgeois citizens were more likely to encounter psychiatry at the turn of the century partly because the erection of a carceral asylum system coincided in time with the heyday of "nervousness," a host of afflictons associated with the stresses of modern, industrial life.[40] The authors of the lunatics' rights movement were steeped in a culture of nerves and mental maladies: most had voluntarily sought out nerve treatments, and unlike the second wave of antipsychiatrists after World War Two, they did not doubt the existence of mental illness.[41] However, nerves and insanity, strictly speaking, belonged to two entirely different worlds of illness. Nerves (though not confined to the middle classes) were a lifestyle, even a leisure activity, an extension of bourgeois identity. The spa, the sanatorium, and the private consulting office were the spaces of nerves; the services they offered: gentility, luxury, and caregiving, a respite from life to be coddled and nurtured. Here (ideally), the doctor-patient relationship

---

[40] Joachim Radkau, *Das Zeitalter der Nervosität* (Munich, 2000), argues that both the discourse and epidemiology of nervousness were more prevalent in Germany than anywhere else.

[41] Though, of course, they disputed their own insanity diagnoses.

built up the ego, respected boundaries, and reinforced class iden-tity.[42] The insanity diagnosis, in radical contrast, belonged to a world that extinguished bourgeois existence – the world of legal incapa-citation and the insane asylum. The problem was that the boundaries between nerves and insanity were not as sharp as one had assumed. According to the pamphlet literature, it was, in fact, entirely possible to consult a doctor for a simple case of nerves but then end up ensnared in the coercive mental health system. "No person is invul-nerable" to the clutches of the asylum, went a typical warning, because of the ubiquitous "nervousness of the age."[43]

Adolf Glöklen, who went on to found the Bund in 1909, was one such unlucky person. His nerves shattered by a daughter's suicide, Glöklen, a *Kaufmann* (businessman) by profession, consulted his physician who recommended that he speak with a specialist at Heidelberg University's psychiatric clinic. Glöklen showed up expecting a short consultation and hoping for a medical certificate to cover the insurance for a stay at a private sanatorium. Instead, he was whisked away to a back room, admitted as a patient, and held against his will. Unable to contact the outside world, he endured five nightmarish days in the asylum until his wife, appearing on visiting day, rescued him.[44]

Except, perhaps, for the stories circulating in the press, nothing in his secure world had prepared Glöklen for what he faced in the asylum. Stripped and placed in a bath, he was astonished to see the attendants "plundering" his clothing and inspecting his briefcase with its "private written things." His body was also invaded, forced to

---

[42] Hegemann-Vorster's description (*Was ist Geisteskrankheit*, pp. 50–54) of her (voluntary) stay at the Rhenish asylum Andernach, which she loved, offers one of the most illuminating accounts of bourgeois expectations and needs in the treatment of nerves. I discuss these issues for an earlier period in Ann Goldberg, "Conventions of Madness: Bürgerlichkeit and the Asylum in the Vormärz," *Central European History* 33 (2000), 173–93.

[43] Ludwig Ernst, *Für die Lebendig Begraben*, 2nd edn (Vienna, 1904), pp. 30–31, 41.

[44] N.a. [Adolf Glöklen], *Zustände in der Heidelberger Universitäts-Irren-Klinik. Oder 5 Tage lebendig begraben* (Heidelberg, 1908). His wife had initially signed the admittance papers, but, Glöklen claimed, she was coerced and did not realize what she was doing.

undergo a cleaning and inspection for vermin and contagious diseases. Dressed in institutional clothing, his possessions taken from him, he was sent to a dorm-like room and, even though it was the middle of the day, ordered to stay in bed. His fellow inmates, he discovered with horror, included criminals (transfered from prison). Glöklen knew a huge mistake had been made, but no one would listen: as "insane," he was a "*Mundtoder*." The attendants barked orders and humiliated him in front of the other patients when he protested the dirtiness of the glass he was assigned for brushing his teeth. He waited impatiently for a doctor – someone, finally, with the education to understand his predicament. But when the professors came by with their students on their daily round, they discussed Glöklen in the third person, as a scientific case, as if he wasn't even present. Glöklen was shaken to his core. Powerless and robbed of his "individuality," he searched for imagery to express the feelings of violation: it was like being treated as a "vagabond," a "recruit in a military barrack," a "prisoner," an "object," an "under-age child."[45]

Glöklen, like other bourgeois patients, had entered the unfamiliar terrain of powerlessness, discipline, declassing, and objectification of Foucault's "carceral society."[46] This experience, and what drove the outrage that turned to authorship and activism, was mediated by bourgeois values and sensibilities, particularly those associated with honor. The writings of these people narrated how the insanity diagnosis (leading to incapacitation or the asylum) tore away at the dignity and respect of the individual, violated the basic rights of the *Staatsbürger*, ruined reputations and careers, and invaded the private sphere of the patriarchal family, turning men into (legal) "children" and promiscuous, avaricious wives into the real power in the home.

This last point needs emphasis. An obsession of the movement, legal incapacitation, being a disaster for both a "lunatic's" honor and his financial interests, was at the same time about losing manhood. It is no accident that gender and parent-child role reversals were not uncommon in this literature. Here, one encountered cases not only of

---

[45] This imagery appears repeatedly in the lunatics' rights literature as a whole.
[46] Michel Foucault, *Discipline and Punish*, trans. Alan Sheridan (New York, 1977).

wives and children using the asylum to get rid of a husband/parent, but even of incapacitated men placed under the guardianship of their wives or (grown) children.[47] *Irrenrechts-Reform* devoted an entire article to a disturbing trend: a kind of "marriage sport" played by "women lacking scruples, conscience or decent morality," who used the asylum to rid themselves of inconvenient husbands.[48] Even when wives had more legitimate motives (i.e. defending themselves against alcoholic husbands), what, apparently, was so alarming about the current situation was a new-found freedom of women through their alliance with psychiatry and the state.[49] Ernst Müller, a Ph.D. and author of agricultural works, knew this from bitter experience, having been shunted off to an asylum after his wife, in fear of her safety, contacted the authorities. In his pamphlet, he blustered about the "assassination of my personal freedom" when what he was talking about was his right to abuse his wife ("tyrannize," as his psychiatrist put it) without interference of the state or the asylum.[50]

The "mad" turned to the public with their stories of wrongful incarceration and incapacitations, in order, paradoxically, to reclaim reputation, honor, and citizenship – in a word, personhood. These authors faced the unenviable task of convincing a public that, contrary to the judgments of officials and experts, they were indeed sane and rational. This presented them with one of the more unusual problems in the history of authorship: the very subject about which they wrote – their experiences as certified lunatics – by definition

---

[47] On the loss of "Vaterrechte," see Rudolf Arndt, *Geisteskrank. Unzurechnungsfähig. Entmündigt* (Greifswald, 1896), p. 12. On cases of wives and daughters appointed as guardians: *Irrenrechts-Reform* 14/15 (1910), 1; 30/31 (1912), 294. Despite its enshrinement of patriarchy, the Civil Code, which went into effect in 1900, permitted the guardianship of men by their wives. *Bürgerliches Gesetzbuch vom 18. August 1896* (Munich, 1902), p. 453.

[48] Paul Elmer, "Die Ehefrau als Schlepperin des Irrenhauses," *Irrenrechts-Reform* 14/15 (1910), 150–52. The wife as evil instigator of her husband's incarceration was central to the discourse of the Fuhrmann case, a national cause célèbre in 1901.

[49] Ibid. The discussion in this article of the alliance of wives and psychiatrists was reminiscent of contemporary anticlerical discourse about pernicious relationships between women and priests.

[50] Ernst Müller, *Drei Monate ohne Grund im Irrenhause* (Dresden, 1898), p. 5.

seemed to invalidate the voice that spoke about it. Thus, while the pamphlets had different agendas, establishing the legitimate status of the writer's voice was always their deeper purpose and subtext. This was the key to erasing the stigma and shame of an insanity diagnosis, to reclaiming legal capacity and honor, and to picking up the pieces of a shattered life. Writing thus went far beyond sympathy pandering (or scandal-mongering); it was an act of claiming a (rational) voice, of shifting the author's social identity and thereby recapturing the person of civil society.

Lunatics' rights pamphlets were predicated on the fact that publicity, and only publicity, could perform this act of social alchemy. One wonders how, in earlier decades and centuries, the "mad" negotiated their way back to honor and personhood. However this occurred, it took place locally, in families and communities. The self-revelatory asylum pamphlet was the extreme exception before the 1880s.[51] This changed with the expansion of the public sphere as a result of national unification and the broadened (Reichstag) franchise, urbanization, a mass press and literacy, and the rise of mass politics.

By the 1890s, the "mad" were learning to use this new public to bypass and subvert the authorities and medical experts, in order to mediate the disputes of private life and the social status of the

---

[51] There was, however, a partial precedent for the Wilhelmine pamphlets that dated back to Karl Philipp Moritz's *Magazin zur Erfahrungsseelenkunde* (1783–1793). This late Enlightenment journal published, among other things, autobiographical stories of educated and well-placed individuals who had undergone experiences of mental derangement and loss of their rational selves. But unlike the Wilhelmine pamphlets, these experiences of mental illness, as far as I can tell, were ephemeral and had not caused the authors to be legally certified as insane. Their authors thus spoke from within the dominant culture, and did so for the purpose of engaging philosophical discussions about the nature of the mind. Their stories were about introspection and self-knowledge. Wilhelmine antipsychiatry stories, by contrast, were about injustice and rights. On the *Magazin* and mental illness in bourgeois culture, see Doris Kaufmann, *Aufklärung, bürgerliche Selbsterfahrung und die 'Erfindung' der Psychiatrie in Deutschland, 1770–1850* (Göttingen, 1995); LeeAnn Hansen, "At the Boundaries of Enlightenment: Definitions of Health, Illness, and Insanity in Karl Philipp Moritz's *Magazin zur Erfahrungsseelenkunde*" (unpublished paper).

psyche.[52] They did this by inventively adapting an existing cultural practice: the personal self-revelatory pamphlet. Having suffered some kind of injustice, Germans took their cases in print to the public, creating a pervasive but ephemeral popular literature of legal self-defenses, confessionals, and exposés of official corruption, which, as discussed in chapter 2, included the pamphlets of the insulted and defamed seeking to recover their honor. Lunatics' rights works took this literature a step further, in effect commodifying the most private of experiences and the psyche itself, offering them up for sale in the literary marketplace.

Raw and improvisational, these publications were a literature in the making, groping for its voice. There were no formal literary rules, because its authors were by definition speaking from a marginalized, non-institutional position. They were thus free to ransack the history of print culture, constrained only by the marketplace and the inner logic of their objectives. The results were inventive new literary hybrids that cannibalized different genres: the novel (high and low), the play, the memoir, the legal brief, the political polemic, and the philosophical tract. The novelistic narration (usually in the first person voice) had the advantage of all drama, especially when the author drew from lowbrow, popular crime and prison novels: the engendering of emotional identification in the reader as well as the appeal to a public greedy for sensational true-life horror stories. Some pamphlets unabashedly sought out this market, prominently displaying the words "sensational!" or "confiscated!"[53] Yet the novel was distinctly incapable of, even harmful to, making claims about the facticity of events and the objectivity of the author. Here is where most authors turned to the legal brief and the primary document, inserting into the

---

[52] Kretzschmar, *Irrenfrage*, p. 253, provided the clearest articulation of the idea, underlying lunatics' rights, that "publicity" was the key to the defense of "personal autonomy" in the face of "state and scientific" malfeasance and injustice.

[53] For example: Ewald Krüner, *Moderne Folterkammern*, 5th edn (Hagen and Zurich, 1913), whose subtitle reveals the mass audience it sought: "Ein Volksbuch zur ..." P. Klos, *Deutsche Beamtenherrschaft in ihrer ganzen Machtentfaltung* (Zurich, 1909), which announced its "confiscated" status, was a politically subversive pamphlet written by a Socialist.

text or in an addendum reproductions of letters, medical opinions, parliamentary petitions, judicial rulings, and legal briefs.

There were infinite variations on the novel-legal-brief-documentary-sourcebook form (and in style and tone), reflecting the differing ways the authors were positioned socially (by occupation, education, gender, and religious, political and philosophical beliefs), their intended audience, and a host of idiosyncratic factors. Male authors in established professions imprinted their pamphlets with writing techniques and an organizational coherence taken from their education. They also favored an "objective" tone and style, including the philosophical proclamation and the didactic survey. Carl Brill, a prominent Magdeburg physician before his troubles, bombarded the reader with court documents, press clippings, medical reports, and footnotes.[54] A legally incapacitated *Rechts-praktikant* felt the need to announce on his title page: "not a novel, [rather] a history based on the official record [*aktenmäßige Geschichte*]."[55] He was claiming a status and voice while distancing himself both from the sensationalism of much of the lunatics' rights literature and its mass audience.[56] (The negative association of this literature – most of which was produced by middle-class authors and publishers – with the gutter press, modernity, and the masses, had been cleverly made a few years earlier by what appears to be a piece of psychiatric propaganda put out to discredit and defuse antipsychiatry sentiment. Its opening pages described how the "author," a quintessential cigar-smoking bourgeois and [happy] former asylum inmate, is disgusted when, in a train station pressed by the "struggle for existence," he discovers that the "booklet" he bought from a "peddlar" is in actuality a scandal-mongering asylum penny dreadful in the manner of the "spirit of the masses" [*Volksgeist*].[57])

---

[54] Carl Brill, *Pflichtwidrigkeiten hiesiger Richter in einem Ehescheidungensprozeß* (Magdeburg, 1906). On the other hand, Anton Maleszka, *Wie man Geisteskranke fabriziert* (Berlin, 1905), a teacher, wrote in pure novelistic form, but used the third person, as if he were talking about someone else.

[55] Georg Platner, *Modernes Standrecht* (Zurich, 1896).

[56] His prefatory remarks make this clear.

[57] Hans Schmidt, *"Das Haus des Schreckens" oder Dichtung und Wahrheit* (Leipzig, 1890), quotes from pp. 3–6.

The lunatics' rights pamphlet was overwhelmingly a male, middle-class phenomenon,[58] the most obvious reason being the empowerment to speak out that social position and education brought. This status also gave bourgeois men expectations of security and privacy which, when violated by experiences of psychiatry and asylum, inflamed feelings of outrage and injustice. This sense of male, bourgeois entitlement is all the more striking in authors who, whether from lack of talent or from a disturbed mental state, lacked mastery over their chosen medium (writing). Their pamphlets were wild, obsessive, and incoherent, capable of, say, bursting into song in the middle of a diatribe against Roman law.[59]

The discord (and inventiveness) of Elise Hegemann's pamphlet came from a different source: as a woman, she lacked the education and training in writing, but she also had greater barriers to surpass in the search for a public voice. She thus sought to pre-empt criticism at the outset with an apology and the reinscription of herself in a traditional female role, begging the reader to view her pamphlet "not as a literary work, but merely as the complaint, questions, and narrative of a mother robbed [of her children]." Likewise, her pamphlet did not begin with a philosophical statement, or even with the facts of her case. Instead, she chose to establish her identity indirectly by surrounding herself with a jumble of images and texts from history, culture, and religion: a picture of the fifteenth-century religious reformer and martyr Jan Huss; Old Testament verse, with accompanying lithograph, of Judith decapitating the Assyrian invader Holofernes; Berlioz on Beethoven; Ernst Moritz Arndt's poem, "Der Gott, der Eisen wachsen ließ"; a Ludwig Auerbach song: 'O Schwarzwald, O Heimat, wie bist Du so schön!'[60] The

---

[58] Despite the fact that most insane asylum inmates were from the lower classes.

[59] One example: Franz Schäfer, *Ein "Schwabenstreich" der Züricher Polizei oder 4 Tage "auf Beobachtung" in der Züricher Irrenanstalt Burghöli* (Belfast, 1897), a dramatist whose "songs" were quotations of passages from his plays.

[60] The inclusion of material on Beethoven and the Schwarzwald signalled to the reader elements of Hegemann's sensibility: the first referred to her love of music and her fond memories of the one psychiatrist (Nasse in Andernach) who treated her with respect; the Schwarzwald was the site of her worst asylum experiences (in

result was pure chaos, but effective, establishing for the reader and reaffirming in the author who she was: a woman of culture, faith, and placeness, but also a fighter.[61]

Hegemann's prefatory pages had another function: to cast the author's perilous and transgressive act of self-revelation in terms of a higher purpose and cause. The old Testament figure Judith, another gutsy widow, had given Hegemann, as she said, "the courage to write." Judith provided a female model of heroism and revenge, elevating and transmuting Hegemann's rancour against men in her life (husband, uncles, and psychiatrists)[62] into a battle for freedom akin to Judith's stand against the Assyrians.[63] This was also the message of Arndt's patriotic poem urging Germans to defend their "rights" against the Napoleonic "tyranny." Directly addressing the reader, Hegemann explained her "duty" to write as follows:

In my view, the individual is not only a member of his own family but of the great family of humanity. 'The truth ... can heal the deepest wounds!' and this brave standing up for the truth can only have a favourable effect on my children's lives.

Lunatics' rights literature recast the particular, the petty, and the base in terms of universal principles and higher causes. Its authors had multiple motives for writing, and revenge and the public shaming of enemies (familial, medical, judicial) were often among them. Yet no matter their motive, authors always purportedly wrote out of a sense

the asylums Illenau and Emmendingen), but also a place that enchanted her with its beauty. (These were her own explanations.) Her use of the Auerbach song can also be linked to the Kaiserreich's Heimat movement, which celebrated the local and linked it to the nation.

[61] Hegemann-Vorster, *Was ist Geisteskrankheit?*

[62] Hegemann sought revenge against both abusive psychiatrists and her husband, who had engineered her incarcerations. In her 1901 petition to the Bundesrat, she called this "publicly explaining the injustice [I] suffered ... due to my husband's intrigues ..." Resp. 86/1273, Bd. 1, Bundesarchiv, Berlin-Lichterfelde (BA); and her remarks in the preface of her pamphlet. Hegemann was also using her pamphlet to publicly shame her uncles, prominent members of the community, into financially providing for her, as well as a son, who retained administrative control over her fortune. See the back cover of her pamphlet.

[63] On the wealth of images and interpretations down the ages of this iconic figure, see Margarita Stocker, *Judith. Sexual Warrior* (New Haven, 1998).

of "duty." In so doing, they linked personal sagas with the fate of the nation. They asserted that personal injustices and violations of their honor had broad implications for questions of law, freedom, and rights. The businessman and former asylum inmate Ewald Krüner saw his life – the injustices and his duty to speak out – through the model of Schiller's Wilhelm Tell courageously battling "tyranny."[64] For the antisemitic Jew Morris de Jonge, whose hatred of his father fits right in to his contemporary Freud's oedipal theories, it was the battle against "international stock market Jewry."[65] More typically, in Hamburg, Ahrens "entered this battle [against city medical officers] ... because it is a question not of an individual person, but of the rights of all ... in our republican free-state [Hamburg]."[66]

The plight of individual "mad" people thus came to be seen in terms of narratives of systemic corruption and the struggle for the freedom and rights of the *Staatsbürger*. Madness, in turn, was nationalized – seen in terms of the fate of the nation (and literally put on the national legislative agenda).[67] The Bund institutionalized this discourse in its journal *Irrenrechts-Reform*, offering a constant stream of articles on sensational wrongful incarcerations and incapacitations (a speciality of the journal) that made the connection between individual cases and nationwide problems in the mental health, judicial, and political systems.[68] It also presented a vision that linked psychiatric abuse to the maladies of modernity: psychiatric power was code for external and threatening forces – science, bureaucracies, police forces, big industry, big cities – that undermined the free burgher, his honor and inviolable private sphere.

At the same time, lunatics' rights were juridifying the insanity question. Forty years earlier, at mid-century, an exposé pamphlet on wrongful incarceration, *Eine Mutter im Irrenhause*, presented the case

---

[64] Krüner, *Moderne Folterkammern*, p. 1.
[65] Morris de Jonge, *Ein Akt moderner Tortur* (Berlin, 1890).
[66] Ad. Ahrens, *Anti-Vernunft. Beweisstücke für die jetzigen ungenügenden Irrengesetze* (Hamburg, 1891).
[67] My point about the "nationalization" of madness is different from the work on national narratives of decline and degeneration at the turn of the century.
[68] Its critique, in particular, of the Prussian three-class voting system.

as an anomaly – a "perhaps unique case, never occurred before [*nie dagewesen*]."[69] By the 1890s, "mad" people were increasingly seeing the individual events of their lives as emblematic of a broader pattern and in terms of national narratives of systemic abuse and corruption. This was both cause and effect of the fact that the "mad" had the ear of the nation: individual cases became public scandals widely reported in the press and the subject of parliamentary debates. This led other "mad" people to reconsider their own experiences in a new light and to contact a network of reformers and publishers specializing in asylum literature.[70] After 1909, they contacted the Bund, which publicized their cases and provided legal and other services, including lobbying parliaments on their behalf. A striking example of the Bund's tactics involved an incarcerated patient who succeeded in smuggling out a letter to the organization. The Bund then went into action, pressuring the institution to transfer the patient to an open-care unit. When this did not work, the Bund turned to the daily press (*Vorwärts*) and the publicity worked. After his transfer, the patient simply walked away, turning up one day at the editorial office of *Irrenrechts-Reform*, which continued to aid him when he was later harassed by the police.[71] Finally, the Bund energetically lobbied for the passage of a federal asylum law to rein in the power of psychiatrists and regulate every facet of insanity.[72]

In 1851, *Eine Mutter* expressed its outrage in the language of morality, castigating the "mother's" persecutors (her children,

---

[69] Anon [Adolph Ebeling], *Eine Mutter im Irrenhause. Beitrag zur Sittengeschichte unserer Zeit* (Bremen, 1851), p. 142. This pamphlet caused a scandal, particularly because its subject, Louise Gabe de Massarellos, belonged to one of Hamburg's leading patrician families. See also, n.a.., *Der Prozeß der Familie Gabe in Hamburg* (Bremen, 1851).

[70] One example of the mobilizing effect of asylum causes célèbres: a civil engineer, whose asylum "nightmare" consisted of trivialities (e.g. bad food and disturbed morning sleep), nevertheless heard about the famous Hegelmaier case (below), began to reconsider his own experiences, and ended up publishing his own pamphlet of complaint. A. De., *Zustände in der Staats-Irrenanstalt Winnenthal* (Stuttgart, 1895), p. 5.

[71] *IR* 24/25 (1912), 239 ff.

[72] Calls for such legislation actually began years before in the early 1890s when the asylum issue was first politicized.

guardian, doctors, asylum) for the violation of their duties and responsibilities. Wilhelmine antipsychiatry, by contrast, spoke the language of law and mass democracy: justice, due process, freedom, the rights of the *Staatsbürger*. The spreading use of the insanity diagnosis, explained one author, threatens the very fabric of society by undermining the basis of "human rights," namely the presumed autonomy and free will of the *rechtsfähig* citizen.[73] Psychiatry was an impenetrable regime of the experts that raised the frightening spectre of an arbitrary power acting outside of the law – what the Bund called *Überpsychiatrie*[74] – invading the private life of citizens[75] and robbing them of their rights. The literature written by the "mad" powerfully evoked the sense of vulnerability in the imagery of the knock-on-the-door-out-of-nowhere, whereby an entirely normal and upright, but somewhat nervous, bourgeois citizen finds his study invaded one day by medical officials who haul him off to the asylum. (He did not realize that, say, his wife or children had been plotting behind his back to steal his fortune.)

Once the mad came to see their plight in legal and political terms – as violations of the rule of law – they acted: beside themselves with anger, they turned to the press; petitioned parliaments and officials to have their cases reversed;[76] wrote open letters to the Kaiser and other officials;[77] cited law codes and filed lawsuits against their doctors. In so doing, they turned the defamation lawsuit into a tool of protest and reform. Doctors who had written allegedly false or incompetent reports declaring insanity diagnoses figured prominently in these lawsuits. One such case involved the leading psychiatrist Emil

---

[73] Kretzschmar, *Die Unvollkommenheit der heutigen Psychiatrie und die Mangelhaftigkeit der deutschen Irrengesetzgebung* (Leipzig, 1891), p. 5.

[74] *IR* 14/15 (1910), 150.

[75] This issue was everywhere in the lunatics' rights literature. For one example that places privacy in a broader political perspective, see "Die geistigen Hinrichtungen in Ostelbien," *IR* 40/41 (Sept. 1913), 368–74.

[76] The BA holds some of the petitions filed in 1895–1906. See Rep. 1501/11909, Nr. 39.

[77] For example, K. v. R. [Oswald Knorr], *Offene Briefe an Seine Majestät den König von Preußen* (Charlottenburg, 1896); Carl Paasch, *Offener Brief an Reichskanzler von Caprivi* (Leipzig, 1891).

Kraepelin, against whom Elise Hegemann, with the help of the Bund, filed suit in 1909.[78]

The "non-insane" in the wider community were likewise motivated to take action. In Tilsit, on the eastern border of Germany, a citizens committee, led by a *Gymnasium* teacher and the editor of a local newspaper, took up the cause of an incapacitated and incarcerated doctor and Lithuanian nationalist (Brozeit), whose case, tapping into ethnic politics, divided the town's inhabitants in the late 1880s and early 1890s.[79] In 1901, at the other end of the Empire, a group of citizens in the Rhenish town of Neuenahr outraged by the "kidnapping" and incarceration of a local businessman, Joseph Fuhrmann, allegedly at the instigation of his wife, wrote an open letter to the *Kölnische Volkszeitung* defending Fuhrmann's character and sanity, while the wife was subject to a boycott and collective attacks against her home.[80] Citizen action could involve instances of individuals "liberating" a patient from an asylum. (The most famous case was that of the innkeeper Mellage, who, in 1894, succeeded in freeing a Scottish priest from a Rhenish Catholic asylum only to face libel charges, as a result of his published exposés on the asylum, in a trial that riveted the nation in 1895.)[81] It also manifested itself in a citizen-sponsored conference on the asylum problem that took place in Göttingen in 1894, as well as in the mounting press coverage and parliamentary debates devoted to asylum scandals.[82]

The Wilhelmine discourse of law and justice on the asylum issue can be found across the political spectrum, from Socialists to right-wing antisemites.[83] This was most spectacularly displayed in one of

---

[78] Bilfinger, "Die Irrenanstalten im Lichte der natürlichen Heilweise," *IR* 3 (1909), 2. Another example is August Menn, *"Hallucinationen" und Gegenbeweise. Ein Rechtsfall* (Salzburg, 1897), whose lawsuit against a *Sanitätsrat* was rejected by the state attorney's office.

[79] Beyer, *Bestrebungen*, pp. 260–74.   [80] Ibid., pp. 290–304.

[81] Goldberg, "Mellage Trial." See also the interesting case of the globe-trotting aristocrat Prince von Sulkowski, whose Hungarian lover helped him escape from an Austrian asylum. Beyer, *Bestrebungen*, pp. 214–21.

[82] The conference brought together (mostly) conservative politicians and concerned citizens from the middle and upper classes.

[83] For a Socialist example among the self-revelatory pamphlets, see Klos, *Deutsche Beamtenherrschaft*.

the great psychiatric causes célèbres of the Kaiserreich: the dismissal, on the basis of an insanity diagnosis, of Heilbronn's mayor Paul Hegelmaier. In the 1880s, Hegelmaier had made himself a hated man with his strong-arm tactics, and opposition to him fed into liberal critiques of Württemberg's anachronistic system of life-long mayoral appointments. Yet, in 1892 "all of Württemberg rose up"[84] in Hegelmaier's defense when it was discovered that the government, seeking to oust Hegelmaier without touching the system of irremovable mayors, had gotten around the law by having the Württemberg medical board declare him insane. The ensuing outcry united all the political parties against this instance of political interference from on high with the judicial process ("Cabinetjustiz"), and the case escalated into a public relations disaster for the government.[85]

The juridical nature of lunatics' rights discourse reflected to an extent the prominent role of lawyers and jurists within the movement.[86] But it was also more broadly rooted in the intensely legalistic and litigious culture of the Kaiserreich that is the subject of this book.[87] Long before their troubles with psychiatry, lunatics' rights authors had been immersed in this litigious culture, and it is this that often led to their insanity diagnoses. The press accounts and pamphlet literature on cases of wrongful incarceration and incapacitation were filled with people who spent huge amounts of time and energy bringing lawsuits, going to court, and filing petitions. They viewed local and familial disputes through the lens of law and rights. As a result, the courts (along with the press) were the institution of choice to vent rage and fight out the petty and not so petty injuries of daily life. Von Bröcker, an artillery officer turned engineer at the Krupp

[84] Kretzschmar, *Irrenfrage*, p. 118.
[85] An overview sympathetic to Hegelmaier, together with some primary sources, can be found ibid., pp. 107–44.
[86] This was related, in turn, to the "boundary disputes" between psychiatrists and the legal profession that resulted from the steadily widening role of psychiatric expertise in the courts.
[87] Margaret Anderson, *Practicing Democracy: Elections and Political Culture in Imperial Germany* (Princeton, 2000) has masterfully analyzed this political culture within electoral politics. Her work, however, does not deal with the justice system.

plant in Essen, filed suit over a maternal inheritance against the father he had long detested. When the case did not go as Bröcker wanted, he turned on the judge, accusing him of "perversion of justice" (*Rechtsbeugung*).[88] In another case, a ship's doctor, who had been fired from his firm, initiated legal proceedings for reimbursement of his fees and ended up being fined for defamation against the court.[89]

Most importantly, the courts were battlegrounds for the defense of honor and reputation. For August Menn, the offense that began his legal imbroglios was a supposed veiled attack against him in the local (Stuttgart) paper.[90] The Magdeburg physician Carl Brill, after losing his divorce case, accused his father's cousin (also a doctor) of having him (Brill) declared insane in order to cover up his adultery with Brill's wife. This led to hearings before a medical disciplinary court and petitions by Brill to the Minister of Justice to intervene. He was subsequently outraged when the authorities failed to prosecute anyone involved in the case, including himself, because it prevented him from defending himself and his reputation in "a public" forum.[91] For years, a power struggle in the conservative party was partly fought out in a series of seemingly petty defamation suits, including those between Adolf Stöcker and the Berlin clergyman Carl Witte, who was eventually declared insane and later became an activist in the lunatics' rights movement.[92]

Originating within the Kaiserreich's culture of honor and law, the legal cases of these bourgeois men, who in many respects were typical of their class and gender, spiraled out of control into furious obsessions,

---

[88] Kretzschmar, *Irrenfrage*, pp. 177–81.
[89] Ibid., pp. 101–02 [90] August Menn, *Hallucinationen*.
[91] Brill, *Pflichtwidrigkeiten*, p. 10.
[92] Carl Witte, *Mein Conflict mit Herrn Hof- und Domprediger Stöcker* (Berlin, 1889); Kretzschmar, *Irrenfrage*, pp. 153–59; Walter Frank, *Hofprediger Adolf Stoecker und die christlichsoziale Bewegung* (Hamburg, 1935). An insanity diagnosis most directly dishonored men by denying them even the ability to sue for defamation. According to Liepmann, "Die Beleidigung," in Mittermaier et al. (eds.), *Vergleichende Darstellung des deutschen und ausländischen Strafrechts: Besonderer Teil* vol. 4 (Berlin, 1906), p. 69, the insane, like children, have "human worth," but they are only in the most limited sense "bearers of honor" (*Ehrenträger*) and thus can only be defamed for an "attack against [their] social position from the period of their health," i.e. before they were declared insane.

personal crusades, and attacks in all directions – most damningly, against judges and other officials. Psychiatrists, called in by alarmed authorities, responded with a diagnosis that was tailor-made for this character type: querulous insanity (*Querulantenwahnsinn*). A species of "moral insanity" and generally hereditary, *Querulantenwahnsinn*, explained the psychiatrist Bernhard Beyer defensively, does not label as ill people who pursue justice (*ihr Recht*), but *how* they do so. According to Heinrich Schüle, co-editor of a leading psychiatric journal,[93] *Querulanten* pathologically imagine themselves to be the victim of a "wrongful injury from external machinations [and] intrigues" and, in a paranoid state, engage in endless written complaints, petitions, and lawsuits. A compulsion [*Zwangsimpuls*] drives them to oppose "subordination," to fight for "human rights," and, in the worst of cases, even to commit "lèse-majesté in open court."[94]

Querulantenwahnsinn was a paradigmatic diagnosis of its time and place – the site where the Kaiserreich's litigiousness intersected with the onslaught of psychiatry, asylum, and the authoritarian state. Fiercely contested, it was also the paradigmatic mental illness of the lunatics' rights movement – not only because of its frequency among authors and activists, but, more importantly, because it embodied in the most extreme form what was felt to be wrong with institutional psychiatry. If the insanity diagnosis stripped citizens of their rights, *Querulantenwahnsinn* went one step further, pathologizing the very act of asserting those rights.[95]

The Bund went after the *Querulantenwahnsinn* diagnosis and other psychiatric abuses with a vengeance, forging in the process a populist special-interest group that brought together a heterogeneous collection

---

[93] The *Allgemeine Zeitschrift für Psychiatrie*. Schüle was also the director of Baden's Illenau asylum.

[94] Heinrich Schüle, *Klinische Psychiatrie* (Leipzig, 1886), quoted in Beyer, *Bestrebungen*, pp. 359–63.

[95] As one author put it, *Querulantenwahnsinn* allows medical practitioners to dismiss as illness "real injustices and conspiracies." Düsing, *Künstlicher Irrsinn. Eine Warnung vor Irrenanstalten* (Leipzig, 1894), p. 24. The Bund's journal, *Irrenrechts-Reform*, was filled with attacks on the concept of *Querulantenwahnsinn* and its use by medical practitioners and the courts.

of former asylum inmates, *Freigeistiger*, Monists, natural-healing adherents, and other sundry social reformers. Class politics were anathema to the Bund's view of itself. Its message, rather, was inclusion – the unity of an aggrieved *Volk* battling the corrupt powers that be. Thus it worked hard to represent itself as a non-partisan, truly "national" organization transcending class, ideological, religious, regional, and even gender divisions in German society.[96] In reality, the Bund was overwhelmingly bourgeois, and primarily male and Protestant.[97]

Its non-partisanship, however, was important and not mere rhetoric. The movement's language of unity flowed from its understanding of psychiatry as a tool of social control in the Kaiserreich – its insight that the insanity diagnosis was dramatically increasing partly because more and more "inconvenient" people, including political outsiders, were arbitrarily labeled as such. This led the Bund to take on and defend cases from people across the political spectrum, irrespective of whether the organization agreed with their personal views. These people included antisemites and their opponents, the Guelph and homosexual von Schulenburg ("private matters" are not the business of the state),[98] and, in 1919, Karl Liebknecht and the Spartacists.[99] It also publicized cases of wrongful incarceration and

---

[96] In its later years, its journal proclaimed this explicitly on its front-page logo.

[97] There were women members in the Bund, and their cases were taken up by the organization from time to time. The Bund also sought to appeal to a female audience by publishing some female-oriented articles. But the organization's leadership, editorial staff, and, seemingly, contributing writers were male, and the general tenor of its articles reflected this. Its Protestant orientation can be seen in its leadership and in its defense of several persecuted Protestant clergyman (including the above-mentioned Witte) against the hierarchy of the Evangelical church. I have not found anything similar for persecuted Catholics.

[98] *IR* 18/19 (1911), 194–95; ibid., 26/27 (1912), 255–62. Schulenburg was a cousin of von Bülow. The Bund argued that Schulenburg's legal incapacitation was the result of persecution for his political views and his homosexuality, as well as the financial machinations of his family.

[99] *IR* 63 (1919), 183–84. The Bund defended them against the "crazy" charge, and, while deploring Liebknecht's "violent methods," called him a "Volksfreund"! Though no friend of the Left, Kretzschmar, *Irrenfrage*, pp. 7–18, was typical in deploring the use of the insanity label against political opponents, including anarchists and Socialists.

incapacitation from all classes and both genders, although those of men from the middle classes predominated. The message, at this level, was not only unity, but tolerance of differences.

The Bund also managed to create a coalition of followers from opposite poles of the political spectrum. On the Right, its ideological roots can be traced to an 1892 antipsychiatry manifesto published by the *Kreuzzeitung* (the organ of Prussian conservatism). But, at the same time, the Bund used the Social Democratic press for many of its exposé pieces, attacked "East Elbian reactionaries," and called for the democratization of the Prussian electoral system.[100] Parliamentary debates saw similar alliances across ideological divisions, with conservatives taking the lead on the asylum issue in the early 1890s, followed, increasingly, by the SPD after the turn of the century.[101]

Neither Right nor Left in any conventional sense, the lunatics' rights movement fits to an extent the "anti-politics" of the "social reform milieu" analyzed recently by Kevin Repp.[102] More broadly, its bourgeois populism was part of the reconfiguration of public life in the Kaiserreich that came with the rise of mass politics in the 1890s. The result was the decline of notable politics (the bastion of ascendant liberalism in the 1860s and 1870s) in the face of challenges both from the Left (SPD) and from a new style of right-wing, bourgeois

---

[100] See, for example, "Die geistigen Hinrichtungen in Ostelbien," *IR* 40/41 (1913), 368–74.

[101] Needless to say, the asylum issue remained peripheral to Socialist politics, and Wilhelm Liebknecht's essential sympathy for psychiatry may have been more representative of the SPD's leadership than that of the antipsychiatry activists Adolf Thiele and Arthur Stadthagen. Liebknecht's basic faith in the scientific and humanitarian value of psychiatry was the position of liberals. However, he did support asylum reform as a civil rights issue.

[102] Kevin Repp, *Reformers Critics, and the Paths of German Modernity* (Cambridge, MA, 2000). On the whole, the lunatics' rights movement shared with this milieu a "discourse of an alternative modernity" (227) that emphasized social unity, nonpartisanship, and the "rejection of existing party-political relationships" (217). Further, individual activists, e.g. Lehmann-Hohenberg, were very much a part of that milieu. But the movement was much more ambivalent about scientific expertise, and its rhetoric of scandal departed significantly from the technocratic pragmatism of the reformers Repp analyzed.

populism that combined radical nationalism and antisemitism with a discourse of democracy.[103]

Accordingly, if the Bund could claim support from Socialists and conservatives, liberals were another matter: they were a "hindrance" to asylum reform, complained the Bund.[104] With their strong faith in science as a force of enlightenment and freedom, liberals were mostly allied with psychiatry in support of the asylum status quo.[105] This position, however, had become severely outdated by the mass ware-housing of deviants and the rising rates of legal incapacitations. The lunatics' rights movement, arising out of this situation, was helping to reshape public discourse on modernity by decoupling the terms liberalism, freedom, and science. Earlier in the century, the new field of psychiatry (in the view of the educated bourgeoisie) was synonymous with liberalism and human rights. The lunatics' rights discourse of the Wilhelmine era, by contrast, represented the defense of civil liberties as a battle, if not against science per se, then against psychiatric expertise, the medical establishment, and, by extension (implicitly) a liberal worldview. In the new "key" of bourgeois populism, it used the language of radical-democracy and liberalism to make claims for the rights of a newly "discovered" disenfranchised group (the mentally ill and wrongfully diagnosed). It did this, as I have shown, by powerfully linking societal ills with private traumas and the class anxieties of the bourgeoisie.

This reconfigured discourse made possible new sorts of alliances (e.g. between Left and Right). It also appealed to the *völkisch* Right, whose presence can be felt in some of *Irrenrechts-Reform*'s articles, as well as in the Bund's leadership.[106] One of its leaders, Johann Lehmann-Hohenberg (1851–1925), a tireless and well-connected social reformer and publisher, who had been fired from his

---

[103] The literature is too large to list here. For an introduction and important analysis, see Geoff Eley, *Reshaping the German Right* (Ann Arbor, MI, 1991).

[104] "Neuorientierung und Irrenrecht," *IR* 56 (1916), 68.

[105] For a more extended discussion of this, see Goldberg, "Mellage Trial."

[106] One article, for example, contrasted "materialist medicine," which it called superficial, female, and oriental, with "German depth" and a "spiritual elite." *IR* 2 (Sept. 1909), 13.

professorial position at Kiel University under suspicion of insanity, was an influential advocate of "Germanic Law" – a favorite idea of the far Right that would gain currency among the likes of Anton Drexler in the Weimar Republic.[107] At its 1914 conference, the Bund adopted Lehmann-Hohenberg's anti-Roman law resolution.[108] For an organization so insistent on the law, the Bund's interest in legal reform is not surprising.[109] It is noteworthy, however, how easily its legalism accommodated a *völkisch* viewpoint. And, while the Bund itself avoided antisemitic rhetoric, some of the loudest lunatics' rights voices in the Kaiserreich were those of rabid antisemites.[110]

Practically speaking, the lunatics' rights movement had very limited effect, never managing to get national reform legislation passed, although some of its activists did later participate in drafting such legislation (never passed) under a more sympathetic regime in the Weimar Republic. The spread of eugenics and the Nazi takeover meant, however, that the next decades would see not civil rights but the mass murder of the insane in the Third Reich. Wilhelmine antipsychiatry participated in the radicalization of bourgeois politics

[107] A very interesting figure, Lehmann-Hohenberg had a career that included numerous publishing ventures, connected an array of causes and social reform "milieus," and moved steadily to the Right. His personal file (Geheimes Staatsarchiv Preußischer Kulturbesitz, Rep. 76 Vf, Lit. L, Nr. 35) contains a wealth of information, as well as many of his writings. His literary archive (BA, N2170) may have been purged of incriminating correspondence by his heirs. See also Schwoch and Schmiedebach, "*Querulantenwahnsinn*," pp. 35ff; Albrecht Götz von Olenhusen, "Zur Entwicklung völkischen Rechtsdenkens. Frühe rechtsradikale Programmatik und bürgerliche Rechtswissenschaft," in Hans Jochen Vogel et al. (eds.), *Die Freiheit des Anderen: Festschrift für Martin Hirsch* (Baden-Baden, 1981), pp. 87–88.

[108] "Allgemeine Irrenrechts-Konferenz," *Vossische Zeitung*, March 8, 1914.

[109] It especially wanted to severely limit (or eliminate) psychiatry's role in the courts, returning the legal judgment of insanity to judges (e.g. *IR* 36/37 [1913], 341) or to civil juries made up of laymen (e.g. F. Kretzschmar, *Die Unvollkommenheit der heutigen Psychiatrie und die Mangelhaftigkeit der deutschen Irrengesetzgebung* [Leipzig, 1891], p. 59).

[110] Indeed, conservatives first seized upon and politicized the asylum issue in the early 1890s by publicizing several cases of antisemites who, it was asserted, had been wrongfully incarcerated or incapacitated. These cases included, among others, the antisemitic leader Karl Paasch. Kretzschmar, *Irrenfrage*, pp. 81–98, 170–94.

after 1890, a phenomenon linked to the later rise of Nazism. Yet, antipsychiatry was, in its own way, emancipatory,[III] stretching our understanding of the uses of the public sphere in the Kaiserreich. Here, the "mad" made the public the medium for the conversion of private traumas into ideology and politics, radically extending its democratic functions in strategies of empowerment aimed at undermining or bypassing the psychiatric and judicial establishments. They invented new ways of addressing the public and in the process constructed a new disenfranchised group – the wrongfully incarcerated and incapacitated, as well as the mentally ill inmate without rights – that became the focus of a politics of rights led by the Bund. Notions of bourgeois privacy, honor, law, and masculinity were central to that politics.

[III] On the socially repressive aspects of the movement, see Goldberg, "Reinvented Public."

Conclusion: Beyond 1914

It was October, 1965. The war in Vietnam was massively escalating under US President Johnson, and a group of German protestors, bearing banners and shouting antiwar slogans, gathered near the US embassy in Bonn. Amid a welter of angry denunciations ("Vietnam: America's Auschwitz," "Negotiations, Not Murder"), one chant caught the authorities attention: "Child Murderer Johnson – Child Murderer Johnson." A slanderous attack against a named head of state, albeit a foreign one, constituted a criminal offense under §103 of the German penal code. An investigation was opened – the leaders of the demonstration, in addition to the above offense, were reputed to have communist connections – and the US State Department contacted about pressing charges. But the US had a very different legal history and no law approaching that of §103. There ensued a moment of diplomatic confusion. Possibly stunned, the US State Department had to confess to the absence in American law of any basis for prosecution. The Germans were thus forced to drop the case.[1] The case is reminiscent of one seventy years earlier when the German authorities under the Kaiser advised their Belgian counterparts of "their right to prosecute" the German Socialist editor Reinhold Stenzel for an article in a German newspaper attacking the Belgian King Leopold II for "his colonial exploits" and other matters.[2] The

---

[1] Rep. 104, Nr. 548, NWHSA. Seven years later, the Nixon administration – not known for its tolerance of dissidents – had a similar response when asked to sign onto a lawsuit against a leftist student group (Spartakus) distributing a pamphlet that called Nixon a "war criminal." Rep. 195, Nr. 1701, NWHSA.

[2] Alex Hall, "The Kaiser, the Wilhelmine State and Lèse-Majesté," *German Life and Letters* 27/2 (1974), p. 108.

outcome in this earlier instance, however, was different: the case went to trial and Stengel was given an eight-month prison sentence.

The persistence of Germany's culture of honor in the courts across every turning point of its history – 1848, 1871, 1918/19, 1933, 1945 – is striking. After World War Two, the numbers of cases brought to trial dropped off and the nature of some of the litigation predictably changed with the new *Zeitgeist* and government. If, under the Third Reich, for example, being a Jew or Jew-like were slanderous charges subject to litigation,[3] after the war the opposite was true. Now, being called an antisemite or a Nazi collaborator were felt to be slanderous, prompting lawsuits.[4] But the culture itself remained very much alive in the West German courts, structuring daily conflicts in ways that appear similiar to earlier times.[5] Across the border, in communist East Germany, lay civil courts, set up to adjudicate daily conflicts, were swamped by honor lawsuits (50–60 percent of all cases). Plaintiffs, like their Second Reich counterparts, sought not money but the restitution of their reputations.[6]

This chapter briefly reviews the post-Kaiserreich history of honor and defamation as they played out in the Weimar Republic, the Third Reich, and the postwar eras. It returns at the end to the historiography and the issues of tradition and continuity in the history.

WEIMAR REPUBLIC

The abdication of the Kaiser and the coming to power of a left-center coalition in the revolution of 1918/19 brought a partial reckoning with the past. Along lines Socialists had long advocated, the Weimar Republic attempted, amidst the chaos of its fourteen short years of

---

[3] For example, the court case against one Frau Seikriet, who in 1939 accused Boris Blacher, a famous composer, of being Jewish. Rep. 17, Nr. 25, NWHSA.

[4] For example, a 1960s case in Rep. 104, Nr. 538, NWHSA.

[5] Hans-Georg Doering, *Beleidigung und Privatklage* (Göttingen, 1971), a criminological study of the years 1957–1965; James Whitman, "Enforcing Civility and Respect: Three Societies," *Yale Law Journal* 109 (2000), 1279–398.

[6] Paul Betts, "Property, Peace and Honor: Neighborhood Justice in Communist Berlin," *Past and Present* 201 (2008), 215–54.

existence, the democratization of libel law and the eradication of some of the worst abuses of the Kaiserreich. In the interest of republican egalitarianism, the lèse-majesté laws, for example, were purposefully not transferred to Weimar's new political leaders, whose honor claims were thereby placed on an equal footing with those of private citizens.[7] §193 remained a topic of heated debate in the press and the legislatures, and led to the placement in 1929 of liberal protections of speech in draft legislation for a revised penal code.

But politics, culture, and the many crises of the Republic put breaks on these reformist impulses. As a result of the explosion of right-wing extremism after 1918 – years of communist uprisings, hyperinflation, right-wing political murders and coup attempts – and in the wake of Foreign Minister Walther Rathenau's assassination, the government issued its July 21, 1922 Law for the Protection of the Republic. The law included a crackdown on antirepublican speech in the form of hefty prison sentences for political defamations. With Rathenau in mind – a public figure who, even after his murder, remained intensely reviled in right-wing propaganda[8] – §7 made it a crime punishable by up to five years in jail to defame an assassinated member of the government. §8 punished with up to five years in prison whomsoever "slandered," "demeaned," or "defamed" the republican state and its members of government, or publicly or in a gathering slandered the flag. Yet, for all its echoes of past censorship via defamation jurisprudence, these laws turned out to be singularly ineffective in the face of an intransigent judicial bureaucracy.

That bureaucracy, a holdover from the Kaiserreich, was dominated by conservative jurists and prosecutors whose antirepublicanism deeply affected defamation jurisprudence. There had been great hopes that the revolution would usher in broad §193 protections of the press in line with the values of republicanism and popular sovereignty. Some courts did begin ruling in favor of greater press

---

[7] H. Haccius, *Die Gesetze zum Schutz der Republik von 1922 und 1930* (Göttingen, 1931), p. 19.
[8] Ibid.

protections. At the top, however, the Reichsgericht maintained its extremely narrow interpretation of §193.[9] Meanwhile, in the lower courts, a pernicious double standard of justice pervaded the treatment of honor. It involved, among other inconsistent applications of the law, the meting out of extremely lenient sentences and acquittals to employer, right-wing, and antisemitic defendants while punishments of leftist, Jewish, and worker defendants tended to be draconic by comparison. The Jewish Hamburg bankers Max Warburg and Carl Melchior, for example, filed suit in 1924 against the antisemitic publisher Theodor Fritsch for an article in his *Hammer* calling them prototypes of a "Jewish world domination." A court refused to convict, affording Fritsch §193 protection. Fritsch's inability to provide proof of the truth of his defamatory statement was not a problem according to the court, since, as the *Berliner Tageblatt* critically summarized, "it is not possible to provide proof of the truth of such value judgments about contemporary events."[10] In sharp contrast, a few weeks earlier, the SPD journalist Martin Gruber was denied §193 protections and sentenced to a fine of 30 days' jail or 3,000RM by a Munich court for calling two right-wing, stab-in-the-back propagandists "fools" and "liars."[11]

The same judges and prosecutors who had sharply limited left-wing dissent under the Kaiserreich were now strangely quiescent in the face of right-wing attacks on the republican state. There was an acute awareness of the problem in the press and parliaments, a problem that, to the dismay of the government, seemed intractable and immune to legislative fixes. Reichstag deputy Kuttner was appalled by the "passivity" of the state attorneys: "In many rabble rousing papers one finds serious insults of the government, but the state attorney never pays any heed, even when they're calling for serious disobedience like refusing to hand over weapons ... The state attorney never once investigates whereas previously [in the Kaiserreich] it zealously studied *Vorwärts* [the Socialist newspaper] in order to find any sort of

---

[9] "Die Tragweite des §193 in der Gegenwart," *Deutsche Zeitung*, October 10, 1926.
[10] "Warburg, Melchior und Theordor Fritsch," *Berliner Tageblatt*, January 28, 1926.
[11] "Das Ende der Dolschstosslegende," *Berliner Tageblatt*, December 9, 1925.

prosecutable expression."[12] Deputy Rosenfeld painted a picture of class warfare in rural Pomerania taking place around defamation lawsuits. The judicial authorities, in deciding which cases to charge with defamation, were making decisions based on whether the defendant was a worker or employer-landowner, so that:

in numerous cases [the authorities proceeded] entirely one-sidedly against employees and indeed often for entirely simple swear words that are common-place in the countryside, whereas in cases of defamation of employees or their representatives in worker associations by lords of the manor [*Rittergutsbesitzer*], the state attorney never gets involved in protecting the insulted party and bringing legal charges.[13]

Meanwhile, Germans continued suing one another at an alarming rate. The contents of the lawsuits were both old and new. Old were the invective and cursings, the feuds and hatreds of daily life. A 1931 list of Berlin *Privatklagen* gives a taste of these:"You old pig, now you're finished, I'll beat the crap out of you," or "kiss my ass."[14] Other cases involved accusations of criminal behavior. The everyday feuds were often bound up with the hard economic times. The most common causes of such lawsuits, explained an experienced Berlin judge, were "fights in pubs, fights between employer and worker, differences over business deals, gossip and, above all, the housing shortage," which forced enemy housemates and "even divorced couples" to remain living in close quarters.[15] One lawsuit alleged that a female defamer had purposefully denounced the complainant to the welfare authorities in order that the latter be deprived of her benefits.[16]

The language and practices of honor were the same, but the new events and circumstances of the Weimar years were also changing the content of defamation lawsuits. In August 1919, the Ober-Präsident of the province of East Prussia wrote in alarm to his superior at the

---

[12] Protokoll des Hauptausschusses über den Haushalt der Justizverwaltung, June 9, 1921. I. HA Rep. 84a, Nr. 8140, GStAPK, p. 81.
[13] Ibid.
[14] "Übersicht über die im Monat März 1931 bei zwei Privatklageabteilungen des Amtsgerichts Berlin eingegangen Privatklagesachen." R22, Nr. 1113, BA, pp. 34, 38.
[15] "Vier Jahre Beleidigungs-Richter," January 27, 1927.   [16] Ibid., p. 35.

Justice Ministry about rising defamations on the part of the civilian population against members of the military. Those attacks were physical; they were also coming in a barrage from the Socialist press, causing a "rising irritability" and demands by the military for government "protection of their honor."[17] The occupation of the industrial Ruhr region by French and Belgian troops in 1923, in order to force the payment in kind of German war reparations, provoked its own set of lawsuits. From Elberfeld came reports of right-wing thugs, masked and armed, breaking into homes and, in a symbolic ritual of sexual retribution recalling the early-modern charivari, cutting off the hair of German women suspected of having "intimate relations" with the French. The victims included the Werners, a married couple in the village of Vohwinkel about whom "there was suspicion among the population of intimate relations with members of the French occupation force." They sued for physical defamation, but lost the case on appeal because, despite Frau Werner swearing she could identify one of the defendants (a neighbor), the court found insufficient proof of his or the other defendants' culpability.[18] In 1926, the wife of a railway worker, one Elisabeth Kreimeier, was tried for anti-French slurs against her landlord. Kreimeier and her husband rented a floor from a police official who, during the Ruhr crisis, had helped out a French family in need. As a "loyal, German-minded woman," Kreimeier explained to the court, she disliked this sort of behavior on the part of her landlord. It came out during a fight over household matters, when she exploded, cussing her landlord out with: "Fatherland-traitor, French friend, separatist …"[19] She was convicted, but her subsequent appeal for clemency was viewed quite sympathetically, the court even scolding the plaintiff – the police official landlord – for his friendly behavior to the French.

Then there were the racial verbal attacks, reflecting the explosion of antisemitism and nationalist xenophobia. The attacks ranged from the simple and unsophisticated – "Polish whore";"filthy Jewish pig"[20] – to

---

[17] August 1, 1919. I. HA Rep. 84a, Nr. 8140, GStPK, p. 62.
[18] Ibid., Rep. 84a, Nr. 58212.   [19] I. HA Rep. 84a, Nr. 58205, GStPK.
[20] R22, Nr. 1113, BA, pp. 30, 34.

the poisonous *völkisch* rhetoric spewing forth from right-wing intellectuals, publicists, and politicians. Its victims fought back with the defamation lawsuit. They were the rich and famous – e.g. Max Warburg, Arnold Zweig – and the entirely obscure. The latter included Dr. Zellner, a Breslau lawyer, who became the object of attack after he had won a civil action for a client in a rental disagreement. The loser, a *Landschaftssekretär*, after being forced to pay the court fees, including an amount to Zellner, turned for revenge to the antisemitic press, where an article appeared ("Judische Kostenberechnung") quoting him accusing Zellner of falsification, as a Jew, of his legal fees. Zellner, feeling his "professional honor offended" and his reputation "debased in public opinion," successfully sued under both the defamation and press laws (though a higher court later reversed the decision).[21]

Like Zellner, there were Jews who were successful in these kinds of lawsuits. (One famous case involved the writer Arnold Zweig who sued the *Deutsches Adelsblatt* in 1929 for a venomously antisemitic review of his book *Der Streit um den Sergeanten Grischa*.)[22] But it was also true that many courts were systematically denying Jews the same honor protections they afforded non-Jews. One hears it in the complaints of the Prussian Minister of Justice in 1922, for example.[23] One sees it in the "hair-splitting" argument of the Reichsgericht in a 1923 decision that reversed a series of lower-court convictions of the far-right Erhardt Brigade for its defamatory song: "We don't need any Jew republic! Shame, Jew republic!"[24] One sees it in the many cases of "prominent Jewish figures in government ... who were refused protection from libel by the courts,"[25] and in unknown, more everyday cases like that of Hermann Grünberg, a Berlin businessman. In 1924, Grünberg went to a police station to lodge a complaint against a coachman. At the station, as he later asserted, he was "mocked and insulted" when the police

---

[21] I. HA Rep. 84a, Nr. 58222, GStPK.

[22] Many of the relevant documents, including clippings of the extensive news coverage generated by the trial, can be found in GStAPK, Rep. 84a, Nr. 53457.

[23] I. HA Rep. 84a, Nr. 8140, GStPK, p. 113.

[24] Ingo Müller, *Hitler's Justice: The Courts of the Third Reich* (Cambridge, MA, 1991), p. 18.

[25] Ibid., p. 19.

sergeant (*Polizeioberwachtmeister*) sneered: "you confounded Jew, you're going to get a few slaps on the face." Grünberg lodged a complaint against the policeman only to find himself indicted, tried, and convicted for the crime of "false accusation."[26]

A racialization of honor in daily life was occurring in a broader sense. One sees this in the way "Jewish" and "Jew" were becoming accepted epithets to be flung against non-Jewish enemies. It is also evident in the distinctions some Germans were making between "Germanic" and "Jewish" honor. In 1925, a Berlin woman was in conflict with a judge, who called her "seriously hysterical." Deeply offended, she had a friend knowledgeable in the law write the judge a letter of complaint:[27]

I am from honorable German stock and no Jew ... I can only say one thing ... in a public courtroom in front of strangers, you so severely insulted me with the words "seriously hysterical" ... if I were immediately sent to prison at least I would have my German honor ... you expect a German woman to put up with such a thing [!] ... The public must be informed.

THE THIRD REICH

Both the entrenched persistence and the plasticity of German honor culture is particularly striking under the Third Reich. The Nazis sought to revolutionize honor, eradicating its individualism and substituting a racially based group honor of the *Volk*. This racialization and nationalization of honor had a profound impact on the laws, courts, and daily life. But the regime's radical zeal encountered barriers, one of which was Germany's entrenched popular honor culture. That culture, while adaptable to the new regime, also served as the basis for resistance to it.

The restoration of "German honor" – from the degradations of the Versailles Treaty and "Jewish" liberal democracy – was, as is well known, central to Nazi rhetoric. Less well known are the legal and social aspects of this obsession. Honor was defined by National Socialist legal experts as a radical break from both Old Regime

---

[26] HA I, Rep. 84a, Nr. 58213 GStAPK.   [27] Rep. 84a, Nr. 58217 GStAPK.

corporatism and liberal individualism. As Walter Buch, chief judge of the Nazi party, put it: previously, German honor was "divided: professional and corporate honor, family honor, national honor ... Today [by contrast] we now know that ... honor is embedded in blood ... and we [Aryan Germans] are all carriers of the same blood of our race and the same honor."[28] Honor derived, in other words, neither from membership in a corporate status group nor from an inherent humanity; it came from membership in a race-based community – the *Volk*. And that membership required as the mark of honor above all: obedience, loyalty, and sacrifice to and for the *Volksgemeinschaft* and the Führer. The submersion of the individual into the *Volk* meant, in turn, that legal questions of honor would now be measured not by individual or universal human standards but according to what benefited or harmed the *Volk*. For, As Roland Freisler, State Secretary of the Reich Ministry of Justice and President of the Volksgerichtshof, explained, "damaging a person's honor is simultaneously an attack on the honor of the nation [*Volkstum*], of which the person is a member."[29] This principle applied more generally to criminal law in the Third Reich, where the purpose of trials "became not so much to determine whether the accused had broken a law, but rather 'whether the wrongdoer still belongs to the community.'"[30]

This fascist egalitarianism, race-based and radically authoritarian, had severe implications for the legal and legislative treatment of honor. Well known, of course, is the Law for the Protection of German Blood and German Honor, which criminalized marriage and sex between Jews and Aryans; those found in violation of the law were tried, literally, for "dishonoring the race."[31] It is not yet clear, however, how these notions affected the ability of Jews and other non-Aryans to bring *Privatklagen* since, theoretically, those

---

[28] Buch, "Des nationalsozialistischen Menschen Ehre und Ehrenschutz," *Deutsche Justiz* (October 21, 1938), 1659.

[29] Roland Freisler, "Gedanken zum Gemeinschaftsehrschutz," *Deutsche Justiz*, September 25, 1936, 1461.

[30] Müller, *Hitler's Justice*, p. 79.   [31] Ibid., p. 100.

"lesser races," in Nazi thought, were not entirely honorless; they simply had a different, inferior kind of honor.[32]

Much of the political policing of speech under the Third Reich occurred under a series of decrees and laws issued in the first years of the regime dealing with the protection of state and party honor. That this was so should not surprise: the practice was a clear continuation of policies, discussed in this book, that went back many decades. The extremity of the repression and the *völkisch* ideology in which it was embedded, however, were new. Newspaper editors were required to censor any statement dishonoring a German. Laws regarding "treacherous attacks" against the government made the intentional spreading of assertions with potential to damage the well-being and respect of the Reich, government, and National Socialist party members punishable by up to two years' jail time. Other laws protected dishonoring comments against Hitler, the flag, and other symbols of the state.[33]

More changes of the honor laws were in the works. A revised penal and procedural code would abolish the *Privatklage* and, reversing the liberal era reform, reinstate the state's monopoly over criminal prosecutions. For, as the Criminal Law Commission (*Strafrechtskommission*) put it, "it is not consistent with the essence of today's state to make the prosecution or not of a crime dependent upon the will of a private person."[34] A 1933 report of the Prussian Minister of Justice, which laid out a set of influential principles for a revised criminal justice system, envisioned a new crime of *Volksverleumdung* (defamation against the national community) that was incorporated into the draft proposal of the proposed penal code.[35] The new thinking affected the juridical status of lèse-majesté. In the Justice Ministry report, attacks against the honor of political leaders came to be equated with attacks against the

---

[32] Brezina, *Ehre und Ehrenschutz im nationalsozialistischen Recht* (Augsburg, 1987), p. 23. Useful information on defamation law in the Third Reich can also be found in Jörg Ernst August Waldow, "Der strafrechtliche Ehrenschutz in der NS-Zeit" (Baden-Baden, 2000), a law-school dissertation.

[33] Ibid., pp. 59–67.

[34] "Aufzeichnungen für die 2. Lesung über Ehrenkränkungen." R22, Nr. 995, BA, p. 147.

[35] Brezina, *Ehre und Ehrenschutz*, p. 121.

Volksgemeinschaft. Thus, early on, when high party and government leaders chose not to prosecute citizens who uttered defamatory statements against them in private, a chief state attorney recommended, by contrast, prosecution for "an attack against the honor of the *Volksgemeinschaft*, to whose leadership the defamed belong."[36]

Nazi notions of duty, nation, and race were also forcing a rethinking of §193 (§295 in the draft proposal). There was a shift taking place from the "liberalist era" focus on "personal interest" as the basis for the legal protection of dishonoring statements to a new standard: the "health of the *Volk*" and "duty" to the state.[37] The result was the simultaneous contracting and expanding of the protection of insulting speech. On the one hand, "now" (as opposed to during the "liberalist era"), according to the Strafrechtskommission, dishonoring speech is tolerated only in "exceptional cases."[38] On the other hand, it became a duty for citizens and party members to report on matters affecting the *Volk*, even if this involved the use of insulting statements, and a clause to this effect was inserted in the penal code draft.[39]

Thus, while newspapers underwent rigid censorship, the notion of duty to the *Volk* ironically gave the press a certain freedom of reportage that had been denied it in the Kaiserreich and the Weimar Republic. In those earlier eras, the Reichsgericht's illiberal interpretation of §193 (which had refused to extend this protection to newspaper stories with insulting content that were published in the public interest) had presumed (and rejected) an oppositional role between state and society via a free press. Now, under the Third Reich, that distinction disappeared, the press being merged with the party state. Newspaper editors, faithful to the party line, were

---

[36] Oberstaatsanwalt Jung to Generalstaatsanwalt Naumburg, Erfurt, August 6, 1934. R22, Nr. 995, BA, p. 17.

[37] "Aufzeichnungen für die 2. Lesung über Ehrenkränkungen" (no date). R22, Nr. 995, BA, p. 144.

[38] Ibid.

[39] Ibid., p. 157. §295, which was to replace §193, gave protections to dishonoring speech made in the "Erfüllung einer rechts- oder sittlicher Pflicht oder sonst zu einem nach gesunder Volksanschauung berechtigtem Zwecke …"

therefore granted §193 protections when the insulting material they published served the greater good of the *Volk*.[40]

These ideas were making their way into the courts, some of whose judgments evinced a new willingness to sacrifice the personal honor of citizens and even officials to the larger needs of the state and *Volk*. In 1936, the Reichsgericht reversed a lower court decision that had denied §193 protection to a citizen who had denounced a state official for abuse of power and been sued by the latter for defamation. The lower court (*Strafkammer*), in ruling against the defendant, had argued that state and party officials enjoy a special honor status and thus protection from defamations. The Reichsgericht, overruling this decision, asserted that (in the words of an approving reporter) it violated the "National Socialist principle that in the interest of upholding the cleanliness [*Sauberkeit*] of public administration, abuses of power both in the party and the other offices" must be communicated to the authorities.[41] The same principle of the higher good of *Volk* and state could in other cases work in the opposite direction to protect party and state officials. Thus a magistrate's ruling against a plaintiff who had brought a *Privatklage* against a low-ranking party officer (*Ortsgruppenleiter*) after the latter, in a speech at a party gathering, called him a "white Jew." The magistrate proclaimed that the defendant's insult was protected speech because it had been uttered in the exercise of his official "duty to realize … the Party program."[42]

There were, however, distinct limits to how far this revolution was able to go, given the chaotic state of Nazi administration, the regime's prioritization of rearmament and war, and the complexities and entrenched nature of the legal traditions at issue.[43] But perhaps the most important barrier resided in popular culture. That culture – its longstanding practices of denunciations and the involvement by citizens of the state in personal honor disputes – was in one sense

---

[40] Brezina, *Ehre und Ehrenschutz*, pp. 86–87.
[41] "Anwendung des §193 StGB, auf Anzeigen gegen Amtsträger," *Deutsche Justiz*, 34 (1936), 1268.
[42] "Abschrift," April 14, 1937. R22, Nr. 996, BA, p. 83.
[43] Brezina, *Ehre und Ehrenschutz*, p. 208, argues that National Socialist honor notions had little practical influence.

remarkably adaptable to the environment of the new regime.[44]
A 1934 state prosecutor's communication from Erfurt spoke of the
"regularity" with which private citizens denounced statements they
overheard that were dishonoring of government officials.[45] In one
case, a citizen denounced a local official for "anti-National Socialist
behavior," and was promptly sued by the latter for false accusation
and libel.[46] These denunciations under the Third Reich, while about
events and political dynamics specific to that era, should also be seen
in terms of the longer-standing legal culture discussed in this book.

But there were a number of ways in which that culture set up
roadblocks for the regime. One was the sheer scale of the number of
suits. Despite repeated attempts to do so, the state seemed helpless to
stop the inundation of the courts by what were considered contempt-
ibly trivial matters that wasted money, time, and administrative
manpower. The state tried imposing a late Weimar (October 6,
1931) regulation that limited and streamlined *Privatklagen*.[47] In
1938, Heinrich Himmler, chief of the SS and police forces, invoking
the overburdening of the police, ordered the courts in *Privatklage*
cases to severely limit the involvement of police organs.[48] During
World War Two, there was a sharp rise in *Privatklagen*, the result
mostly of an epidemic of fights breaking out in air-raid shelters
during allied bombings.[49] Orders again went out for judges to
shorten these procedures and to refuse hearings altogether in "trivial" cases.[50] But this hardline generated so much anger on the part of
the citizenry (the "population complain that comrades are no longer
being protected from insults") that the authorities found themselves

---

[44] On denunciation in Europe and the Third Reich, see Sheila Fitzpatrick and Robert
Gellately (eds.), *Accusatory Practices: Denunciation in Modern European History,
1789–1989* (Chicago, 1996).

[45] R22, Nr. 995, BA, p. 17.

[46] "§164 StGB. Zum Begriff der falschen Anschuldigung," *Deutsche Justiz*, 49 (1936),
1855.

[47] January 22, 1941. R22, Nr. 1113, BA, p. 104.   [48] R22, Nr. 1113, BA, p. 63.

[49] Figures for 1938–1940 are listed in R22, Nr. 1113, BA, p. 149. They show a marked
increase in lawsuits in the third quarter of 1940.

[50] Berlin, October 28, 1940. R22, Nr. 1113, BA, p. 144.

having to backtrack and reconsider their position.[51] The problem of *Privatklagen* burdening the courts continued, and a decree of August 13, 1942, tried once again to limit them by shifting these cases to a system of civil arbitration and, among other measures, requiring a one-month waiting (or cooling-off) period between the defamatory incident and the filing of a legal action.[52]

The depth of popular sentiment for the *Privatklage*, shared in part by some jurists, was also why the initial aim of abolishing the institution was far from successful, and the new draft legislation ended up looking a lot like the one it was to replace. Concessions had to made. Thus, citizens were given the right, if not to initiate and file a criminal suit themselves, then to function as a co-plaintiff (*Nebenkläger*) if and when the state prosecuted their case. The proceedings before a *Friedensrichter* (a local magistrate) in those cases deemed inappropriate for state criminal proceedings were not dissimilar to the old *Privatklage*.[53]

Not only would the legal culture that underlay popular opinion not go away, it empowered a kind of autonomous action and resistance on the part of citizens. When the April 7, 1933 Law for the Restoration of the Professional Civil Service resulted in the firings of Jewish and politically undesirable civil servants (including teachers, professors, and judges), the reaction was a barrage of *Privatklagen*. They initiated criminal proceedings for false accusation or defamation or filed *Privatklagen* against people whom they held responsible for the loss of their jobs.[54] During the war, a doctor's wife, Edit Rudofsky, sued the party *Kreisleiter* (district leader) in Bischofteinitz for defamation after the latter, having accused Rudofsky in a formal hearing for "forbidden contact" with a French prisoner of war (for giving him cigarettes), went on to smear her character, calling her underhanded, self-important, an alien to the community, work-shy, and other derogatory things.[55]

---

[51] Nuremberg, September 6, 1941. R22, Nr. 1113, BA, p. 254.
[52] Waldow, "Strafrechtliche Ehrenschutz," pp. 497–98.
[53] Brezina, *Ehre und Ehrenschutz*, p. 145.   [54] R22, Nr. 995, BA, pp. 23–26.
[55] Ibid., Nr. 3097, p. 2.

This was not an isolated case. So frequent, in fact, were "unwanted *Privatklagen* proceedings against bearers of the highest or especially high responsibility in the party and state" that they produced another round of discussions, decrees, and rethinking of draft legislation for the new procedural code.[56]

THE POSTWAR ERA

Partly in reaction to the Nazi years, some significant changes in German defamation law in the interests of freeing political speech occurred in postwar West Germany. Political defamation (§187 StGB) was downgraded to a *Privatklage* offense. The legal discourse of honor came to be stamped by the notion, dating back to the nineteenth century, of "personal rights" (*Persönlichkeitsrechts*) and the value of protecting a universal right of the individual to "free self-determination."[57] Judges, moreover, began incorporating civil-law remedies in the form of less punitive monetary rewards to plaintiffs.[58] The development of European-wide institutions is potentially crucial, pushing Germany and other European countries with restrictive libel laws in the direction of greater freedom of expression. Article 10 of the European Convention on Human Rights (ECHR) guarantees the "right to freedom of expression," a provision potentially at odds with features of German libel law. Indeed, beginning in the mid-1980s, the European Commission[59] has been issuing "a series of decisions either upholding or quashing criminal libel convictions against journalists accused of publishing defamatory political stories."[60] The legal principle now being enforced by the European Commission

---

[56] Ibid., Nr. 996, p. 248.

[57] Dieter Leuze, *Die Entwicklung der Persönlichkeitsrechts im 19. Jahrhundert* (Bielefeld, 1962).

[58] Rüdiger Koewius, *Die Rechtswirklichkeit der Privatklage* (Berlin, 1974), pp. 169–74.

[59] Its precise name: European Commission and Court of Human Rights.

[60] Ian Loveland, *Political Libels* (Oxford, 2000), p. 108. Previously, its rulings, as in the 1975 *X v. Germany*, had tended to support the limitation of political speech with libel laws. Ibid., p. 104, and passim. For a comparative discussion of West German, US, and EU law, see Georg Nolte, *Beleidigungsschutz in der freiheitlichen Demokratie* (Berlin, 1992).

(and by post-*Sullivan* jurisprudence in the US) is exactly the opposite of the era discussed in this book. In the Kaiserreich (and in other nineteenth-century European countries),[61] public figures, particularly government officials and civil servants, were afforded more protections against libel than private citizens, the latter being forced to pursue their cases as *Privatklagen*. By contrast, the European Commission now privileges free speech on "matters of legitimate public interest" over protecting the reputations of public persons, offering "substantially more effective defences than those available to purveyors of 'private' information."[62]

Still, as the legal scholar James Whitman cogently shows, the power of a German "insult culture" – of honor and its defense in the courts – remains strong to this day.[63] Its impact can be felt in the way the legal system treats hate speech against Turks and sexual harassment of women as forms of disrespect rather than as discrimination against outsider minority or "traditionally inferior" groups. (Special laws, by contrast, protect Jews against hate speech.) "German jurists ask [in cases of insults against Turks or women] whether there has been an *outward show of individual disrespect*, not whether the larger climate of equal dignity has been endangered."[64] The result is anachronistic court rulings, as in a *Privatklage* brought by a female law student against a male stranger who groped her breast as he passed her on a Frankfurt street. She was told by the public prosecutor that such conduct did not constitute sexual harassment because there was no intent on the part of the perpetrator to demean her dignity, since respect for a woman "can include treating her as attractive and desirable" and this may involve "unwanted sexual advances."[65] Clearly, the anachronistic "traditions" of honor, to the extent that, as Whitman argues, they continue to prevail in the German courts, provide an inadequate legal basis for modern claims of equal treatment and anti-discrimination.

---

[61] See, for example, on French law: Lilienthal, "Üble Nachrede und Verleumdung", in Mittermaier et al. (eds.), *Vergleichende Darstellung des deutschen und ausländischen Strafrechts: Besonderer Teil* vol. 4 (Berlin, 1906), pp. 413–14.

[62] Loveland, *Political Libels*, p. 155.   [63] Whitman, "Enforcing Civility."

[64] Ibid., p. 1311. Emphasis in the original.   [65] Ibid., p. 1307.

How one defines those traditions – their nature, origins, and transmission over time – however, makes an important difference. Whitman, using mostly prescriptive sources such as law codes, argues that Germany's traditions derive from a premodern aristocratic culture of deference, hierarchy, and dueling justice. In his argument, this culture, still exclusive to the upper classes in the nineteenth century, was gradually diffused throughout the population. In the nineteenth century the upper bourgeoisie, mirroring the values of their social superiors and empowered by changes in the legal codes, adopted the *Privatklage* as an extension of the aristocratic dueling concept of "private prosecutions."[66] The *Privatklage* was thus a redoubt of the *satisfaktionsfähig* upper classes. Ironically, it was not until the Nazi era that honor, in the egalitarian form of the national *Volksgemeinschaft*, was fully democratized and inclusive of the entire population, a process continued in an altered, liberal-democratic key after World War Two.

This book is likewise about the democratization of German honor traditions, but it tells a very different story. Those traditions were never homogeneous nor exclusively aristocratic. They did, however, originate in a premodern corporate society, where, not in the 1930s, but as early as the late Middle Ages, lower- and middle-status people took their honor claims to court. Those lawsuits, limited by the legal and social hierarchies of a corporate, premodern world, were confined to horizontal suits within same-ranked people or vertical ones of superiors against inferiors. That situation changed in the nineteenth century when the law itself was liberalized and citizens were placed on a footing of formal legal equality. This opened up a new set of possibilities as traditionally inferior and excluded people began to utilize the defamation lawsuit to make new claims for respect and rights. It was in this context that the premodern *Privatklage* gained a new lease on life. It was a renewal that derived from liberal battles against the absolutist state, not the victory of aristocratic traditions. To be sure, corporate identities remained strong in middle-class honor, and those identities were influenced by aristocratic traditions

---

[66] Ibid., p. 1321.

(most clearly in the duel). But corporate and hierarchical notions of honor were themselves merging with and being transformed by liberalism, universal male suffrage, and mass politics. The Kaiserreich, in this sense, developed a hybrid legal culture of honor that fused old and new, and furthered the continuity of corporate traditions while modernizing and partly democratizing them. In discussing the democratic and/or populist practices of honor, this book has looked at a range of actors – workers, peasants, women, Socialists – devoting particular attention to the examples of Jews and lunatics. It has also shown the very modern politicization of honor in Germany's parliamentary politics around debates – §193, *Beamtenbeleidigung*, the *Wahrheitsbeweis*, the lèse-majesté bill – about free speech rights and state power. Indeed, parliamentary politics itself functioned in many ways within a (contested) honor idiom. This hybridity challenges the dichotomy, built into many studies of German history, between modernity and tradition, progress and backwardness.

Finally, the Nazis, it is true, developed a racialized honor that transcended earlier corporate distinctions. But the lessening hold of those distinctions was already far advanced in the nineteenth century, and the Nazis, rather than opening up the *Privatklage* to the masses, tried their best (in vain) to shut that legal device down, while shifting trivial honor cases to a system of civil arbitration.

Honor and its legal practices were extremely adaptable to new historical circumstances, political regimes, and socio-economic realities. Rather than a static set of values or traditions handed down and diffused through the population, they constituted, in the argument of this book, a language and strategy within which many of the battles of German history – large and small; personal and political – took place. The staying power of this honor culture across the upheavals and regime changes of German history lay precisely in its multipurpose and malleable character. If honor was a tradition, it was constantly being (re)"invented" and appropriated in different contexts that involved disputes over power, status, identity, and rights.[67]

---

[67] Eric Hobsbawm and Terence Ranger (eds.), *The Invention of Tradition* (Cambridge, 1983). One wonders, in this context, about the "traditional" notions

By paying close attention to those contexts, this book reveals how the practices of defamation litigation could, strangely, function simultaneously as methods of government repression and tools of empowerment; as a means of defending corporate interests and preserving the stratified social order and of challenging that order. The obsessive litigation around honor derived from and reinforced a society of intense status anxiety. Yet, it also partially worked as a dissolvent of traditional status differences. This was the reality of modernization.

Germany was far from alone in the importance it accorded honor and in its use of defamation law to repress speech (see, Introduction and chapter 1). The protection of the honor of heads of state via lèse-majesté laws was the norm in nineteenth-century Europe. The French and Italians dueled with the same passion as their German upper- and upper-middle-class counterparts. But Germany developed a quite distinctive legal culture around honor, which encouraged an explosion of litigation of all manner of personal and political conflicts. This was a culture of surveillance – from above and below – in which diginity, respect, and reputation often trumped free speech. It was also a culture that propped up the state by treating civil servants and other officials as a specially protected class. I do not believe, however, that the evidence produced in this book supports the idea (long debated among historians) of a German *Sonderweg* (special path), at least not in the older sense of the 1960s and 1970s. Built upon modernization theory, that idea of German exceptionalism argued that Germany in the nineteenth century began to pathologically diverge from Western democratic norms, culminating in twentieth-century fascism, because of the weakness of German liberalism and the survival of premodern elites and attitudes. I hope that this study contributes to a renewed focus on continuities in German history.[68] But in the history of law, as this

of gender honor that, according to Whitman, were (are) embedded in postwar court rulings against female claims of sexual harassment. Certainly, the nineteenth-century tradition, as shown in this book (chapter 2), was anything but tolerant of sexually demeaning aggression against women.

[68] See, for example, Helmut Walser Smith, *The Continuities of German History: Nation, Religion, and Race across the Long Nineteenth Century* (Cambridge, 2008).

and other recent studies show,[69] the picture does not conform to that earlier way of conceiving continuity. Rather than constituting a hinderance to modernization, Germany's honor culture was in part an instrument of it, and in complex ways that nation's famous litigiousness and legalism could support both repressive and reformist impulses. That double-sidedness – authoritarianism and democracy – is the history I have tried to tell in this book.

[69] Benjamin Carter Hett, *Death in the Tiergarten: Murder and Criminal Justice in the Kaiser's Berlin* (Cambridge, MA, 2004); Ian McNeely, *The Emancipation of Writing: German Civil Society in the Making, 1790s–1820s* (Berkeley, 2003); Kenneth Ledford, "Formalizing the Rule of Law in Prussia: The Supreme Administrative Law Court, 1876–1914," *Central European History* 37 (2004), 203–24; Richard Wetzell, *Inventing the Criminal: A History of German Criminology, 1880–1945* (Chapel Hill, 2000).

Index

Anderson, Margaret, 13
antisemitism, 18, 77, 132, 157ff., 189–90, 196, 198ff.
Arnim, Achim von, 161
Arnim, Bettina von, 161
Arnim, Harry von, 84
Aschaffenburg, Gustav, 159

Beamtenbeleidigung, 16, 17, 34, 82, 96ff., 115ff., 132–33, 210, 211
Bebel, August, 74, 88, 121
Beseler, Max von, 95, 139–40
Bethmann Hollweg, 86, 94–96
Bismarck, Otto von, 15, 16, 29, 83–85, 87, 100, 121
Bismarck–Becker Affair, 135
Bochumer Steuerprozess, 79–80, 129, 132
Bruhn, Wilhelm, 75
Bülow, Bernhard von, 86, 138, 139
Bund für Irrenrecht und Irrenfürsorge (Bund), 169, 180–81, 183, 186–90

Campe, von, 144
Caprivi, Leo von, 86, 88
censorship, 8, 13, 16–17, 81ff., 115, 117, 145
    in Third Reich, 202ff.
Center Party, 29, 123–24, 139, 144–146, 151ff.
Centralverein deutscher Staatsbürger jüdischen Glaubens (CV), 164–66, 170
Conservatives, 144, 146
    and lunatics' rights, 188
    and political debates, 128ff.
courts 9, 17, 41, 107 ff. (*see also* Reichsgericht)
    divisions within, 112ff.
    in Weimar Republic, 195ff.
Crosby, Eileen, 72

Dallwitz, Johann von, 92ff., 121
defamation law 3–4, 19 (*see also* defamation lawsuits; courts; *Privatklage*; Reichsgericht)
    Allgemeines Landrecht, Prussia, 20ff.
    Criminal Code (StGB), 28, 32ff., 40, 116, 133, 140
    early modern, 19ff.

in England, 2, 3, 32, 34
in France, 3, 35
in Kaiserreich, 4
liberalization, 9, 14, 19, 22ff., 36, 116–17
policies for top Prussian officials, 83ff., 97
Privatgenugtuung, 21, 23
postwar Germany, 4, 207–08
Procedural Code (StPO), 26, 29, 30, 32
in Third Reich, 201ff.
in US, 3, 34
in Weimar Republic, 195ff.
defamation lawsuits, 3, 8, 19
    and class, 41, 59ff., 187
    as form of state rule, 8, 16, 50ff., 81ff., 211
    horizontal and vertical, 11, 209
    statistics,
        in East Germany, 194
        in France, 5 n. 16
        in Kaiserreich, 4–5
    uses in daily life, 14
        in Kaiserreich 37ff.
        in Third Reich, 205ff.
        in Weimar Republic, 197ff.
denunciations, 149, 204ff
Drexler, Anton, 190
dueling, 2, 7–8, 31, 41, 45, 47–48, 51, 87–88, 113, 120, 209
    and conservatives, 133
    in *Effi Briest*, 134–35

Eulenburg Affair, 17, 89, 116, 124, 129, 131, 136ff., 142–45
European Convention on Human Rights, 207–08
Eysoldt, Friedrich, 29

Fichte, Johann 12
Fontane, Theodor, 134
Foucault, Michel, 169
Freisler, Roland, 201
Fritsch, Theodor, 196

Gowing, Laura, 71

Harden, Maximilian, 137, 138
Hegelmaier, Paul, 184
Heine, Wolfgang, 125, 145, 147, 150
Herzl, Theodor, 163–64
Himmler, Heinrich, 205
Hirschfeld, Magnus, 138
honor, 2, 10–11
    and anthropology, 6–7, 11, 43
    and anti-socialism, 152ff.
    bourgeois, 10, 12, 45–46, 64, 173–74
    business, 14, 56ff., 64
    and class, 41, 44ff., 72, 77
    and conservatism, 130–31, 76, 209–10
    corporate, 5, 8, 10, 11–12, 17, 20ff., 51, 58, 64
    of the courts, 113, 126
    and culture, 2, 4, 8–9, 11, 13, 14, 18, 43ff., 210–12
    democratization, 10–11, 14, 123ff., 157ff.
    Enlightenment, 12, 46
    and free speech, 59, 65, 80, 112, 203ff., 207
    gender, 15, 66ff., 143, 154–55, 173–74, 178–79
    labor relations, 14, 59ff., 104–05
    legal opinion, 40–41, 47, 143 n. 93
    liberals, 14, 30ff., 123ff.
    literature, 46
    lunatics, 18
    nationalism, 152ff.
    officialdom, 14, 16, 45, 50ff., 83ff, 98–99
    politics, 74ff., 93, 115ff.
    pre-modern, 7, 45, 60–61, 71–72, 158, 162, 209
    the professions, 9, 15, 61ff.
    and disciplinary courts, 8, 62–63, 64
    racialization of, 198ff.
    Socialists, 17, 48, 123ff. (*see also* SPD)
    status anxiety, 10, 14, 52

Jacoby, Johann, 22
Jews, 10, 12, 17–18, 77, 157–68, 180;
    and the Arnim–Itzig Affair, 161–62
    and the duel, 159, 163
    post-World War II, 208
    and Reichsgericht decision on
        Kollektivbeleidigung, 167–68
    under Third Reich, 198–200;
Johnson, Lyndon, 193

Kaiser Wilhelm II, 139, 149–50
Kaiserreich, 12–13
    political system and developments, 15–16, 139
Koch, Adolf, 42
Kollektivbeleidigung, 167
Königsberg lèse–majesté trial, 152ff.
Kulturkampf, 29 (*see also* religious politics)

Laing, R. D., 169
legal culture, 4, 8–9, 11, 13, 19, 30
"legitimate interest" clause, 17, 33, 83, 108ff. (*see also* Paragraph 193)
Lehmann-Hohenberg, Johann, 189–90, 190 n. 107
lèse-majesté, 22, 82, 83, 86, 210, 211
    1908 bill, 17, 116, 148, 150ff.
    statutes, 33, 149
    in Weimar Republic, 195
Levy, Sara, 161
Lex Eulenburg, 116, 141ff.
Liberals, 126, 128, 129, 142, 144, 151ff., 155, 189
    and political debates, 117ff.
Liebknecht, Karl, 103, 187
Liepmann, Moritz, 47
Lilienthal, Karl von, 40
Lindenberger, Thomas, 92
Luise, Queen (of Prussia), 152ff.
lunatics, 17–18, 50, 168ff.
    use of defamation lawsuit, 182–86
lunatics' rights, 169–70

Melchior, Carl, 196
Moabit uprising, 89–90, 101, 106
    and libel litigation, 90ff., 95
modernization, 10–11, 14, 19
    theory,
Moltke, Kuno Count von, 137

Natural-healing movement, 64–65
New York Times v. Sullivan, 3 n. 9, 208
Nieberding, Rudolf Arnold, 140ff., 149

Osann, Artur, 154

pamphlet literature, 10, 14, 18, 48–50, 171, 174–82
Paragraph 193, 17, 33–34, 61, 82, 83, 97, 105, 115, 210
    (*see also* "legitimate interest" clause)
    and 1881 ruling, 108ff.
    under Third Reich 203ff.
    in Weimar Republic, 195–97
Peristiany, J. G., 6
Peters, Karl, 52
Pitt-Rivers, Julian, 43
Polish question, 78, 89
post-World War II, 193–94, 207–09
Privatklage, 9–10, 25, 32, 35–36 (*see also* defamation lawsuits)
    comparative law, 34ff.
    and daily life in Kaiserreich, 9, 37ff.
    historical development, 19, 25ff.
    and liberalism, 25ff., 123–24, 127, 209–10
    mechanics, 35–36, 38–39, 41, 104
    as political tool, 74ff., 104
    premodern, 25

"principal", 27
"subsidiary", 27–28
in Third Reich, 202–07
in view of Whitman, 209
women, 67ff.
Progressive Party, 29, 153–54, 155
Prussian Ministry of State, 16, 83, 88ff.

Querulantenwahnsinn, 186

Rathenau, Walther, 195
Reichsgericht (Supreme Court), 17, 83, 107ff., 167
    1881 ruling on "legitimate interests," 108ff
    in Third Reich, 204
    in Weimar Republic, 199
religious politics, 15, 29, 75, 79–80 (*see also*
    Kulturkampf)
Revolution (1848), 22, 23
Richter, Eugen, 74
Ruge, Arnold, 42

Schiffer, Eugen, 122
Sonderweg, 8, 211–12
SPD, 15–16, 84, 86, 87, 88, 92ff., 145ff., 147–48,
    150ff., 152
    and lunatics' rights, 188
    and political debates, 117ff
    subject to defamation prosecutions, 101, 102–06
    in Weimar Republic, 194–96
Sperber, Jonathan, 56
state attorney's office, 30
    development of, 23, 24ff.
    prosecutorial monopoly controversy, 24ff.
Steakley, James, 137

Stewart, Frank H., 11
Stöcker, Adolf, 118–19
Stuart, Kathy, 7
Szasz, Thomas, 169

Third Reich, 200ff., 209, 210
Twesten, Karl, 22, 84

Verband Deutscher Journalisten- und
    Schriftstellervereine (VDJS),
    62–63
Vietnam War, 193
Vincke, Freiherr von, 28

Wagner, Edward, 155
Wahrheitsbeweis, 87, 88, 95, 115ff., 131
    and the Eulenburg Affair, 137
    in European comparison, 145
    legislation to restrict it, 140ff.
Waldeck, Benedikt, 28
Warburg, Max, 196, 199
Weber, Marianne, 42
Weber, Max, 5–6, 42
Weimar Republic, 18, 190, 194–200
Wendorff, Hugo, 75
Whitman, James, 8, 208–09
Windthorst, Ludwig, 29
women, 10, 67ff.
    and chastity, 66ff.
    as "mad" pamphlet writers, 178–79
    post-World War Two, 208
    and sexual harassment, 68ff.

Zweig, Arnold, 199